PENGUIN BOOKS

SEX, ART, AND AMERICAN CULTURE

'*Sex, Art and American Culture* **reveals her as she is now ...
in full unflustered command of her extraordinary powers. It
is a book chock-full of brilliant animadversions and unerring
disdain**' – *The Times Literary Supplement*

'Paglia strikes with a glorious insight that seduces even the most reluc-
tant or argumentative reader ... one must be awed by her vast
energy, erudition and wit' – *Washington Post Book World*

'**Rarely has a woman of letters been such a motormouth, so
unashamedly upset so many people, been so unafraid to hold
unfashionable views ... Her style is up-front, aggressive,
funny and infuriating; her views a bewildering mixture of the
profound and the simply provocative**' – *The List*

'Paglia's a marvellous corrective to PC cant and has sketched a brilliant urgent plan of educational reform in *Sex, Art and American Culture*'
– *Time Out*

'**She has a lot of very provocative, interesting and necessary
things to say ... Her work has the immensely beneficial
aspect of rescuing fashion, beauty and instinct from their
consignment to the dustbin of the ideologically unsound**'
– *Irish Times*

D0920082

ABOUT THE AUTHOR

Camille Paglia is Professor of Humanities at the University of the Arts in Philadelphia. She graduated in 1968 from Harpur College of the State University of New York at Binghamton and received her doctorate in English literature in 1974 from Yale University, where she studied with Harold Bloom. She has taught at Bennington College and Wesleyan University, as well as Yale. She is the author of the critically acclaimed *Sexual Personae*, also published by Penguin.

CAMILLE PAGLIA

———

SEX, ART AND AMERICAN CULTURE

ESSAYS

PENGUIN BOOKS

PENGUIN BOOKS

Published by the Penguin Group
Penguin Books Ltd, 27 Wrights Lane, London W8 5TZ, England
Penguin Books USA Inc., 375 Hudson Street, New York, New York 10014, USA
Penguin Books Australia Ltd, Ringwood, Victoria, Australia
Penguin Books Canada Ltd, 10 Alcorn Avenue, Toronto, Ontario, Canada M4V 3B2
Penguin Books (NZ) Ltd, 182–190 Wairau Road, Auckland 10, New Zealand

Penguin Books Ltd, Registered Offices: Harmondsworth, Middlesex, England

First published in the USA by Vintage Books, a division of Random House Inc. 1992
Published simultaneously in Canada by Random House of Canada Ltd
First published in Great Britain by Viking 1993
Published in Penguin Books 1993
1 3 5 7 9 10 8 6 4 2

Printed in England by Clays Ltd, St Ives plc

CONTENTS

INTRODUCTION

The essays in this collection are united by common themes. I want to rethink American cultural history in order to clarify the heritage of my generation of the Sixties, which heroically broke through Fifties conformism but which failed in many ways to harness or sustain its own energies.

Popular culture is my passion. It created Sixties imagination. I define pop culture as an eruption of the never-defeated paganism of the West. Its brazen aggression and pornographic sexuality are at odds with current feminism, whose public proponents are in a reactionary phase of hysterical moralism and prudery, like that of the Temperance movement a century ago. We need a new kind of feminism, one that stresses personal responsibility and is open to art and sex in all their dark, unconsoling mysteries. The feminist of the *fin de siècle* will be bawdy, streetwise, and on-the-spot confrontational, in the prankish Sixties way.

My essays often address the impasse in contemporary politics between "liberal" and "conservative," a polarity that I contend lost its meaning after the Sixties. There should be an examination of the way Sixties innovators were openly hostile to the establishment liberals of the time. In today's impoverished dialogue, critiques of liberalism are often naïvely labeled "conservative," as if twenty-five hundred years of Western intellectual history presented no other alternatives. My thinking tends to be libertarian. That is, I oppose intrusions of the state into the private realm—as in abortion, sodomy, prostitution, pornography, drug use, or suicide, all of which I would strongly defend as matters of free choice in a representative democracy. Similarly,

I oppose the meddling of campus grievance committees in the issue of date rape. We should teach general ethics to both men and women, but sexual relationships themselves must not be policed. Sex, like the city streets, would be risk-free only in a totalitarian regime.

We need a new point of view that would combine the inspiring progressive principles and global consciousness of the Sixties with the hard political lessons of the Seventies and Eighties, sobering decades of rational reaction against the arrogant excesses of my generation, who thought we could change the world overnight. In other words, we need a fusion of idealism and realism. Social justice and compassion are compatible with an intelligent respect for private enterprise and law and order. But first, history and economics must be directly studied, without the posturing and simplistic clichés that masquerade as political thinking these days among liberals in and out of academe. I sometimes call my new system "Italian pagan Catholicism," but it could more accurately be called "pragmatic liberalism," with roots in Enlightenment political philosophy. It is a synthesis of the enduring dual elements in our culture, pagan and Judeo-Christian, Romantic and Classic.

One of my central concerns is the reform of education, which has degenerated since my generation made "relevance" a quickie standard of judgment. Education has become a prisoner of contemporaneity. It is the great past, not the dizzy present, that is the best door to the future. While I often felt stultified and imprisoned by my elementary and high-school instruction (I was always plotting to get out of the classroom and roam the halls), I now recognize that it was the basis of my present skills as a thinker, researcher, and writer. The rigorous, no-nonsense American public schools that provided free education for a hundred years to the immigrants, including my mother, have been allowed to degenerate.

Contemporaneity is an even worse plague upon the "best" higher education. The most interesting and daring minds of my generation did not, as a rule, go on to graduate school or succeed in the academic system. Hence our major universities are now stuck with an army of pedestrian, toadying careerists, Fifties types

who wave around Sixties banners to conceal the
less, beaverlike tunneling to the top. That the New
in its exclusion of history and psychoanalysis, insup
perfectly obvious in the Sixties. But there was an Am
out of its dilemma. I found it in Allen Ginsberg, No
Brown, Leslie Fiedler, and Harold Bloom. We did n   need
French post-structuralism, whose pedantic jargon, clumsy con-
volutions, and prissy abstractions have spread throughout aca-
deme and the arts and are now blighting the most promising
minds of the next generation. This is a major crisis if there ever
was one, and every sensible person must help bring it to an end.

A serious problem in America is the gap between academe
and the mass media, which *is* our culture. Professors of human-
ities, with all their leftist fantasies, have little direct knowledge
of American life and no impact whatever on public policy. Ac-
ademic commentary on popular culture is either ghettoized as
lackluster "communications," tarted up with semiotics, or loaded
down with grim, quasi-Marxist, Frankfurt School censoriousness:
the pitifully witless masses are always being brainwashed by
money-grubbing capitalist pigs. But mass media is completely,
even servilely commercial. It is a mirror of the popular mind.
All the P.R. in the world cannot make a hit movie or sitcom. The
people vote with ratings and dollars. Academic Marxists, with
their elitist sense of superiority to popular taste, are the biggest
snobs in America.

The American intellectual should mediate between aca-
deme and media, the past and the present. Language should be
lucid, concrete, direct, with the brash candor of the American
people and the brusque, can-do rhythms of American life. I was
always attracted to Thirties voices—to the Algonquin wits, like
Dorothy Parker, with her caustic one-liners, and to pugnacious
literary journalists like Edmund Wilson and Mary McCarthy.
Ever since the triumph of television and rock music (both of which
I worship), American intellectual life has been in the doldrums.
It needs to be jump-started with the energy of mass media. Ac-
ademics have got to get out of the Parisian paper matchbox and
back into the cultural mainstream, the American roaring rapids,
with their daily excitement and bracing vulgarity.

The pieces in this volume, with one exception, were written during the last two years. Most of them were concentrated in the year following the appearance of my controversial op-ed article on Madonna in *The New York Times* in December 1990. That piece opens the book, followed by a longer essay on Madonna commissioned by *The Independent* for the British premiere of *Truth or Dare* (called *In Bed with Madonna* overseas) and published as the cover story of its Sunday magazine. Next is "Hollywood's Pagan Queen," a confession of my lifelong adoration of Elizabeth Taylor, which was published in *Penthouse*. Finally, there is another op-ed piece from *The New York Times* calling for rock music to be taken seriously as an art form.

Following these four articles on popular culture is a group of essays on sex in America: my analysis, from *Esquire*, of homosexuality as a central cultural force at the close of the century; a review, commissioned by Andrew Sullivan for *The New Republic*, of the Presbyterian report on human sexuality; a defense of Robert Mapplethorpe for *Tikkun;* an op-ed piece, from *The Philadelphia Inquirer*, on the Clarence Thomas/Anita Hill crisis; and my op-ed piece on date rape from *New York Newsday*.

The *Newsday* article, carried nationally by the wire services, was immediately denounced by many feminists for its heresy. At the same time, I received letters from parents and teachers all over the country, thanking me for restoring common sense to the date-rape question. Since then, reporters have regularly asked me to clarify and expand on the remarks I made in *Newsday*. My references to rape in those interviews have been widely cited and reprinted elsewhere, often hostilely and sometimes in unrecognizably garbled form. Because there have been so many self-perpetuating misquotes, I am excerpting here, as "The Rape Debate, Continued," the most substantive passages on rape from my media interviews. Normally, I don't think it appropriate for authors to reproduce their own interview material, but this particular subject is clearly of overriding concern in the current public agenda.

Next is a series of book reviews that I wrote for *The New York Times*, *The Washington Post*, *The Boston Globe*, and *The Philadelphia Inquirer*. Book reviewing, through which literary critics form taste and communicate with the general audience, has languished. Bland, cautious, back-scratching reviews have become the norm. Over the past twenty years, the trend has been that if a review is likely to be negative, a reviewer will refuse to do it. Two years ago, I was thrilled by the hilariously satirical British reviews of *Sexual Personae,* which, though largely negative, overflowed with contentious intellectual vitality.* They reinforced my desire to reintroduce the scathing voices of Dorothy Parker and Mary McCarthy to American letters. Hence my very rude, no-holds-barred reviews, which so many aggrieved letter writers, invoking sepulchral Victorian pieties, have condemned. When in doubt, I read Oscar Wilde. His battles are my battles, and there are echoes of his strategies and formulations throughout my work. Like Wilde, I try to use all the modalities of language, from lyric to comic and martial, to do yeoman's service in the culture wars.

There are three lengthy unpublished pieces in this volume. The first is the cancelled preface of *Sexual Personae.* Newspaper and magazine profiles have chronicled the disastrous twenty-year history of my career, the job problems and rowdy incidents, the isolation and poverty, the frustrating inability to get published. *Sexual Personae* (including the second volume on popular culture) was completed in February 1981, but the first volume was not released until 1990. Seven major New York publishers rejected the book before it was accepted, thanks to the editor Ellen Graham, by Yale University Press.

Because of the extreme and expensive length of the first volume of *Sexual Personae,* which moves from prehistory to the end of the nineteenth century, the Yale editors felt that the preface, which details my critical sources and methods, could be dispensed with. I shifted some material from the preface to the body of the book (for example, the infamous sentence, "If civilization had been left in female hands, we would still be living in grass huts") and drastically compressed the rest to one page.

---

* Sample headlines from the British reviews: "Flesh and Dread," "Blame it All on Mother Nature," "Apollo and Di," "One in the Eye for the Beholder," "A Bit Much," "The Pathetic Phalluses of Art," "A Bishop Slapped Her."

I now reproduce the original preface, with the cuts smoothed over.

Following that is a memoir of my great college teacher, the poet Milton Kessler, which appeared in *Sulfur*. Next is "East and West," an unpublished day-by-day account of an experimental, multicultural course that I co-taught in 1991 at the University of the Arts with Lily Yeh, a Philadelphia artist active in community affairs.

The last section of the book addresses the state of academe today. First is a long, polemical essay, "Junk Bonds and Corporate Raiders," that began as a routine review for the classics journal *Arion*. Then there is the unpublished transcript of a lecture I gave in September 1991 at the Massachusetts Institute of Technology, "Crisis in the American Universities."

Ending this collection is a three-part appendix. "A Media History" is a chronological record of my first media appearances, documenting my strange quick passage from obscurity to notoriety. What has happened is not my doing but that of the Zeitgeist. I was not in control of my career when it was a disaster, and I am not in control of it now. My explanation is that, at the end of the century and millennium, the culture has suddenly changed. There is a hunger for new ways of seeing and thinking. Anti-establishment mavericks like me are back in fashion. It's a classically American story, the loner riding out of the desert to shoot up the saloon and run the rats out of town.

Next, the appendix reproduces several cartoons that amusingly satirize either me or my ideas. Finally, there is a selected bibliography of newspaper and magazine articles on me. One reason for the proliferation of such articles is probably that, as a lifelong devotee of mass media, I like reporters and enjoy talking to them. With most academics, I feel bored and restless. I have to speak very slowly and hold back my energy level. With reporters, on the other hand, I'm in my element, like Roz Russell in *His Girl Friday*, a boisterous, wisecracking, machine-gun American verbal style. My manic personality, which frightens and repels academics, seems perfectly normal to media people, who are always in a rush and on a deadline.

Furthermore, I get as much back from reporters as I give them. That is, by their questions and objections, I gain priceless information about evolving public thought on crucial issues. Reporters are on the front lines, grilling major figures and hypersensitive to breaking news. Talking with them, I feel connected to a vast communications network. My conversations with the foreign press have been especially valuable in proving to me that Anglo-American feminism is caught in a white, middle-class cul-de-sac and that my theories about sex are more in tune with world culture.

Most of the previously published articles and book reviews in this volume have been given new titles, since the original headlines were not composed by me. The pieces are verbatim as they appeared in print except where I have reinserted material cut by last-minute deadline editing at the newspaper or magazine, most of the time with my permission but sometimes not. There were significant losses, for example, in *The Independent*'s Madonna essay, which was lavishly illustrated with paper-doll drawings, the sizing of which devoured some of my text. All dropped material has now been restored.

I would like to thank my editor, LuAnn Walther, for proposing the idea for this collection and for her invaluable professional advice and guidance, and my publicist, Katy Barrett, for her shrewd counsel and warm support in my media sallies and jousts.

Camille Paglia
Philadelphia, June 1992

SEX, ART, AND

AMERICAN CULTURE

MADONNA I:

ANIMALITY AND ARTIFICE

Madonna, don't preach.

Defending her controversial new video, "Justify My Love," on *Nightline* last week, Madonna stumbled, rambled, and ended up seeming far less intelligent than she really is.

Madonna, 'fess up.

The video is pornographic. It's decadent. And it's fabulous. MTV was right to ban it, a corporate resolve long overdue. Parents cannot possibly control television, with its titanic omnipresence.

Prodded by correspondent Forrest Sawyer for

[*The New York Times*, December 14, 1990]

evidence of her responsibility as an artist, Madonna hotly proclaimed her love of children, her social activism, and her condom endorsements. Wrong answer. As Baudelaire and Oscar Wilde knew, neither art nor the artist has a moral responsibility to liberal social causes.

"Justify My Love" is truly avant-garde, at a time when that word has lost its meaning in the flabby art world. It represents a sophisticated European sexuality of a kind we have not seen since the great foreign films of the 1950s and 1960s. But it does not belong on a mainstream music channel watched around the clock by children.

On *Nightline*, Madonna bizarrely called the video a "celebration of sex." She imagined happy educational scenes where curious children would ask their parents about the video. Oh, sure! Picture it: "Mommy, please tell me about the tired, tied-up man in the leather harness and the mean, bare-chested lady in the Nazi cap." Okay, dear, right after the milk and cookies.

Sawyer asked for Madonna's reaction to feminist charges that, in the neck manacle and floor-crawling of an earlier video, "Express Yourself," she condoned the "degradation" and "humiliation" of women. Madonna waffled: "But I chained myself! I'm in charge." Well, no. Madonna the producer may have chosen the chain, but Madonna the sexual persona in the video is alternately a cross-dressing dominatrix and a slave of male desire.

But who cares what the feminists say anyhow? They have been outrageously negative about Madonna from the start. In 1985, *Ms.* magazine pointedly feted quirky, cuddly singer Cyndi Lauper as its woman of the year. Great judgment: gimmicky Lauper went nowhere, while Madonna grew, flourished, metamorphosed, and became an international star of staggering dimensions. She is also a shrewd business tycoon, a modern new woman of all-around talent.

Madonna is the true feminist. She exposes the puritanism and suffocating ideology of American feminism, which is stuck in an adolescent whining mode. Madonna has taught young women to be fully female and sexual while still exercising control over their lives. She shows girls how to be attractive, sensual, energetic, ambitious, aggressive, and funny—all at the same time.

American feminism has a man problem. The beaming Betty Crockers, hangdog dowdies, and parochial prudes who call themselves feminists want men to be like women. They fear and despise the masculine. The academic feminists think their nerdy bookworm husbands are the ideal model of human manhood.

But Madonna loves real men. She sees the beauty of masculinity, in all its rough vigor and sweaty athletic perfection. She also admires the men who are actually like women: transsexuals and flamboyant drag queens, the heroes of the 1969 Stonewall rebellion, which started the gay liberation movement.

"Justify My Love" is an eerie, sultry tableau of jaded androgynous creatures, trapped in a decadent sexual underground. Its hypnotic images are drawn from such sadomasochistic films as Liliana Cavani's *The Night Porter* and Luchino Visconti's *The Damned*. It's the perverse and knowing world of the photographers Helmut Newton and Robert Mapplethorpe.

Contemporary American feminism, which began by rejecting Freud because of his alleged sexism, has shut itself off from his ideas of ambiguity, contradiction, conflict, ambivalence. Its simplistic psychology is illustrated by the new cliché of the date-rape furor: " 'No' always means 'no.' " Will we ever graduate from the Girl Scouts? "No" has always been, and always will be, part of the dangerous, alluring courtship ritual of sex and seduction, observable even in the animal kingdom.

Madonna has a far profounder vision of sex than do the feminists. She sees both the animality and the artifice. Changing her costume style and hair color virtually every month, Madonna embodies the eternal values of beauty and pleasure. Feminism says, "No more masks." Madonna says we are nothing but masks.

Through her enormous impact on young women around the world, Madonna is the future of feminism.

MADONNA II:

VENUS OF THE RADIO

WAVES

I'm a dyed-in-the-wool, true-blue Madonna fan.

It all started in 1984, when Madonna exploded onto MTV with a brazen, insolent, in-your-face American street style, which she had taken from urban blacks, Hispanics, and her own middle-class but turbulent and charismatic Italian-American family. From the start, there was a flamboyant and parodistic element to her sexuality, a hard glamour she had learned from Hollywood cinema and from its devotees, gay men and drag queens.

Madonna is a dancer. She thinks and expresses

[*The Independent on Sunday Review*, London, July 21, 1991]

herself through dance, which exists in the eternal Dionysian realm of music. Dance, which she studied with a gay man in her home state of Michigan, was her avenue of escape from the conventions of religion and bourgeois society. The sensual language of her body allowed her to transcend the over-verbalized codes of her class and time.

Madonna's great instinctive intelligence was evident to me from her earliest videos. My first fights about her had to do with whether she was a good dancer or merely a well-coached one. As year by year she built up the remarkable body of her video work, with its dazzling number of dance styles, I have had to fight about that less and less. However, I am still at war about her with feminists and religious conservatives (an illuminating alliance of contemporary puritans).

Most people who denigrate Madonna do so out of ignorance. The postwar baby-boom generation in America, to which I belong, has been deeply immersed in popular culture for thirty-five years. Our minds were formed by rock music, which has poured for twenty-four hours a day from hundreds of noisy, competitive independent radio stations around the country.

Madonna, like Venus stepping from the radio waves, emerged from this giant river of music. Her artistic imagination ripples and eddies with the inner currents in American music. She is at her best when she follows her intuition and speaks to the world in the universal language of music and dance. She is at her worst when she tries to define and defend herself in words, which she borrows from louche, cynical pals and shallow, single-issue political activists.

Madonna consolidates and fuses several traditions of pop music, but the major one she typifies is disco, which emerged in the Seventies and, under the bland commercial rubric "dance music," is still going strong. It has a terrible reputation: when you say the word *disco,* people think "Bee Gees." But I view disco, at its serious best, as a dark, grand Dionysian music with roots in African earth-cult.

Madonna's command of massive, resonant bass lines, which she heard in the funky dance clubs of Detroit and New York, has always impressed me. As an Italian Catholic, she uses them liturgically. Like me, she sensed the buried pagan religiosity in disco. I recall my stunned admiration as I sat in the theater in 1987 and first experienced the crashing, descending chords of Madonna's "Causing a Commotion," which opened her dreadful movie, *Who's That Girl?* If you want to hear the essence of modernity, listen to those chords, infernal, apocalyptic, and grossly sensual. This is the authentic voice of the *fin de siècle*.

Madonna's first video, for her superb, drivingly lascivious disco hit "Burnin' Up," did not make much of an impression. The platinum-blonde girl kneeling and emoting in the middle of a midnight highway just seemed to be a band member's floozie. In retrospect, the video, with its rapid, cryptic surrealism, prefigures Madonna's signature themes and contains moments of eerie erotic poetry.

"Lucky Star" was Madonna's breakthrough video. Against a luminous, white abstract background, she and two impassive dancers perform a synchronized series of jagged, modern kicks and steps. Wearing the ragtag outfit of all-black bows, see-through netting, fingerless lace gloves, bangle bracelets, dangle earrings, chains, crucifixes, and punk booties that would set off a gigantic fashion craze among American adolescent girls, Madonna flaunts her belly button and vamps the camera with a smoky, piercing, come-hither-but-keep-your-distance stare. Here she first suggests her striking talent for improvisational floor work, which she would spectacularly demonstrate at the first MTV awards show, when, wrapped in a white-lace wedding dress, she campily rolled and undulated snakelike on the stage, to the baffled consternation of the first rows of spectators.

I remember sitting in a bar when "Lucky Star," just out, appeared on TV. The stranger perched next to me, a heavyset, middle-aged working-class woman, watched the writhing Madonna and, wide-eyed and slightly frowning, blankly said, her beer held motionless halfway to her lips, "Will you look at this." There was a sense that Madonna was doing something so new and so strange that one didn't know whether to call it beautiful or grotesque. Through MTV, Madonna was transmitting an avant-garde downtown New York sensibility to the American masses.

In "Lucky Star," Madonna is raffish, gamine, still full of the street-urchin mischief that she would portray in her first and best film, Susan Seidelman's *Desperately Seeking Susan* (1984). In "Borderline," she shows her burgeoning star quality. As the girl-friend of Hispanic toughs who is picked up by a British photographer and makes her first magazine cover, she presents the new dualities of her life: the gritty, multiracial street and club scene that she had haunted in obscurity and poverty, and her new slick, fast world of popularity and success.

In one shot of "Borderline," as she chummily chews gum with kidding girlfriends on the corner, you can see the nondescript plainness of Madonna's real face, which she again exposes, with admirable candor, in *Truth or Dare* when, slurping soup and sporting a shower cap over hair rollers, she fences with her conservative Italian father over the phone. Posing for the photographer in "Borderline," Madonna in full cry fixes the camera lens with challenging, molten eyes, in a bold ritual display of sex and aggression. This early video impressed me with Madonna's sophisticated view of the fabrications of femininity, that exquisite theater which feminism condemns as oppression but which I see as a supreme artifact of civilization. I sensed then, and now know for certain, that Madonna, like me, is drawn to drag queens for their daring, flamboyant insight into sex roles, which they see far more clearly and historically than do our endlessly complaining feminists.

Madonna's first major video, in artistic terms, was "Like a Virgin," where she began to release her flood of inner sexual personae, which appear and disappear like the painted creatures of masque. Madonna is an orchid-heavy Veronese duchess in white, a febrile Fassbinder courtesan in black, a slutty nun-turned-harlequin flapping a gold cross and posturing, bum in air, like a demonic phantom in the nose of a gondola. This video alone, with its coruscating polarities of evil and innocence, would be enough to establish Madonna's artistic distinction for the next century.

In "Material Girl," where she sashays around in Marilyn Monroe's strapless red gown and archly flashes her fan at a pack of men in tuxedos, Madonna first showed her flair for comedy.

Despite popular opinion, there are no important parallels between Madonna and Monroe, who was a virtuoso comedienne
but who was insecure, depressive, passive-aggressive, and infu-
riatingly obstructionist in her career habits. Madonna is manic,
perfectionist, workaholic. Monroe abused alcohol and drugs,
while Madonna shuns them. Monroe had a tentative, melting,
dreamy solipsism; Madonna has Judy Holliday's wisecracking
smart mouth and Joan Crawford's steel will and bossy, circus-
master managerial competence.

In 1985 the cultural resistance to Madonna became overt.
Despite the fact that her "Into the Groove," the mesmerizing
theme song of *Desperately Seeking Susan,* had saturated our lives
for nearly a year, the Grammy Awards outrageously ignored her.
The feminist and moralist sniping began in earnest. Madonna
"degraded" womanhood; she was vulgar, sacrilegious, stupid,
shallow, opportunistic. A nasty mass quarrel broke out in one of
my classes between the dancers, who adored Madonna, and the
actresses, who scorned her.

I knew the quality of what I was seeing: "Open Your
Heart," with its risqué peep-show format, remains for me not
only Madonna's greatest video but one of the three or four best
videos ever made. In the black bustier she made famous (transforming the American lingerie industry overnight), Madonna,
bathed in blue-white light, plays Marlene Dietrich straddling a
chair. Her eyes are cold, distant, all-seeing. She is ringed, as if
in a sea-green aquarium, by windows of lewd or longing voyeurs:
sad sacks, brooding misfits, rowdy studs, dreamy gay twins, a
melancholy lesbian.

"Open Your Heart" is a brilliant mimed psychodrama of
the interconnections between art and pornography, love and lust.
Madonna won my undying loyalty by reviving and re-creating
the hard glamour of the studio-era Hollywood movie queens,
figures of mythological grandeur. Contemporary feminism cut
itself off from history and bankrupted itself when it spun its
puerile, paranoid fantasy of male oppressors and female sex-
object victims. Woman is the dominant sex. Woman's sexual
glamour has bewitched and destroyed men since Delilah and
Helen of Troy. Madonna, role model to millions of girls world-

wide, has cured the ills of feminism by reasserting woman's command of the sexual realm.

Responding to the spiritual tensions within Italian Catholicism, Madonna discovered the buried paganism within the church. The torture of Christ and the martyrdom of the saints, represented in lurid polychrome images, dramatize the passions of the body, repressed in art-fearing puritan Protestantism of the kind that still lingers in America. Playing with the outlaw personae of prostitute and dominatrix, Madonna has made a major contribution to the history of women. She has rejoined and healed the split halves of woman: Mary, the Blessed Virgin and holy mother, and Mary Magdalene, the harlot.

The old-guard establishment feminists who still loathe Madonna have a sexual ideology problem. I am radically pro-pornography and pro-prostitution. Hence I perceive Madonna's strutting sexual exhibitionism not as cheapness or triviality but as the full, florid expression of the whore's ancient rule over men. Incompetent amateurs have given prostitution a bad name. In my university office in Philadelphia hangs a pagan shrine: a life-size full-color cardboard display of Joanne Whalley-Kilmer and Bridget Fonda naughtily smiling in scanty, skintight gowns as Christine Keeler and Mandy Rice-Davies in the film *Scandal*. I tell visitors it is "my political science exhibit." For me, the Profumo affair symbolizes the evanescence of male government compared to woman's cosmic power.

In a number of videos, Madonna has played with bisexual innuendos, reaching their culmination in the solemn woman-to-woman kiss of "Justify My Love," a deliciously decadent sarabande of transvestite and sadomasochistic personae that was banned by MTV. Madonna is again pioneering here, this time in restoring lesbian eroticism to the continuum of heterosexual response, from which it was unfortunately removed twenty years ago by lesbian feminist separatists of the most boring, humorless, strident kind. "Justify My Love" springs from the sophisticated European art films of the Fifties and Sixties that shaped my sexual imagination in college. It shows bisexuality and all experimentation as a liberation from false, narrow categories.

Madonna's inner emotional life can be heard in the smooth,

transparent "La Isla Bonita," one of her most perfect songs, with its haunting memory of paradise lost. No one ever mentions it. Publicity has tended to focus instead on the more blatantly message-heavy videos, like "Papa Don't Preach," with its teen pregnancy, or "Express Yourself," where feminist cheerleading lyrics hammer on over crisp, glossy images of bedroom bondage, dungeon torture, and epicene, crotch-grabbing Weimar elegance.

"Like a Prayer" gave Pepsi-Cola dyspepsia: Madonna receives the stigmata, makes love with the animated statue of a black saint, and dances in a rumpled silk slip in front of a field of burning crosses. This last item, with its uncontrolled racial allusions, shocked even me. But Madonna has a strange ability to remake symbolism in her own image. Kitsch and trash are transformed by her high-energy dancer's touch, her earnest yet over-the-top drag-queen satire.

The "Vogue" video approaches "Open Your Heart" in quality. Modelling her glowing, languorous postures on the great high-glamour photographs of Hurrell, Madonna reprises the epiphanic iconography of our modern Age of Hollywood. Feminism is infested with white, middle-class, literary twits ignorant of art and smugly hostile to fashion photography and advertisement, which contain the whole history of art. In the dramatic chiaroscuro compositions of "Vogue," black and Hispanic New York drag queens, directly inspired by fashion magazines, display the arrogant aristocracy of beauty, recognized as divine by Plato and, before him, by the princes of Egypt.

In my own theoretical terms, Madonna has both the dynamic Dionysian power of dance and the static Apollonian power of iconicism. Part of her fantastic success has been her ability to communicate with the still camera, a talent quite separate from any other. To project to a camera, you must have an autoerotic autonomy, a sharp self-conceptualization, even a fetishistic perversity: the camera is a machine you make love to. Madonna has been fortunate in finding Herb Ritts, who has recorded the dazzling profusion of her mercurial sexual personae. Through still photography, she has blanketed the world press with her image between videos and concert tours. But Madonna, I contend, never does anything just for publicity. Rather, publicity is the language naturally used by the great stars to communicate with their vast modern audience. Through publicity, we live in the star's flowing consciousness.

Madonna has evolved physically. In a charming early live video, "Dress You Up," she is warm, plump, and flirty under pink and powder-blue light. Her voice is enthusiastic but thin and breathy. She began to train both voice and body, so that her present silhouette, with some erotic loss, is wiry and muscular, hyperkinetic for acrobatic dance routines based on the martial arts. Madonna is notorious for monthly or even weekly changes of hair color and style, by which she embodies the restless individualism of Western personality. Children love her. As with the Beatles, this is always the sign of a monumental pop phenomenon.

Madonna has her weak moments: for example, I have no tolerance for the giggling baby talk that she periodically hauls out of the closet, as over the final credits of *Truth or Dare*. She is a complex modern woman. Indeed, that is the main theme of her extraordinary achievement. She is exploring the problems and tensions of being an ambitious woman today. Like the potent Barbra Streisand, whose maverick female style had a great impact on American girls in the Sixties, Madonna is confronting the romantic dilemma of the strong woman looking for a man but uncertain whether she wants a tyrant or slave. The tigress in heat is drawn to surrender but may kill her conqueror.

In "Open Your Heart," Madonna is woman superbly alone, master of her own fate. Offstage at the end, she mutates into an androgynous boy-self and runs off. "What a Tramp!," thundered the *New York Post* in a recent full-page headline. Yes, Madonna has restored the Whore of Babylon, the pagan goddess banned by the last book of the Bible. With an instinct for world-domination gained from Italian Catholicism, she has rolled like a juggernaut over the multitude of her carping critics. This is a kaleidoscopic career still in progress. But Madonna's most enduring cultural contribution may be that she has introduced ravishing visual beauty and a lush Mediterranean sensuality into parched, pinched, word-drunk Anglo-Saxon feminism.

ELIZABETH TAYLOR

HOLLYWOOD'S PAGAN

QUEEN

Hollywood, America's greatest modern contribution to world culture, is a business, a religion, an art form, and a state of mind. It has only one living queen: Elizabeth Taylor.

My devotion to Elizabeth Taylor began in the late Fifties, when I was in junior high school and when Taylor was in her heyday as a tabloid diva. I was suffering sustained oppression in the Age of Perky Blondes: day after day, I reeled from the assaults of Doris Day, Debbie Reynolds, Sandra Dee. All that parochial pleasantness! So chirpy, peppy, and pink,

[*Penthouse*, March 1992]

so well-scrubbed, making the world safe for democracy.

In 1958, Elizabeth Taylor, raven-haired vixen and temptress, took Eddie Fisher away from Debbie Reynolds and became a pariah of the American press. I cheered. What joy to see Liz rattle Debbie's braids and bring a scowl to that smooth, girlish forehead! As an Italian, I saw that a battle of cultures was under way: antiseptic American blondeness was being swamped by a rising tide of sensuality, a new force that would sweep my Sixties generation into open rebellion.

Three years later, adulteress Taylor was forgiven by the American public when she caught near-fatal pneumonia in London. She was photographed being rushed unconscious on a stretcher into a hospital for an emergency tracheotomy. This brush with death seems, in some strange mythic way, to have divinized her. A worldwide surge of popular sympathy helped her win the Oscar in 1961 for *Butterfield 8*. There was a brilliant series of glossy color pictures of her in *Look* magazine that year in which her melting beauty was frankly set off by the unconcealed pale white scar on her throat.

Suffocating in the tranquil, bourgeois Fifties, I escaped by studying ancient Egypt and Greece—and worshipping Elizabeth Taylor. At one point, I had collected 599 pictures of her. I sensed that she was a universal archetype of woman. At the very moment that I was rebelling against the coercive role of femininity and modelling myself on my other heroine, the intrepid, masculine Amelia Earhart, I also recognized that Taylor's mystery and glamour were coming from nature, not culture.

Elizabeth Taylor is pre-feminist woman. This is the source of her continuing greatness and relevance. She wields the sexual power that feminism cannot explain and has tried to destroy. Through stars like Taylor, we sense the world-disordering impact of legendary women like Delilah, Salome, and Helen of Troy. Feminism has tried to dismiss the femme fatale as a misogynist libel, a hoary cliché. But the femme fatale expresses woman's ancient and eternal control of the sexual realm. The specter of the femme fatale stalks all of men's relations with women.

There is an absurd assumption in the air that Meryl Streep is the greatest American actress. Meryl Streep is a good, intelligent actress who has never given a great performance in her life. Her reputation is wildly out of sync with her actual achievement. Cerebral Streep was the ideal high-WASP actress for the fast-track yuppie era, bright, slick, and self-conscious.

Elizabeth Taylor is, in my opinion, the greatest actress in film history. She instinctively understands the camera and its nonverbal intimacies. Opening her violet eyes, she takes us into the liquid realm of emotion, which she inhabits by Pisces intuition. Richard Burton said that Taylor showed him how to act for the camera. Economy and understatement are essential. At her best, Elizabeth Taylor simply *is*. An electric, erotic charge vibrates the space between her face and the lens. It is an extrasensory, pagan phenomenon.

Meryl Streep, in the Protestant way, is stuck on words; she flashes clever accents as a mask for her deeper failures. (And she cannot deliver a Jewish line; she destroyed Nora Ephron's snappy dialogue in *Heartburn*.) Streep's work doesn't travel. Try dubbing her for movie houses in India: there'd be nothing left, just that bony, earnest horse face moving its lips. Imagine, on the other hand, lesser technicians like Hedy Lamarr, Rita Hayworth, Lana Turner: these women have an international and universal appeal, crossing the centuries. They would have been beautiful in Egypt, Greece, Rome, medieval Burgundy, or eighteenth-century Paris. Susan Hayward played Bathsheba. Try to picture Meryl Streep in a Bible epic! Streep is incapable of playing the great legendary or mythological roles. She has no elemental power, no smouldering sensuality.

Elizabeth Taylor, it is true, lacks stage training; in live theater, she shrinks. Her weakest moments on film are when, as in *Cleopatra*, she pushes her voice for grand effects and ends up sounding shrill. But she already is grand. Her mere presence is regality enough. In retrospect, the terrible irony of *Cleopatra* is that the fall of the love-sick Antony, played by Richard Burton, mirrors that of Burton himself, who threw his brilliant stage career away to follow Elizabeth Taylor around the world. Taylor is too attractive to play the real Cleopatra, who from our scanty evidence seems to have had a large nose and weak chin. But the scenes of this film are magnificent in their own right: the subdued, dignified Cleopatra, austerely cloaked, escaping from Rome by torch-lit boat after Caesar's assassination; Cleopatra, magically garbed as Venus, arriving by fabulous royal yacht to meet Antony at Tarsus.

Over the span of her long career, Elizabeth Taylor has produced a remarkable body of work. Her great performances include those, as in *Elephant Walk* (1954) and *Giant* (1956), of lovely, sensitive young wives painfully isolated in a harsh world of men. In *Suddenly, Last Summer* (1959), Taylor did in a single, punishing, protracted take Catherine's cathartic memory of the death-by-cannibalism of her cousin Sebastian Venable. Her superb, fiery performance as Maggie in *Cat on a Hot Tin Roof* (1958) remains for me the definitive reading of that role. When the highly touted Jessica Lange did Maggie for a television production, I could not contain my scorn. Lange, in this role as in her others, is a pallid wax doll with as much substance as a Ping-Pong ball. Finally, everyone has to admit that Taylor, daringly haggard and all slatternly, gritty vigor, chewed up the scenery in *Who's Afraid of Virginia Woolf?* (1966).

Because so much of her mythic power is nonverbal, Taylor flourishes in iconic images, ideal for movie posters. For *Suddenly, Last Summer,* she kneels in a white bathing suit, like Venus rising from the sea. Her face is anxious, averted; her legs are pressed tightly together; her full breasts, half-exposed, fall forward for our gaze. It is an astonishingly rich picture, full of the paradoxes of concealment and exhibitionism that make woman so elusive and so dominant.

In both *Cat on a Hot Tin Roof* and *Butterfield 8,* Taylor appears in a tight white silk slip that looks as if it were sewed onto her body. What a gorgeous object she is! Feminists are currently adither over woman's status as sex object, but let them rave on in their little mental cells. For me, sexual objectification is a supreme human talent that is indistinguishable from the art impulse. Elizabeth Taylor, voluptuous in her sleek slip, stands like an ivory goddess, triumphantly alone. Her smooth shoulders and round curves, echoing those of mother earth, are gifts of nature, beyond the reach of female impersonators. *Butterfield 8,* with its call-girl heroine working her way down the alphabet of men from

Amherst to Yale, appeared at a very formative moment in my adolescence and impressed me forever with the persona of the prostitute, whom I continue to revere. The prostitute is not, as feminists claim, the victim of men but rather their conqueror, an outlaw who controls the sexual channel between nature and culture.

One of the most spectacular moments of my moviegoing career occurred in college as I watched Joseph Losey's bizarre *Secret Ceremony* (1968). Halfway through the film, inexplicably and without warning, Elizabeth Taylor in a violet velvet suit and turban suddenly walks across the screen in front of a wall of sea-green tiles. It is an overcast London day; the steel-gray light makes the violet and green iridescent. This is Elizabeth Taylor at her most vibrant, mysterious, and alluring, at the peak of her mature fleshy glamour. I happened to be sitting with a male friend, one of the gay aesthetes who had such a profound impact on my imagination. We both cried out at the same time, alarming other theatergoers. This vivid, silent tableau is for me one of the classic scenes in the history of cinema.

Elizabeth Taylor is a creation of show business, within which she has lived since she began as a child star. She has the hyper-reality of a dream vision. Meryl Streep, with her boring decorum, is welcome to her pose of unpretentious working actor. I'll take trashy, glitzy Old Hollywood any day. Elizabeth Taylor, heartily eating, drinking, lusting, laughing, cursing, changing husbands, and buying diamonds by the barrel, is a personality on the grand scale. She is a monarch in an age of glum liberals. As a star, she has, unlike Greta Garbo, Marlene Dietrich, and Katharine Hepburn, no sexual ambiguity in her persona. Earthy and sensual, passionate and willful, yet tender and empathetic, Elizabeth Taylor is woman in her many lunar phases, admired by all the world.

ROCK AS ART

Rock is eating its young. Rock musicians are America's most wasted natural resource.

Popular music and film are the two great art forms of the twentieth century. In the past twenty-five years, cinema has gained academic prestige. Film courses are now a standard part of the college curriculum and grants are routinely available to noncommercial directors.

But rock music has yet to win the respect it deserves as the authentic voice of our time. Where rock goes, democracy follows. The dark poetry and surging

[*The New York Times,* April 16, 1992]

Dionysian rhythms of rock have transformed the consciousness and permanently altered the sensoriums of two generations of Americans born after World War Two.

Rock music should not be left to the Darwinian laws of the marketplace. This natively American art form deserves national support. Foundations, corporations and Federal and state agencies that award grants in the arts should take rock musicians as seriously as composers and sculptors. Colleges and universities should designate special scholarships for talented rock musicians. Performers who have made fortunes out of rock are ethically obligated to finance such scholarships or to underwrite independent agencies to support needy musicians.

In rock, Romanticism still flourishes. All the Romantic archetypes of energy, passion, rebellion and demonism are still evident in the brawling, boozing bad boys of rock, storming from city to city on their lusty, groupie-dogged trail.

But the Romantic outlaw must have something to rebel against. The pioneers of rock were freaks, dreamers and malcontents who drew their lyricism and emotional power from the gritty rural traditions of white folk music and African-American blues.

Rock is a victim of its own success. What once signified rebellion is now only a high-school affectation. White suburban youth, rock's main audience, is trapped in creature comforts. Everything comes to them secondhand, through TV. And they no longer have direct contact with folk music and blues, the oral repository of centuries of love, hate, suffering and redemption.

In the Sixties, rock became the dominant musical form in America. And with the shift from singles to albums, which allowed for the marketing of personalities, it also became big business. The gilded formula froze into place. Today, scouts beat the bushes for young talent, squeeze a quick album out of the band, and put them on the road. "New" material is stressed. Albums featuring cover tunes of classics, as in the early Rolling Stones records, are discouraged.

From the moment the Beatles could not hear themselves sing over the shrieking at Shea Stadium in the mid-Sixties, the rock concert format has become progressively less conducive to music-making. The enormous expense of huge sound systems and grandiose special effects has left no room for individualism and improvisation, no opportunity for the performers to respond to a particular audience or to their own moods. The show, with its army of technicians, is as fixed and rehearsed as the Ziegfeld Follies. Furthermore, the concert experience has degenerated. The focus has switched from the performance to raucous partying in the audience.

These days, rock musicians are set upon by vulture managers, who sanitize and repackage them and strip them of their unruly free will. Like sports stars, musicians are milked to the max, then dropped and cast aside when their first album doesn't sell.

Managers offer all the temptations of Mammon to young rock bands: wealth, fame, and easy sex. There is not a single public voice in the culture to say to the musician: You are an artist, not a money machine. Don't sign the contract. Don't tour. Record only when you are ready. Go off on your own, like Jimi Hendrix, and live with your guitar until it becomes part of your body.

How should an artist be trained? Many English rock musicians in the Sixties and early Seventies, including John Lennon and Keith Richards, emerged from art schools. We must tell the young musician: Your peers are other artists, past and future. Don't become a slave to the audience, with its smug hedonism, short attention span and hunger for hits.

Artists should immerse themselves in art. Two decades ago, rock musicians read poetry, studied Hinduism, and drew psychedelic visions in watercolors. For rock to move forward as an art form, our musicians must be given the opportunity for spiritual development. They should be encouraged to read, to look at paintings and foreign films, to listen to jazz and classical music.

Artists with a strong sense of vocation can survive life's disasters and triumphs with their inner lives intact. Our musicians need to be rescued from the carpetbaggers and gold-diggers who attack them when they are young and naïve. Long, productive careers don't happen by chance.

HOMOSEXUALITY AT THE

FIN DE SIÈCLE

Thinking about sex as the century closes, we must give the question of homosexuality centrality. Modern homosexuality is, in my view, a product of the intolerable pressures and repressions of the affluent, ambitious nuclear family, marooned by the breakdown of the vast, multigenerational extended family, still powerful only among the working class.

The fate of masculinity is intimately tied to homosexuality. Worldwide, in Greece and Rome as in the Near East, China, and Japan, pretty boys have usually been considered by men to be as sexually

[*Esquire*, October 1991]

desirable as women. This seems to me perfectly natural. Judeo-Christianity is unusual in finding the practice of boy-love abhorrent.

Exclusive sex or love affairs between adult males is another matter. This phenomenon is so rare, when we consider history as a whole, that it requires explanation. I see two principal kinds of male homosexuality. The first and most ancient is rooted in identification with the mother, perceived as a goddess. The castrated, transvestite priests of Cybele, honored in disco-like rites of orgiastic dance, survive in today's glamourous, flamboyant drag queens.

The second kind of homosexuality represents a turning away from the mother and a heroic rebellion against her omnipotence. Such homosexuality disdains femaleness and esteems perfected masculinity, which it symbolizes in the "hunk," the tautly muscular, arrogantly architectural male form first fully imagined by the Greeks. Greek athletics were a religious spectacle of the beauty of masculinity, formalized in the kouros sculptures that began the Western high-art tradition.

There is nothing deviant or effeminate in this kind of homosexuality. On the contrary, I view the modern gay male as occupying the ultimate point on a track of intensifying masculinity shooting away from the mother, who begins every life story. Gay men and straight men have much more in common than do gay men with lesbians or straight men with straight women. Every man must define his identity against his mother. If he does not, he just falls back into her and is swallowed up. This is the agonizing myth-pattern in the comic, matricidal *Psycho* (1960), one of the hauntingly emblematic films of our time.

Contemporary feminists, who are generally poor or narrowly trained scholars, insist on viewing history as a weepy scenario of male oppression and female victimization. But it ismore accurate to see men, driven by sexual anxiety away from their mothers, forming group alliances by male bonding to create the complex structures of society, art, science, and technology.

Every gay man pursuing another man is recapitulating that civilization-forging movement away from the mother. Lesbians, in contrast, refuse to leave the mother. Gay men may seek sex without emotion; lesbians often end up in emotion without sex. Male homosexuality, pushing outward into risky, alien territory, is progressive and, overall, intellectually stimulating. Lesbianism, seeking a lost state of blissful union with the mother, is cozy, regressive, and, I'm sorry to say, too often intellectually enervating, tending toward the inert.

Male lust, I have written elsewhere, is the energizing factor in culture. Men are the reality principle. They created the world we live in and the luxuries we enjoy. When women cut themselves off from men, they sink backward into psychological and spiritual stagnancy.

When I was young, I thought teenage boys were the most awkward, miserable, antsy, bratty, scuzzy, snickering creatures on God's green earth. Now at midlife and, as it were, *hors de combat,* I see them quite differently. Watching them rampage on the street or at the shopping mall, I find them extraordinarily moving, for they represent the masculine principle struggling to free itself from woman's cosmic dominance.

Teenage boys, goaded by their surging hormones (at maximum strength at this time), run in packs like the primal horde. They have only a brief season of exhilarating liberty between control by their mothers and control by their wives. The agon of male identity springs from men's humiliating sense of dependence upon women. It is women who control the emotional and sexual realms, and men know it.

One of the problems that most vexed me in my meditation on sex is the promiscuity of gay men. Again and again, I was astonished to learn from gay friends of hot spots in notorious toilets at the diner, the bus terminal, or, Minerva help us, the Yale library. What gives? Women, straight or gay, do not make a life-style of offering themselves without cost to random strangers in sleazy public settings.

At last, I saw it. Gay men are guardians of the masculine impulse. To have anonymous sex in a dark alleyway is to pay homage to the dream of male freedom. The unknown stranger is a wandering pagan god. The altar, as in prehistory, is anywhere you kneel. Similarly, straight men who visit prostitutes are valiantly striving to keep sex free from emotion, duty, family—in other words, from society, religion, and procreative Mother Nature.

THE JOY OF

PRESBYTERIAN SEX

Last February, after three years of preparation, the Special Committee on Human Sexuality of the Presbyterian Church (U.S.A.) released a 200-page report, *Keeping Body and Soul Together,* which calls for radical change in traditional Christian attitudes toward sexual behavior and which specifically endorses extramarital relationships and homosexuality. Two members of the committee, disturbed by its liberalism, resigned in protest early in its deliberations. In the months after its release, the report was condemned by conservative individuals and congregations. In June the report was

[*The New Republic,* December 2, 1991]

overwhelmingly rejected (by a vote of 534 to 31) at the 203rd General Assembly of the Presbyterian Church in Baltimore.

Keeping Body and Soul Together offers itself as a profound, compassionate, and expertly researched statement on contemporary sexuality. But it is in fact a repressive, reactionary document. Its language is banal, its ideas simplistic, its view of human nature naïve and sentimental. Above all, its claims of sexual liberalism are false. It reduces the complexities and mysteries of eroticism to a clumsy, outmoded social-welfare ideology. The old-style Protestant suppression of the passions, torments, and untidy physicalities of the body is still abundantly evident in the report, which, in its opening premise of "the basic goodness of sexuality," projects a happy, bouncy vision of human life that would have made Doris Day and Debbie Reynolds—those Fifties blonde divas—proud.

Keeping Body and Soul Together dramatically demonstrates the chaos and intellectual ineptitude in the fashionable liberal discourse on sex that now fills the media and the academic and political worlds. All human problems are blamed on an unjust social system, a "patriarchy" of gigantic and demonized dimensions, blanketing history like a river of molasses. The report paints a grotesque picture of America. "Wife-battering is rampant and almost 40 percent of rapes happen inside heterosexual marriages," it declares. Married women suffer "control and violation through sexualized terror." We hear of "the wife with the blackened eye or broken bones, the rape survivor with semen discernible in her vagina, . . . the new woman on the assembly line whose colleagues drive her from her job by placing snakes in her lunch box each day." There is a lurid, hallucinatory paranoia about contemporary culture, portrayed as passive to the greedy mass media. "Harassment and battering increase daily," proclaims the report, oblivious to the distinction between number of incidents and frequency of reporting. "Sexual violence"—bizarrely dubbed the "incarnational heresy"—takes "diverse forms, many of them not overtly 'sexual,'" including "catcalls, cartoons, snide asides," rock videos, and *Playboy*. Humor, irony, satire, and bawdiness are evidently politically incorrect in the eyes of the new sexual commissars.

The report assails the "influential tradition of radical asceticism" in "Western Christianity" that expresses "body-alienation," "fear of sex and, in particular, of women." It assumes that eremites and monks were not contemplatives but killjoys, neurotics, and misogynists, scowling while the rest of the world caroused, footloose and fancy free. The report complains of "our cultural captivity to a patriarchal model of sexuality and its ethic of sexual control," as if sexual rules and taboos were not prevalent in every culture. There is no sense whatever that asceticism exists in other religions, like Hinduism and Buddhism, where it has the highest spiritual status. There is no reference even to pre-Christian thought in our own tradition: Greco-Roman philosophy regularly addresses moderation, restraint, and abstinence. Socrates, after all, remained chaste through his tempting night with the beautiful Alcibiades.

The committee members seem to have read nothing in their lives but feminist tracts churned out since 1969. Kate Millett and Carolyn Heilbrun, those intellectual giants, are approvingly quoted. Alice Walker is pushed forward to symbolize modern literature. There is no reference to any major writer in history except Dante, whose theory of love is inaccurately and superficially summarized. Naturally, Dante's great episodes of Francesca da Rimini and Brunetto Latini are not mentioned, since these would reveal his actual view of the sins of lust, adultery, and homosexuality.

The report makes saccharine pronouncements ("Sexuality is . . . a form of vulnerability," says one expert) and solves vexing philosophic problems in the blink of an eye: the Christian dualism of body and spirit falsely "sets up an antagonistic relation between these intrinsic and unified components of our personhood." If body and spirit were so obviously unified, we could all move to Tahiti. And where does this reassuring unification leave the soul—dead when the body dies? Apparently, the committee has never heard of Greek metaphors for the conflict between reason and passion, such as Plato's image of charioteer and steeds or, even earlier, the battle between Lapiths and Centaurs on the temple pediment at Olympia.

But there is something deeper at work in the report than

contemporary platitudes and ignorance of world history and culture. It is the revival of the old Protestant ethic, masquerading in hip new clothes. Like so much current feminist ideology, this supposedly liberal statement on sexuality represents not progressive thinking but a throwback to pre-Sixties conventionalism, rigid, narrow, and puritanical. It is a new tyranny of the group, pretending to speak for individuals while it crushes them. Humanitarian jargon phrases are used to pin us in pious attitudes of compulsory brotherhood. The smug, sunny tone of the report reminds me of my enslavement at the hands of elementary-school teachers who, with beaming faces, forced us to sing Christmas carols to auditoriums of beaming parents. The harsh, raunchy cacophony of rock and roll was my generation's answer to all that.

Thirty years ago, as a teenager in upstate New York, I was smouldering with rebellion against what was then the WASP hegemony in American culture. From the Girl Scout troop to the country club, Protestant looks, Protestant manners, Protestant values were the order of the day. In downtown Syracuse, the stately Presbyterian church was not just a religious but a social citadel. Its congregation was the richest and the toniest, a hub of old-guard business networking. To a Catholic, this world was profoundly alien.

The primary problem of Protestantism is word-fixation: Scripture-study is at its heart. No fleshly mediator is needed between the soul and God; no images of saints, Mary, or God are permitted, though portraits of the Good Shepherd began to slip into some denominations within the last century. In highly ritualized Italian and Spanish Catholicism, by contrast, there is a constant, direct appeal to the senses. One of my earliest memories is of staring transfixed at a brightly painted statue in a niche near the altar of my baptismal church: boyishly appealing, prettily posed Saint Sebastian, arrows sticking from his bleeding, seminude body. I interpret the ravishing sadomasochistic sensuality of such iconography as evidence of the ancient, buried paganism of Roman Catholicism. Catholic crucifixes and gory depictions of the martyrdom of ecstatic saints preserve the pagan intuition that our lives in the body are submerged in the Dionysian continuum of pleasure-pain.

...can Protestantism, outside the Evangelical ...atically repressed both sex and emotion as part ... bequest. That repression continues in current ...iberalism, which is simply Protestantism in disguise. ...sbyterian report tries to paper over with words the raw ...iental experiences and conflicts of our mortality. "Eros," says ine report's glossary, is "a zest for life." Is this a soap commercial? Eros, like Dionysus, is a great and dangerous god. The report gives us vanilla sex, smothered with artificial butterscotch syrup. In its liberal zeal to understand, to accept, to heal, it reduces the grand tragicomedy of love and lust to a Hallmark card. Its unctuous normalizing of dissident sex is imperialistic and oppressive. The gay world is stripped of its outlaw adventures in toilets, alleyways, trucks, and orgy rooms. There are no leathermen, hustlers, or drag queens. Gay love is reduced to a nice, neat, middle-class couple moving in next door on *Father Knows Best*. It's *Guess Who's Coming to Dinner?* all over again, with Sidney Poitier, Mr. Smooth and Perfect, recast in gay form. This is censorship in the name of liberal benevolence.

The committee seems to have jumped directly from the soft-spoken, lily-white pre-Freudian WASP world into the strident, petulant post-Freudian feminist camp without doing its homework in between. To understand the dark drama of sex, you must absorb not only Freud, with his crucial theories of aggression, conflict, and ambivalence, but Krafft-Ebing, who catalogs the eternal perversities and crimes of sexual desire. There is a century of rich commentary on sex—including important work by women like Melanie Klein and Karen Horney—that women's studies, mired in the shallow present, has ignored. Above all, to understand sex and emotion, you must study the world history of art, music, and literature, which is the precious record of the strange, kaleidoscopic human imagination. The placid, high-minded thinking of the Presbyterian committee descends from the 1950s, when Freud was still linked to pushy, crass, or bohemian ethnic types. Sexual self-analysis or psychobiography was resisted as vulgar. In the Protestant corporate, managerial way, the report is based instead on the arrogant, condescending welfare-agency model of life: there are all those poor, troubled souls out there

whom we privileged, superior, all-knowing people must
But no one—least of all, liberal Presbyterians—can ever s
the problem of love.

The committee's prescription for an enlightened Christianity is "learning from the marginalized." This new liberal cliché
is repeated so often that I began to misread it as "margarinized."
We are told that "those of us with varying degrees of social power
and status must now move away from the center, so that other,
more marginalized voices . . . may be heard." But the report
picks and chooses its marginalized outcasts as snobbishly as
Proust's Duchesse de Guermantes. We can move tender, safe,
clean, hand-holding gays and lesbians to the center—but not, of
course, pederasts, prostitutes, strippers, pornographers, or sadomasochists. And if we're going to learn from the marginalized,
what about drug dealers, moonshiners, Elvis impersonators,
string collectors, Mafiosi, foot fetishists, serial murderers, can-
nibals, Satanists, and the Ku Klux Klan? I'm sure they'll all
have a lot to say. The committee gets real prudish real fast when
it has to deal with sexuality outside its feminist frame of reference:
"Incest is abhorrent and abhorred," it flatly declares. I wrote in
the margin, "No lobbyists, I guess!"

The committee members seem to have a foggy idea that all
guilt and shame in human life come from either a lack of "loving
full of joyful caring" or from cold patriarchal institutions, those
useless, totalitarian structures that we must, as part of a glorious
"global struggle," dismantle as quickly as possible to achieve a
blissful "egalitarian" society. To which one must reply: go read
King Lear to see the anarchy and wolfishness, the primitive regression that result from a sentimental deconstruction of social institutions. Stormy nature, in our hearts and beyond the gates, is
ready to consume us all. Next read the *Oresteia* to reflect on the
evolution of law and order out of barbarism and vengeful pri-
vatism. The egalitarian fantasy is an Arcadian myth revived and
propagated in the past twenty years by feminist politicos. This
is the kind of nonsense you get when you spend more time reading
fifth-rate contemporary women writers than you do dead white
males like Aeschylus and Shakespeare.

Freud is the deepest thinker on guilt in modern Western

culture. To his intricate analysis of the necessity of instinctual repression in civilized life, we must add anthropology's documentation of the elaborate codes of shame-based cultures. Life without guilt or shame would be found only in sociopaths and the lobotomized. In our culture, guilt may automatically accompany the construction and reinforcement of identity in earliest infancy, from which comes our entire ability to function as autonomous adults. As I got into my car recently on the way to work, I was greeted by a two-year-old neighbor boy who had wandered out of the house without his pants on. Waving cheerfully, he stood on the curb nude from the waist down and with his sister's purse on his arm. Contemplating his enviable happiness, I could not help but reflect that bare-bottomed purse-carrying would be short-lived in his future. But he will gain and not lose identity by his instruction in our particular social codes. Rules governing sex and gender are always relative but are not necessarily authoritarian.

Cultures with what appears to be greater permissiveness about sexual behavior are usually small, tribal, and agricultural, without the economic and technological complexities and advantages of our civilization. What egalitarian feminist ideology fails to realize is that tribal cultures suppress individuality. The group rules. Our distinct, combative, introspective, conflicted, and highly verbal and creative personalities are a product of Western culture. Feminism itself has been produced by Western culture. Even the idea of social reform is Western. The Presbyterian report lunges around crassly, insulting oppressive patriarchy, but it doesn't seem to have a clue about anything in the world outside its own cloyingly contemporary stereotypes. In airy, vacuous New Age tones, it exalts "intimacy and interpersonal communication" without awareness of the unexamined local assumptions in these clichéd terms. Perhaps eroticism has a right to live *without* intimacy and may in fact be most itself, most free in that state. But to come to that view, you would have to study the ancient art of pornography, and that is something the Presbyterian report firmly condemns.

In its laudable desire to remove the stigma from homosexuality, this document follows a strategy of distorting history. The

Seventh Commandment forbidding adultery is never mentioned, while the overwhelming evidence that the Bible condemns homosexuality is blandly argued away, piece by piece. This technique of disinformation has got to stop. Rational claims for social justice, as well as the crucial search for a modern gay identity, cannot rest on lies. We must accept history for what it is, neither lightening nor darkening it to fit a ready-made political agenda. Like the current proponents of academic speech codes, the Presbyterian committee wants to soften, to cushion, to shield minority groups from any rebuff or blow to their self-esteem. Such pampering is ultimately demeaning. Let us hear the worst that can be said, then define and know ourselves in relation to it. Opposition and pressure enlarge and intensify personality. In my opinion, the most powerful, energetic personalities in America are not WASPs but blacks, Jews, and gays, all of whom are in combat with larger, perhaps unconquerable historical forces. Ease and privilege may exact their price in torpor.

The report segues from "justice–love"—its banal, incoherent model for sexual relations—into an orgy of lugubrious soap opera. We are introduced to shy Michelle, who learns she is a lesbian in her college class on sexuality, then begins "blossoming" and meeting "other wonderful people" who are gay. Next there's Fred, a victim of cerebral palsy confined to a wheelchair, who gains "self-esteem" through masturbation with an electric vibrator. And Harold, "permanently on a respirator in the hospital," who wants his wife, Marge, to perform oral sex on him "to express their sexual intimacy" and who gets the chaplain, in a happy ending, to wangle privacy for them. Over all these bathetic tales hover, with their aggressive compassion, the Presbyterian committee members, like Blake's vulture Yahweh smothering the newborn Adam. The hospital as a metaphor for society belongs to a vanished era, the tranquilized 1950s of Confessional poetry, with its strained, silent marriages and nervous breakdowns.

The primary error of the report is its collapsing of the social sphere of life into the overlapping but quite different sexual, spiritual, and emotional sphere. Hinduism, Buddhism, and Christianity all teach us that we are much larger than merely social beings. The Presbyterian report assumes that spirituality is linked to or predicated on social reform. Like many feminists, the committee believes that adjusting the social mechanism, whether through reeducation or passing more regulations, will eliminate the turbulence that is going on between the sexes. But most of the sexual and emotional sphere of life is unreachable by legislation or by verbal formulas of any kind. Christian misogyny cannot be blamed for the suffering of the love-sick Sappho, six centuries before the birth of Christ, or for the humiliation of Catullus, obsessed with the faithless, promiscuous Clodia. Homer's portraits of the femmes fatales Helen, Circe, and Calypso tell us much more about the magic irrationalism of sex than do the bitterly anti-male tracts of current feminism that underlie the Presbyterian report.

Following blindly along the anti-authority track laid down by my generation in its failed rebellion, the report tries to free sex from its delimitation by tradition. But if sex is removed from religious and social institutions, then it must be considered in the context of nature, about which the report is completely silent. In Western culture we already have a complex intellectual critique of nature and sexuality: it's a long argument that begins with Rousseau, with his benevolent mother nature, and continues through the Marquis de Sade, Gautier, Baudelaire, and Swinburne to Oscar Wilde, who brings it to bear on homosexuality. The Presbyterian report waffles, calling sexuality "always culturally encoded" or "socially constructed" on one page and "God's gracious gift" elsewhere. It is a critical confusion.

In this regard, gays have two choices. First, if they want to think of themselves as a distinct group worthy of the special protection of civil rights, they should perhaps accept the Judeo-Christian position that homosexuality is against nature (which has tyrannically designed our bodies for procreation) and then celebrate gay love as a seditious and necessary act of human freedom and imagination, in the Sade, Baudelaire, and Wilde way. The scornful term *breeders*, used by some urban gays about heterosexual couples with children, suggests that this strategy is still possible. Another solution is to blur homosexual and heterosexual desire and to see all of eroticism as a dynamic continuum, in constant flux from hour to hour and day to day. This would logically end in withholding legal recognition from gays as a distinct category but would argue instead for protection of all nonconformist sexual behavior on the pagan grounds of pansexuality. In insisting, for political purposes, on a sharp division between gay and straight, gay activism, like much of feminism, has become as rigid and repressive as the old order it sought to replace.

The Presbyterian report, confronted with conflict, tries to smother it with all-absolving salve. It wants acceptance for its victimized groups without real understanding. The word *gay* is used here in a way that cuts off historical inquiry. It assumes that there has always been a gay class of persons and that they have been uniformly oppressed. I view exclusive homosexuality among adults as a relatively recent phenomenon related to the emergence of the isolated nuclear family, with its destabilized and disintegrating sex roles. Our best tool to chart the internal pressures of bourgeois culture is Freud's theory of family romance—but of course Freud has been consigned to outer darkness by feminism, so his insights were lost to the Presbyterian committee. Instead the report confidently predicts that the ideal future will be "nonpatriarchal" and will function "on a friendship model." In wonderful "countercultural zones," we are told, "Such families will exhibit both closeness and spaciousness, and offer its members room and resources for stretching and growing." Sound familiar? It's the chipper Chamber of Commerce language of a country-club brochure, the authentic voice of 1950s American Protestantism, with its trimmed-lawn view of sex and emotion. Pardon me: I happen to think that Italian opera and African-American rhythm and blues contain the real truth about sex, with its Dionysian energies and ungovernable intensities.

The Presbyterian report is so skittish about the physical facts of our mortal life that it argues, "The tendency in our culture to consider birth children more authentically related to their parents than adopted children are to theirs is rooted in a fundamentally patriarchal understanding of family in which children are seen as possessions." This is Orwellian logic approaching lunacy. Birth children emerge from their mother's body, a primal, concrete, sensory relatedness unconnected to and prior to patriarchy. In its political scheme, the Presbyterian report exalts love but represses biology, through which love gains material expression. Though in the uncontroversial section on adolescence there is a fleeting reference to drastic hormonal changes, the only sex differences the report admits are those that make woman the victim of men—when she is in fact their mysterious creator, eerily dominating world mythology.

The report is so eager to argue away the inconvenient facts of Christian morality about sex that one has to ask the committee members, Why remain Christian at all? Why not leave Judeo-Christianity for our other great Western tradition, the Greco-Roman, in which philosophic discourse about ethics is possible without reference to a transcendental deity? As a lapsed Catholic of wavering sexual orientation, I have never understood the pressure for ordination of gay clergy or even the creation of gay Catholic groups. They seem to me to indicate a need for parental approval, an inability to take personal responsibility for one's own identity. The institutional religions, Catholic and Protestant, carry with them the majesty of history. Their theology is impressive and coherent. Efforts to revise or dilute that theology for present convenience seem to me misguided. My generation left its own society and religion behind in its quest for expanded consciousness. This self-reliant lesson of the 1960s has not been fully absorbed.

We are living, at the close of the second Christian millennium, in a Hellenistic era, cosmopolitan, diverse, eclectic. Syncretism may be our lot. The Presbyterian report, so mawkish and muddled, dramatizes the pressing need for education in the great world religions, the repository of thousands of years of spiritual experience and wisdom. When feminism and gay activism set themselves against organized religion, they have the obligation to put something better in its place. Hostile intrusions into church services, as undertaken by gay groups in New York and Philadelphia, are infantile, damaging the image of gays and bringing their cause into disrepute. All sacred spaces, pagan or Christian, should be honored, not because there is or is not a God but because these are quiet points of contact between the individual and the macrocosm. Gays must face the fact that, unlike other minority groups, they cannot reproduce themselves. Like artists, their only continuity is through culture, which they have been instrumental in building. Therefore when, by guerrilla tactics, they attack the institutions of culture (including religion), they are sabotaging their own future.

While I was reading the Presbyterian report, the Rolling Stones' "Sympathy for the Devil" came on the radio. As I listened to its jaunty epic saga of a force of evil spiraling through history, inciting riots, wars, and assassinations, I was struck by how much more truthful the song seemed than the document before me, with its optimistic patter about "empowerment" and "mutuality" and its blissful obliviousness to human perversity. The Presbyterian committee, seeing evil only in institutions and society rather than in our hearts, strips from us the possibility of heroic conflict. The saints, many of them women, warred with themselves as well as God. The body has its own animal urges, just as there are attractions and repulsions in sex that modern liberalism cannot face.

Virtually everything the Presbyterian report says about society is wrong. Our problem is not patriarchy but, in the urban industrialized world, collapsing manhood, which male homosexuality properly remedies by its glamourous cult of the masculine. The report laments "the erosion of intimacy." Alas, we have not too little intimacy but too much. Once there was the world of men and the world of women. Now the sexes, freely mingling, know each other too well, and both have lost their allure. In this twilight zone, gays should be freethinkers, self-created and self-sustained, hostile to dogma even among themselves. There may never be a world in which gay men are completely tolerated and in which women are completely safe. We must learn to accept limitation, duality, paradox. The culture has split but not fragmented. In an ideal syncretism, all institutions would be strengthened and honored, from the sex industry, with its pornographic pagan truths, to organized religion, with its austere, enduring legacy.

THE BEAUTIFUL

DECADENCE

OF ROBERT MAPPLETHORPE

A RESPONSE TO ROCHELLE GURSTEIN

Rochelle Gurstein is absolutely correct in her diagnosis of the ineptitude, sanctimony, and crass politicizing of last year's campaign by liberals and activists on behalf of Robert Mapplethorpe. However, I disagree with her in her negative assessment of Mapplethorpe's talent and cultural significance. In this essay, I will comment on Gurstein's vigorous critique and give my own view of Mapplethorpe, whom I consider my spiritual brother.

First of all, the struggle between radical or avant-garde artists and writers against a conservative estab-

[*Tikkun*, November/December 1991]

lishment does not, as Gurstein says, date from "the close of the nineteenth century." It is the inner dynamic of Romanticism itself, a movement that began over 200 years ago and still has not run its course. We see this pattern of cultural combat in the abortive public career of the Marquis de Sade, whose writings were banned, or the younger English High Romantic poets, who died in exile. It is in the official judicial censoring of Baudelaire's *Les Fleurs du mal* and in the public outcry over Whitman's *Leaves of Grass,* Swinburne's *Poems and Ballads,* and Oscar Wilde's homoerotic *The Picture of Dorian Gray.* In the visual arts, the battle in Paris between bohemian painters and the old-guard Salon juries was formalized by the middle of the nineteenth century, although the Romantic desire to affront and scandalize is visible as early as 1826, in Delacroix's lushly pornographic *Death of Sardanapalus.*

Gurstein's curt denial that Mapplethorpe's sadomasochistic photos shock in the manner of Manet's notorious *Le Déjeuner sur l'herbe* (1863) seems to me unsupported and unpersuasive. Manet's innovations in that painting, it can be argued, are precisely parallel to Mapplethorpe's. While rosy nudity was permissible in academic Salon paintings of Greek and Roman themes, the flat, sallow flesh tones of Manet's nude female picnicker disturbed first viewers by a harsh contemporary realism and immediacy. There is no attempt to soften or idealize. This sexual flesh is frankly available and unromanticized. The casual air with which Manet juxtaposes brazen open-air nudity with the raffish workaday costume of the two young intellectuals, lost in discourse, is exactly the tone of many of Mapplethorpe's photos, where libertines pose in relaxed moods amid the bizarre discontinuities of their sexual underworld. The original shock of Manet's painting is surely reproduced, with the greater explicitness of our age, in Mapplethorpe's extraordinary photograph, *Man in Polyester Suit,* with its large black penis poking from an otherwise fully clothed torso. Finally, Manet goaded respectable sensibilities by the cool, appraising look on the face of his nude woman, who, like his self-possessed courtesan Olympia, meets our eyes without apology or embarrassment. She is practical, efficient, a bawdy woman of the world who knows her market value. She has, I submit, the same unsentimental sexual efficiency as Mapplethorpe's jaunty, jaded sadomasochists.

I agree with Gurstein that the defense of Mapplethorpe piously and sometimes hysterically invoked the terminology of old avant-garde combat in a way no longer applicable to a society that, as she says, "now tolerates and even encourages explicit images and inordinate amounts of talk about sex." The avant-garde tradition was terminated in the Sixties by pop art, which closed the gap between high and low culture. The art world since then has, in my view, sunk into naked hucksterism and puerile mini-fads, a toy-train rat race of mediocrity and irrelevance. American creative energy is flowing instead into popular culture, which is sweeping the world. Mapplethorpe's distinction is that he revived the idea of the avant-garde at a moment when it seemed buried forever. He showed that there are still deep cultural taboos for the serious artist to expose. In this respect, he has nothing in common with people like Karen Finley and Holly Hughes, who pretend to be avant-garde but who are just peddling tired twenty-year-old feminist clichés.

Gurstein asks why, if "the forces of reaction" were as threatening as some liberals claim, there were no conservative protests prior to the Mapplethorpe show at the Corcoran Art Gallery in Washington. America, unlike England and France, suffers from a split between its cultural and political capitals. What goes on in small private galleries or even the Whitney Museum in New York is not likely to register on the national political radar screen. Most people in the country have a low opinion of New York City and don't give a hoot about what's going on there—a fact to which arrogant Manhattanites, inside and outside the media, are completely oblivious. New York, like San Francisco and Los Angeles, occupies its own mental zone.

As for the Mapplethorpe show at the Institute of Contemporary Art in Philadelphia, I can speak to that, since I attended it. First of all, the Institute is on the grounds of a private academic institution, the University of Pennsylvania. Secondly, it was very difficult to find, recessed like a burrow at the edge of a huge, crowded, leafy quadrangle. The hidden, removed placement of the show seemed to fit it exactly. I had a feeling of entering Pompeii's Villa of the Mysteries. It was a descent to the nether realm, from which one emerged blinking in the sunlight.

The small, informal Institute of Contemporary Art was the ideal setting for Mapplethorpe's photographs. The majestic Corcoran Gallery, one block from the White House, was not. Official Washington, whether we like it or not, is the nation's public stage, the site of its historical identity and highest political values. Visitors—citizens or foreigners—know perfectly well they are touring a theater set. Mapplethorpe was an avant-garde outsider, a sexual outlaw, a night rider. It dilutes him to enshrine him in a national landmark. For me, one of the supreme moments in contemporary art was the night protest that projected slides of Mapplethorpe's pictures against the wall of the Corcoran. There is Mapplethorpe's essence, his spectral identity as a suffering Romantic artist forever outside the pale. The demonstration ingeniously replayed, without knowing it, the cinema of Blake's great poem "London," where solitary, excluded voices smear or mar the cold stone walls of society's institutions.

Let me offer an analogy from my own life. The Philadelphia Museum of Art, that grand Greek temple dominating the city's sightlines from river and parkway, has most graciously allowed photographers from various magazines to take my picture in its galleries. When *Playboy* recently asked about possible settings for a photo shoot, I automatically suggested the museum. The museum's public relations department agreed as usual but then, a day later, called the magazine to say it had been overruled from above. *Playboy* was somewhat miffed to be denied access, but I, after an initial moment of surprise, was pleased, even exhilarated. Both *Playboy* and the Philadelphia Museum of Art gain by their mutual exclusion. Each is an American institution, with its own tradition and destiny. A strong, vigorous society has the will and ability to draw lines, to make demarcations, to set limits. Identity thrives by conflict and opposition.

Gurstein next says "most" of Mapplethorpe's photographs are "unexceptional" and fall within the "mainstream" of contemporary art. She cites as an example his "high-contrast, artsy" portraits of celebrities, which she rightly says would be at home in "tony magazines" like *Vogue* and *Vanity Fair*. But chic upscale magazines are hardly the "mainstream" of contemporary art, which likes to adopt hip gestures of funky pseudo-leftism. Later,

Gurstein again dismisses this important element of Mapplethorpe's photos: "To make something 'fashionable' guarantees
that it most definitely will not be taken seriously." I disagree.
The fashionable style has its own powerful history in Western,
as in Chinese and Japanese, art. It is glossy, artificial, sophisticated, the aristocratic pose of "late" or decadent phases of style.
We see it in bas-reliefs of New Kingdom Egypt, in Hellenistic
sculpture, in Roman imperial busts, in the Mannerist paintings
of Bronzino, Pontormo, and El Greco, in the stylized portraits of
Ingres, Romaine Brooks, and Tamara de Lempicka.

Mapplethorpe has a long and varied artistic lineage. Like
me, he was also an admirer of Andy Warhol, whose silver-lined
Factory overflowing with tramps, studs, transvestites, and Superstars I regarded, from the far distance of an upstate New York
college, as my spiritual home in the Sixties. Warhol, Mapplethorpe, and I were born and raised Catholic. The Warhol cult
of celebrity is a transposition of Catholic iconography, with gilded
saints become glittering stars. I see this erotic process of modern
idolatry as an eruption of Catholicism's ancient, latent paganism.

Gurstein dismisses Mapplethorpe's flower photographs as,
to use my word, conventional. I heartily concur. I find the flower
pictures insipid, formulaic, and uninspired, compared to Georgia
O'Keeffe's menacingly turgid and authentically sexual studies of
the same theme. Mapplethorpe is too timid here. For consistency
with his other work, he should have given us real *fleurs du mal*,
poison flowers straight out of Joris-Karl Huysmans's *Against Nature*, with its seething, primeval hothouse garden. Huysmans, with
his peculiar, over-ripe French, successfully creates in words the
biomorphic analogies that Mapplethorpe only reaches for. The
soft, shapely penises of Mapplethorpe's photos are far more fully
seen and rendered as organic presences than his effete, too-pretty
flowers, which wouldn't turn a hair in Phyllis Schlafly's kitchen.

Gurstein raises the question of "violent sex" in Mapplethorpe's photos and laments the fact that "stark records of sexual
violence have come to qualify as art." But very few of the photos
do in fact directly depict such violence, which is in any case
central to the tradition of Christian art, with its bloody, seminude,
tortured saints in transports of martyrdom. Crucifixes in Medi-

terranean and Mexican Catholicism have a sensual, writhing, polychrome violence that Mapplethorpe, with his calm, austere black and white, never came near. In short, Mapplethorpe's photos cannot be dismissed on the grounds of violence alone.

However, Gurstein rightly showers contempt on the efforts by "experts" at the Cincinnati trial to laud things like "the centrality of the forearm" in a Mapplethorpe photo of one man "fisting" another. I agree that such obtuse attempts to aestheticize intentionally shocking content are, as Gurstein puts it, "insults to common sense." It injures Mapplethorpe to whitewash him, to deny his cunningly perverse motives, to turn him into a gay Norman Rockwell. I have been heavily influenced by the art for art's sake tradition, created by Gautier and descending through Walter Pater to Oscar Wilde. But pure aestheticism of the abstract-tending Whistler kind has only a limited application to Mapplethorpe, who more closely resembles Baudelaire in his conscious fusion of cool, classical form and squalid, decadent, in-your-face content. Mapplethorpe's offhand comment about the beauty of his photo of "a guy with a finger up a cock" should be taken with a grain of salt. As my mentor Harold Bloom has intricately demonstrated, artists cannot be trusted in remarks about their own work or that of their rivals or predecessors. Such statements are merely strategies in a larger game.

The obsequiousness to amnesiac formalism has stripped Mapplethorpe of his ultimate meanings. We must frankly face the mutilations and horrors in Mapplethorpe's sexual world and stop trying to blandly argue them away as fun and frolics of "an alternative lifestyle." His grim sadomasochists are not lovable, boppy Venice Beach eccentrics on roller skates. Gurstein correctly speaks of the "brutality" and "degradation" in Mapplethorpe's pictures. Degradation is at the heart of his eroticism. To deny the degradation in the photos of one man urinating into the mouth of another is to remove all their erotic charge. Such acts have never been sanctioned in any culture. This is why they are now and will remain radical.

It is foolish and naïve to claim, as has repeatedly been done, that the discomforting or painful features of Mapplethorpe's sexual tastes reflect the unjust oppression of a homophobic society.

This reduces Mapplethorpe's work to a tedious, one-issue, social-welfare activism; it imprisons him in the contemporary; it destroys him as an artist. I would argue, on the contrary, that the stringent sexual repressions and yet high sensory stimulation of Catholicism gave Robert Mapplethorpe his special vision; these tensions and limitations allowed him to look directly into universal sexual reality. He saw and accepted the cruelty and aggression in our animal nature, our unevolved link with the pagan and primeval past. Mapplethorpe was not a liberal. Sadomasochism is not liberal. It is rigorously hierarchical and coldly ritualistic. In my analysis of history, sadomasochism always returns when moral codes and social institutions weaken. It returns because it is our deepest nature. Mapplethorpe's liberal supporters do not understand him. His work is a scandal to all their progressive humanitarian ideals.

Gurstein, more honestly than Mapplethorpe's apologists, confronts the obvious sexual facts of the photographs: human beings reduced to "the status of things" (as, I would add, in barbarous prehistory), turned into "living fetishes," like the man half-mummified and near-asphyxiated in a sealed black rubber bodysuit. The desolate sexual personae of these horror-show scenarios quest for metaphysical truth. Mere physical gratification is no longer the issue. Sadomasochism is a sacred cult, a pagan religion that reveals the dark secrets of nature. The bondage of sadomasochism expresses our own bondage by the body, our subservience to its brute laws, concealed by our myths of romantic love. Mapplethorpe's work, like Swinburne's, demolishes the liberal world-view, with its optimistic faith in benevolent, egalitarian social and sexual relationships.

Gurstein correctly exposes the indulgent, sentimental nonsense that has been said and written about Robert Mapplethorpe. The intrusion of strident liberal politics into the assessment of Mapplethorpe has done a great disservice to this remarkable artist. I was outraged, for example, at an early *Nightline* program on the controversy in which the ABC correspondent ostentatiously posed in a room lined with propped-up examples of Mapplethorpe's photos of black men. It was a blatantly biased attempt to suggest that Jesse Helms's opposition to Mapplethorpe was simply racially motivated. I continued to be outraged, as weeks and then months passed, by the suppression in sympathetic media reports of the most horrific of Mapplethorpe's pictures. Gurstein describes one of them as a "before-and-after picture" of a man's genitals trapped and protruding from three holes in a wooden plank like a "guillotine." She neglects to say that blood is spattered like paint all over it. When I first saw this grisly, almost incomprehensible photograph in Philadelphia, I was stunned and overwhelmed. It seemed to symbolize everything I had found in the turbulent sexual history of mankind and tried to express in my own book. Mapplethorpe, in his life and his work, shows the harsh truths faced by our Sixties generation, whose quest for sexual freedom ended in disaster. It is nature, not society, that is our greatest oppressor.

I have loved Robert Mapplethorpe ever since I saw his bleak, half-transvestite portrait of Patti Smith, posing like an anorexic Frank Sinatra on her first album, *Horses* (1975). I think it is one of the greatest pictures ever taken of a woman. I esteem Mapplethorpe for his learned recapitulation of the history of art, his allusions to and corruption of classic and Renaissance style. As an heir to the gay artist Tom of Finland and the German photographer Helmut Newton, he sees the hard, militant, sculptural quality of Western personality, which tends toward the imperialistic and fascist. He unites sharp-edged Apollonian form with melting Dionysian content. In his celebrations of homoerotic beauty, which is one of the most ancient and enduring inspirations of Western art, Mapplethorpe retrains our eye to see the penis and scrotum at their real size. Male genitals, except in outlandish comic orgy scenes in Greek art, have never before been so truthfully integrated into the high-art tradition. I accept Mapplethorpe as a pornographer, but for me Donatello, Michelangelo, and Caravaggio were also pornographers. I do not think Mapplethorpe ever produced a masterpiece, but then neither did another of my favorite artists, Dante-Gabriel Rossetti. I believe that, in the general emptiness of the present art world, Robert Mapplethorpe's photographs will indeed live on to eloquently represent the modern imagination at the *fin de siècle*.

THE STRANGE CASE OF

CLARENCE THOMAS

AND ANITA HILL

Anita Hill is no feminist heroine. A week ago, in the tense climax of the Senate Judiciary Committee's hearings into the nomination of Clarence Thomas to the Supreme Court, the important issue of sexual harassment, one of the solid innovations of contemporary feminism, was used and abused for political purposes.

In an atrocious public spectacle worthy of the show trials of a totalitarian regime, uncorroborated allegations about verbal exchanges ten years old were paraded on the nation's television screens. The Judiciary Committee should have thoroughly investigated

[*Philadelphia Inquirer,* October 21, 1991]

the charges but conducted the proceedings privately. It was an appalling injustice to both Anita Hill and Clarence Thomas to pit them and their supporters against each other. The Senate turned itself into the Roman Colosseum, with decadent, jaded patricians waving thumbs down over a blood-drenched arena.

Five years ago, because of the absence of a sexual harassment policy at my university, I initiated a workshop on the question in my women's studies class. I collected sexual harassment guidelines and documents from Philadelphia-area universities, distributed them to the class, and guided the formulation of proposals, which we presented to the dean. Such guidelines are crucial not only to warn potential offenders but to help women stand their ground in specific encounters. In our democratic society, however, we must also protect the rights of the accused. Frivolous claims of misconduct do occur.

I listened carefully to Anita Hill's testimony at the Senate hearings. I found her to be sincere and intelligent. But I reject her claim of sexual harassment. What exactly transpired between her and Clarence Thomas we can never know. That Hill was distressed by references to sex may indeed be the case. But since they were never threatening and never led to pressure for a date, I fail to see how they constitute sexual harassment. Many religious men, as well as women, find conversations about sex or pornography inappropriate and unacceptable. This is not a gender issue. It is our personal responsibility to define what we will and will not tolerate.

The sexual revolution of my Sixties generation broke the ancient codes of decorum that protected respectable ladies from profanation by foul language. We demanded an end to the double standard. What troubles me about the "hostile workplace" category of sexual harassment policy is that women are being returned to their old status of delicate flowers who must be protected from assault by male lechers. It is anti-feminist to ask for special treatment for women.

America is still burdened by its Puritan past, which erupts again and again in public scenarios of sexual inquisition, as in Hawthorne's *The Scarlet Letter*. If Anita Hill was thrown for a loop by sexual banter, that's her problem. If by the age of twenty-six, as a graduate of the Yale Law School, she could find no convincing way to signal her displeasure and disinterest, that's her deficiency. We cannot rely on rigid rules and regulations to structure everything in our lives. There is a blurry line between our professional and private selves. We are sexual beings, and as Freud demonstrated, eroticism pervades every aspect of our consciousness.

Hill woodenly related the content of conversations without any reference to their context or tone. The senators never asked about joking, smiles, facial expressions, hers as well as his. Every social encounter is a game being played by two parties. I suspect Hill's behavior was compliant and, to use her own word about a recent exchange with a Thomas friend, "passive." Judging by her subsequent cordial behavior toward Thomas, Hill chose to put her career interests above feminist principle. She went along to get along. Hence it is hypocritical of her, ten years later, to invoke feminist principle when she did not have the courage to stand on it before. For feminists to make a heroine out of Hill is to insult all those other women who have taken a bolder, more confrontational course and forfeited career advantage.

In this case, the sexual harassment issue was a smoke screen, cynically exploited to serve another issue, abortion rights. Although I am firmly pro-choice, I think there should be no single-issue litmus test for nominees to the Supreme Court. And the strategy backfired. Thomas, who had seemed bland and evasive for the prior hundred days of the hearings, emerged under fire with vastly increased stature. He was passionate, forceful, dignified.

Make no mistake: it was not a White House conspiracy that saved this nomination. It was Clarence Thomas himself. After eight hours of Hill's testimony, he was driven as low as any man could be. But step by step, with sober, measured phrases, he regained his position and turned the momentum against his accusers. It was one of the most powerful moments I have ever witnessed on television. Giving birth to himself, Thomas reenacted his own credo of the self-made man.

RAPE AND

MODERN SEX WAR

Rape is an outrage that cannot be tolerated in civilized society. Yet feminism, which has waged a crusade for rape to be taken more seriously, has put young women in danger by hiding the truth about sex from them.

In dramatizing the pervasiveness of rape, feminists have told young women that before they have sex with a man, they must give consent as explicit as a legal contract's. In this way, young women have been convinced that they have been the victims of rape. On elite campuses in the Northeast and on the

[*New York Newsday,* January 27, 1991]

West Coast, they have held consciousness-raising sessions, peti-
tioned administrations, demanded inquests. At Brown University, outraged, panicky "victims" have scrawled the names of
alleged attackers on the walls of women's rest rooms. What mar-
ital rape was to the Seventies, "date rape" is to the Nineties.

The incidence and seriousness of rape do not require this
kind of exaggeration. Real acquaintance rape is nothing new. It
has been a horrible problem for women for all of recorded history.
Once fathers and brothers protected women from rape. Once the
penalty for rape was death. I come from a fierce Italian tradition
where, not so long ago in the motherland, a rapist would end up
knifed, castrated, and hung out to dry.

But the old clans and small rural communities have broken
down. In our cities, on our campuses far from home, young
women are vulnerable and defenseless. Feminism has not prepared them for this. Feminism keeps saying the sexes are the
same. It keeps telling women they can do anything, go anywhere,
say anything, wear anything. No, they can't. Women will always
be in sexual danger.

One of my male students recently slept overnight with a
friend in a passageway of the Great Pyramid in Egypt. He described the moon and sand, the ancient silence and eerie echoes.
I will never experience that. I am a woman. I am not stupid
enough to believe I could ever be safe there. There is a world of
solitary adventure I will never have. Women have always known
these somber truths. But feminism, with its pie-in-the-sky fantasies about the perfect world, keeps young women from seeing
life as it is.

We must remedy social injustice whenever we can. But there
are some things we cannot change. There are sexual differences
that are based in biology. Academic feminism is lost in a fog of
social constructionism. It believes we are totally the product of
our environment. This idea was invented by Rousseau. He was
wrong. Emboldened by dumb French language theory, academic
feminists repeat the same hollow slogans over and over to each
other. Their view of sex is naïve and prudish. Leaving sex to the
feminists is like letting your dog vacation at the taxidermist's.

The sexes are at war. Men must struggle for identity against the overwhelming power of their mothers. Women have menstruation to tell them they are women. Men must do or risk something to be men. Men become masculine only when other men say they are. Having sex with a woman is one way a boy becomes a man.

College men are at their hormonal peak. They have just left their mothers and are questing for their male identity. In groups, they are dangerous. A woman going to a fraternity party is walking into Testosterone Flats, full of prickly cacti and blazing guns. If she goes, she should be armed with resolute alertness. She should arrive with girlfriends and leave with them. A girl who lets herself get dead drunk at a fraternity party is a fool. A girl who goes upstairs alone with a brother at a fraternity party is an idiot. Feminists call this "blaming the victim." I call it common sense.

For a decade, feminists have drilled their disciples to say, "Rape is a crime of violence but not of sex." This sugar-coated Shirley Temple nonsense has exposed young women to disaster. Misled by feminism, they do not expect rape from the nice boys from good homes who sit next to them in class.

Aggression and eroticism are deeply intertwined. Hunt, pursuit, and capture are biologically programmed into male sexuality. Generation after generation, men must be educated, refined, and ethically persuaded away from their tendency toward anarchy and brutishness. Society is not the enemy, as feminism ignorantly claims. Society is woman's protection against rape. Feminism, with its solemn Carry Nation repressiveness, does not see what is for men the eroticism or fun element in rape, especially the wild, infectious delirium of gang rape. Women who do not understand rape cannot defend themselves against it.

The date-rape controversy shows feminism hitting the wall of its own broken promises. The women of my Sixties generation were the first respectable girls in history to swear like sailors, get drunk, stay out all night—in short, to act like men. We sought total sexual freedom and equality. But as time passed, we woke up to cold reality. The old double standard protected women. When anything goes, it's women who lose.

Today's young women don't know what they want. They

see that feminism has not brought sexual happiness. The theatrics of public rage over date rape are their way of restoring the old sexual rules that were shattered by my generation. Because nothing about the sexes has really changed. The comic film *Where the Boys Are* (1960), the ultimate expression of Fifties man-chasing, still speaks directly to our time. It shows smart, lively women skillfully anticipating and fending off the dozens of strategies with which horny men try to get them into bed. The agonizing date-rape subplot and climax are brilliantly done. The victim, Yvette Mimieux, makes mistake after mistake, obvious to the other girls. She allows herself to be lured away from her girlfriends and into isolation with boys whose character and intentions she misreads. *Where the Boys Are* tells the truth. It shows courtship as a dangerous game in which the signals are not verbal but subliminal.

Neither militant feminism, which is obsessed with politically correct language, nor academic feminism, which believes that knowledge and experience are "constituted by" language, can understand preverbal or nonverbal communication. Feminism, focusing on sexual politics, cannot see that sex exists in and through the body. Sexual desire and arousal cannot be fully translated into verbal terms. This is why men and women misunderstand each other.

Trying to remake the future, feminism cut itself off from sexual history. It discarded and suppressed the sexual myths of literature, art, and religion. Those myths show us the turbulence, the mysteries and passions of sex. In mythology we see men's sexual anxiety, their fear of woman's dominance. Much sexual violence is rooted in men's sense of psychological weakness toward women. It takes many men to deal with one woman. Woman's voracity is a persistent motif. Clara Bow, it was rumored, took on the USC football team on weekends. Marilyn Monroe, singing "Diamonds Are a Girl's Best Friend," rules a conga line of men in tuxes. Half-clad Cher, in the video for "If I Could Turn Back Time," deranges a battleship of screaming sailors and straddles a pink-lit cannon. Feminism, coveting social power, is blind to woman's cosmic sexual power.

To understand rape, you must study the past. There never was and never will be sexual harmony. Every woman must take personal responsibility for her sexuality, which is nature's red flame. She must be prudent and cautious about where she goes and with whom. When she makes a mistake, she must accept the consequences and, through self-criticism, resolve never to make that mistake again. Running to Mommy and Daddy on the campus grievance committee is unworthy of strong women. Posting lists of guilty men in the toilet is cowardly, infantile stuff.

The Italian philosophy of life espouses high-energy confrontation. A male student makes a vulgar remark about your breasts? Don't slink off to whimper and simper with the campus shrinking violets. Deal with it. On the spot. Say, "Shut up, you jerk! And crawl back to the barnyard where you belong!" In general, women who project this take-charge attitude toward life get harassed less often. I see too many dopey, immature, self-pitying women walking around like melting sticks of butter. It's the Yvette Mimieux syndrome: make me happy. And listen to me weep when I'm not.

The date-rape debate is already smothering in propaganda churned out by the expensive Northeastern colleges and universities, with their overconcentration of boring, uptight academic feminists and spoiled, affluent students. Beware of the deep manipulativeness of rich students who were neglected by their parents. They love to turn the campus into hysterical psychodramas of sexual transgression, followed by assertions of parental authority and concern. And don't look for sexual enlightenment from academe, which spews out mountains of books but never looks at life directly.

As a fan of football and rock music, I see in the simple, swaggering masculinity of the jock and in the noisy posturing of the heavy-metal guitarist certain fundamental, unchanging truths about sex. Masculinity is aggressive, unstable, combustible. It is also the most creative cultural force in history. Women must reorient themselves toward the elemental powers of sex, which can strengthen or destroy.

The only solution to date rape is female self-awareness and self-control. A woman's number one line of defense is herself. When a real rape occurs, she should report it to the police. Complaining to college committees because the courts "take too long" is ridiculous. College administrations are not a branch of the judiciary. They are not equipped or trained for legal inquiry. Colleges must alert incoming students to the problems and dangers of adulthood. Then colleges must stand back and get out of the sex game.

THE RAPE DEBATE,

CONTINUED

A selection of my public remarks about the issue of rape, in the year following the appearance of my op-ed piece on date rape in *Newsday*.

———

I wrote the following letter to the editor of *The New York Times Magazine* in response to a column by Susan Jacoby criticizing my view of rape (May 19; June 9, 1991).

I'm sure Susan Jacoby means well, but I must correct her simplistic caricature of my position on date rape, upon which I have been writing and speaking extensively. First of all, I am not, as she claims, an "antifeminist." I am a feminist who wants to radically reform current feminism, to bring it back to common sense about life.

Jacoby's article is a good example of the warm, fuzzy, genteel thinking about sex that has been emanating for twenty years from privileged, white, middle-class feminists. The dream man in this scenario is literate, sensitive, introspective, cooperative. Such men are a minority in America, much less in the world. Intelligent, ambitious, but overprotected young women, brainwashed by this view of life, are arriving at college and screaming bloody murder when reality doesn't jibe with their expectations.

When I entered college in 1964, women were locked in the dorm at 11:00 P.M. My generation rebelled against and shattered these paternalistic rules. But with freedom come risk and responsibility. We accepted the risk in order to explore and learn about life. My kind of feminism stresses independence and personal responsibility for women.

Blaming the victim makes perfect sense if the victim has behaved stupidly. I doubt that Susan Jacoby would leave her purse on the street or sleep with her doors wide open at night. Theft, rape, and murder are facts of life in large societies, except in police states.

Feminism has got to wake up and look at life as it is. Sex is a dark and turbulent power that may not be controllable by pat verbal formulas and chirpy hopes.

———

From interview with David Talbot, the *San Francisco Examiner*, July 7, 1991.

Dating is a very recent phenomenon in world history. Throughout history, women have been chaperoned. As late as 1964, when I arrived in college, we had strict rules. We had to be in the dorm under lock and key by eleven o'clock. My generation was the one that broke these rules. We said, "We want freedom— no more double standard!" When I went to stay at a male friend's apartment in New York, my aunts flew into a frenzy: "You can't do that, it's dangerous!" But I said, "No, we're not going to be like that anymore." Still, we understood in the Sixties that we were taking a risk.

Today, these young women want the freedom that we won, but they don't want to acknowledge the risk. That's the problem. The minute you go out with a man, the minute you go to a bar to have a drink, there is a risk. You have to accept the fact that part of the sizzle of sex comes from the danger of sex. You can be overpowered.

So it is woman's personal responsibility to be aware of the dangers of the world. But these young feminists today are deluded. They come from a protected, white, middle-class world, and they expect everything to be safe. Notice it's not black or Hispanic women who are making a fuss about this—they come from cultures that are fully sexual and they are fully realistic about sex. But these other women are sexually repressed girls, coming out of pampered homes, and when they arrive at these colleges and suddenly hit male lust, they go, "Oh, no!"

These girls say, "Well, I should be able to get drunk at a fraternity party and go upstairs to a guy's room without anything happening." And I say, "Oh, really? And when you drive your car to New York City, do you leave your keys on the hood?" My point is that if your car is stolen after you do something like that, yes, the police should pursue the thief and he should be punished. But at the same time, the police— and I—have the right to say to you, "You stupid idiot, what the hell were you thinking?"

I mean, wake up to reality. This is male sex. Guess what, it's hot. Male sex is hot. There's an attraction between the sexes that we're not totally in control of. The idea that we can regulate it by passing campus grievance committee rules is madness. My kind of feminism stresses personal responsibility. I've never been raped, but I've been very vigilant—I'm constantly reading the signals. If I ever got into a dating situation where I was overpowered and raped, I would say, "Oh, well, I misread the signals." But I don't think I would ever press charges.

The girl in the Kennedy rape case is an idiot. You go back to the Kennedy compound late at night and you're surprised at what happens? She's the one who should be charged—with ignorance. Because everyone knows that Kennedy is spelled S-E-X. Give me a break, this is not rape. And it's going to erode the real outrage that we should feel about actual rape. This is just overprivileged people saying they want the world to be a bowl of cherries. Guess what? It's not and it never will be.

———

From article on date rape in *YM* magazine, September 1991. Various "experts" were asked the same questions. My replies were 180 degrees opposed to the others.

Is it rape if you don't say no?
Absolutely not. This kind of thing is turning women into jokes. All the responsibility is being shunted onto men. And besides, it's ridiculous to think that saying no always means no. We all know how it goes in the heat of the moment: it's "no" now, it's "maybe" later, and it changes again.

Is it rape if a couple is making out and the girl decides she doesn't want to go all the way, but the guy forces her to?
You can't make rules to legislate this kind of behavior. These girls don't understand the risks of adulthood and sex. Don't put yourself in that situation and then

go crying to authority figures—stay home if you can't handle it.

Is it rape if she's too drunk to object?
If she's drunk, she's complicitous. If someone gets behind the wheel of a car drunk and mows down three people, you wouldn't excuse him because he started whining that he didn't mean it.

From interview with Warren Kalbacker, *Playboy*, October 1991.

Playboy: You've noted with delight that your views on rape have inspired feminist fury.

Paglia: I am being vilified by feminists for merely having a common-sense attitude about rape. I loathe this thing about date rape. Have twelve tequilas at a fraternity party and a guy asks you to go up to his room, and then you're surprised when he assaults you? Most women want to be seduced or lured. The more you study literature and art, the more you see it. Listen to *Don Giovanni.* Read *The Faerie Queene.* Pursuit and seduction are the essence of sexuality. It's part of the sizzle. Girls hurl themselves at guitarists, right down to the lowest bar band here. The guys are strutting. If you live in rock and roll, as I do, you see the reality of sex, of male lust and women being aroused by male lust. It attracts women. It doesn't repel them. Women have the right to freely choose and to say yes or no. Everyone should be personally responsible for what happens in life. I see the sexual impulse as egotistical and dominating, and therefore I have no problem understanding rape. Women have to understand this correctly and they'll protect themselves better. If a real rape occurs, it's got to go to the police. The business of having a campus grievance committee decide whether or not a rape is committed is an outrageous infringement of civil liberties. Today, on an Ivy League campus, if a guy tells a girl she's got great tits, she can charge him with sexual harassment. Chickenshit stuff. Is this what strong women do?

————

From two-part interview with Celia Farber, *SPIN*, September and October 1991.

Part One

Paglia: I'm noticing that many people coming into the media now are people whose minds have been poisoned by their training at Yale and other Ivy League places. For example, I see where this whole date-rape thing is coming from. I recognize the language of these smart girls who are entering the media; they are coming from these schools. They have this stupid, pathetic, completely-removed-from-reality view of things that they've gotten from these academics who are totally off the wall, totally removed. Whereas my views on sex are coming from the fact that I am a football fan and I am a rock fan. Rock and football are revealing something true and permanent and eternal about male energy and sexuality. They are revealing the fact that women, in fact, *like* the idea of flaunting, strutting, wild masculine energy. The people who criticize me, these establishment feminists, these white upper-middle-class feminists in New York, especially, who think of themselves as so literate, the kind of music they like, is, like Suzanne Vega—you know, women's music.

SPIN: Yuck.

Paglia: This date-rape propaganda has been primarily coming out of the elite schools, where the guys are all these cooperative, literate, introspective, sit-on-their-ass guys, whereas you're not getting it that much down in the football schools where people accept the fact of the beauty and strength of masculinity. You see jocks on the campus all the time—they understand what manhood is down there. It's only up here where there is this idea that they can get men on a leash. It's these guys in the Ivy League schools who get used to obeying women. They're sedentary guys. It's ironic that you're getting the biggest bitching about men from the schools where the men are just eunuchs and bookworms.

SPIN: That point about primordial male sexuality is also at odds with much contemporary pop psychology. I'm referring to the twelve-step, women-who-love-too-much school of thought, which insists that a woman's attraction to an "untamed" man, as it were, is necessarily a sign of sickness—a sign of a warped emotional life that invariably traces back to childhood, and the attention span of the father. It never considers such an attraction to be a naturally occurring phenomenon—a force of nature. I think the approach to remedying the problem is simplistic, even dangerously so at times.

Paglia: I agree. I'm a Freudian. I like Freud very much, even though I adapt him and add things to him. But his system of analysis is extremely accurate. It's a conflict-based system that allows for paradox. It's also very self-critical and self-analytical. I've watched therapy getting more and more mushy in the past fifteen years in America. . . . It's become what I call coercive compassion. It's disgusting, it's condescending, it's insulting, it's coddling, it keeps everyone in an infantile condition rather than in the adult condition that was postulated as the ultimate goal of Freudian analysis. You were meant to be totally self-aware as a Freudian. Now, it's everyone who will help you, the group will help you. It's awful. It's a return to the Fifties conformist model of things. It's this victim-centered view of the world, which is very pernicious. We cannot have a world where everyone is a victim. "I'm this way because my father made me this way. I'm this way because my husband made me this way." Yes, we are indeed formed by traumas that happened to us. But then you must take charge, you must take over, you are responsible. Personal responsibility is at the heart of my system. But today's system is this whining thing, "Why won't you help me, Mommy and Daddy?" It's like this whole thing with date rape.

SPIN: One point that hasn't been made in the whole rape debate is women's role over men, sexually. In the case of a rape, a man has to use brute force to obtain something that a woman has—her very sex. So naturally she's weaker physically, and will always be oppressed by him physically. But in that moment when he decides that the only way he can get what he wants from her emotionally, or sexually, or whatever, is to rape her, he is confessing to a weakness that is all-encompassing. She is abused, but he is utterly tragic and pathetic. One is temporary and the other is permanent. I was raped once and it helped me to think of it like that. Not at all to apologize for him, but to focus on my power instead of my helplessness. It was a horrible experience, but it certainly didn't destroy my whole life or my psyche, as much as contemporary wisdom insisted it must have.

Paglia: Right, we *have* what they want. I think woman is the dominant sex. Men have to do all sorts of stuff to prove that they are worthy of a woman's attention. It's very interesting what you said about the rape, because one of the German magazine reporters who came to talk to me—she's been living in New York for ten years—she came to talk to me about two weeks ago and she told me a very interesting story, very similar to yours. She lives in Brooklyn, and she let this guy in whom she shouldn't have, and she got raped. She said that, because she's a feminist, of course she had to go for counseling. She said it was awful, that the minute she arrived there, the rape counselors were saying, "You will never recover from this, what's happened to you is so terrible." She said, what the hell, it was a terrible experience, but she was going to pick herself up, and it wasn't that big a deal. The whole system now is designed to make you feel that you are maimed and mutilated forever if something like that happens. She said it made her feel worse. It's absolutely American—it is not European—and the whole system is filled with these clichés about sex. I think there is a fundamental prudery about sex in all this. Rape is one of the risk factors in getting involved with men. It's a risk factor. It's like driving a car. My attitude is, it's like gambling. If you go to Atlantic City—these girls are going to Atlantic City, and when they lose, it's like "Oh, Mommy and Daddy, I lost." My answer is stay home and do your nails, if that's the kind of person you are. My Sixties attitude is, yes, go for it, take the risk, take the challenge—if you get raped, if you get beat up in a dark alley in a street, it's okay. That was part of the risk of freedom, that's part of what we've demanded as women. Go with it. Pick yourself up, dust yourself off, and go on. We cannot regulate male sexuality. The uncontrollable aspect of male sexuality is part of what makes sex interesting. And yes, it can lead to rape in some situations. What feminists are asking for is for men to be castrated, to make eunuchs out of them. The powerful, uncontrollable force of male sexuality has been censored out of white middle-class homes. But it's still there in black culture, and in Spanish culture.

Part Two

SPIN: In the first part of our interview, the section about rape upset every single woman who read it—in the offices at *SPIN* and even at the typesetters. They all seemed to feel that you were defending the rapist.
Paglia: No, that's not it at all. The point is, these white,

upper-middle-class feminists believe that a pain-free world is achievable. I'm saying that a pain-free world will be achievable only under totalitarianism. There is no such thing as risk-free anything. In fact, all valuable human things come to us from risk and loss. Therefore we value beauty and youth because they are transient. Part of the sizzle of sex is the danger, the risk of loss of identity in love. That's part of the drama of love. My generation demanded no more overprotection of women. We wanted women to be able to freely choose sex, to freely have all the adventures that men could have. So women began to hike on mountain paths and do all sorts of dangerous things. That's the risk of freedom. If women break their legs on mountain bikes, that's the risk factor. I'm not defending the rapist—I'm defending the freedom to risk rape. I don't want sexual experience to be protected by society. A part of it is that since women are physically weaker than men, in our sexual freedom, women are going to get raped. We should be angry about it, but it's a woman's personal responsibility now, in this age of sexual liberation, to make herself physically fit, so that she can fight off as best she can man's advances. She needs to be alert in her own mind to any potential danger. It's up to the woman to give clear signals of what her wishes are. If she does not want to be out of control of the situation, she should not get drunk, she should not be in a private space with a man whom she does not know. Rape does not destroy you forever. It's like getting beaten up. Men get beat up all the time.

SPIN: But don't you think that people see a man getting beat up and a woman getting raped as completely different? Do you think rape should be considered as serious a crime as murder?

Paglia: That's absurd. I dislike anything that treats women as if they are special, frail little creatures. We don't need special protection. Rape is an assault. If it is a totally devastating psychological experience for a woman, then she doesn't have a proper attitude toward sex. It's this whole stupid feminist thing about how we are basically nurturing, benevolent people, and sex is a wonderful thing between two equals. With that kind of attitude, then of course rape is going to be a total violation of your entire life, because you have had a stupid, naïve, Mary Poppins view of life to begin with. Sex is a turbulent power that we are not in control of; it's a dark force. The sexes are at war with each other. That's part of the excitement and interest of sex. It's the dark realm of the night. When you enter the realm of the night, horrible things can happen there. You can be attacked on a dark street. Does that mean we should never go into dark streets? Part of my excitement as a college student in the Sixties was coming out of the very protective Fifties. I was wandering those dark streets understanding that not only could I be raped, I could be killed. It's like the gay men going down to the docks and having sex in alleyways and trucks; it's the danger. Feminists have no idea that some women like to flirt with danger because there is a sizzle in it. You know what gets me sick and tired? The battered-woman motif. It's so misinterpreted, the way we have to constantly look at it in terms of male oppression and tyranny, and female victimization. When, in fact, everyone knows throughout the world that many of these working-class relationships where women get beat up have hot sex. They ask why she won't leave him? Maybe she won't leave him because the sex is very hot. I say we should start looking at the battered-wife motif in terms of sex. If gay men go down to bars and like to get tied up, beaten up, and have their asses whipped, how come we can't allow that a lot of wives like the kind of sex they are getting in these battered-wife relationships? We can't consider that women might have kinky tastes, can we? No, because women are naturally benevolent and nurturing, aren't they?

Everything is so damn Mary Poppins and sanitized.

SPIN: What do you think is the main quality that women have within them that they aren't using?

Paglia: What women have to realize is their dominance as a sex. That women's sexual powers are enormous. All cultures have seen it. Men know it. Women know it. The only people who don't know it are feminists. Desensualized, desexualized, neurotic women. I wouldn't have said this twenty years ago because I was militant feminist myself. But as the years have gone on, I begin to see more and more that the perverse, neurotic psychodrama projected by these women is coming from their own problems with sex.

———

From interview with Margaret LeBrun, *Syracuse Herald American,* November 3, 1991.

How do your views differ from today's feminists'?
Today's feminists want the government to pass rules to protect them. They all want approval. I don't look for approval. I believe we do everything by ourselves. I identify today's feminists as Rousseauists. That is, they belong to this tradition of liberalism which sees mankind as naturally good and thinks an evil society makes us bad.

The feminists would say sex is naturally good. It's nice and happy, Betty Crocker time. And therefore, anything that's bad or abusive in sex is, like, rape. "Well," they say, "rape can't be coming from sex, because sex is good. And we're naturally good. So, rape has to be coming from—pornography!" Now I, as a Catholic and also as a Freudian, have the opposite view. I believe it's society that trains us not to be aggressive, that trains us to be ethical.

I hear you have outspoken views on date rape.
What's happening with this date-rape thing is a crock. There is rape, which is an outrage, or there is not rape.

I'm not excusing men. That's stupid. Ethical men have always been opposed to rape. If a man commits a crime, punish him. If a rape occurs, go to the police. Men have responsibility too. But we as women cannot constantly be putting ourselves in this infantile position of, you know, this floating victim status, as if we were like these accidents waiting to happen. It's like defensive driving. I'm calling for defensive dating. We allow for the fact that some people can be stupid. Other people can break the law. Other people can be drunk. Other people could have a failure of their brakes. I'm not excusing the driver who runs the red light. But I'm saying, if women want to protect themselves, if women want to be rational and realistic about the world as it is, okay, we must allow for the fact that we cannot constantly be trusting.

Unfortunately, most victims of date rape are young and inexperienced—they haven't thought about these things.
That's correct. That's what I'm saying also. I'm saying this endless prolongation of childhood in this country, this endless coddling and pampering of people who are in fact adult, is another paternalistic way of turning back the clock. What we have in this country is this absurd idea that we are not an adult until, what? In the middle of our twenties. Even Anita Hill, she was, what? Twenty-six when this [alleged sexual harassment] happened. Please, that's ridiculous.

It seems you give men "permission" to behave like animals. That it's okay for men to flaunt violence and aggression, because that's their nature.
People have misread it that way. People say, oh, she's a biological determinist. But that's not what I'm saying at all. I say again and again: it is necessary for us to behave as civilized beings. Ethics is something we learn. We've made an enormous transition out of barbarism and dog-eat-dog toward abstract law and order. My entire book is about civilization.

From interview with Emily Culbertson, *The Daily Pennsylvanian*
(University of Pennsylvania), March 3, 1992.

I am saying that many of the problems between
the sexes are coming from something prior to socialization, a turbulence that has to do with every boy's
origin in a woman's body, a mother's body, and the
way he is overwhelmed by this huge, matriarchal
shadow of a goddess figure in his childhood. And I
feel, after so many decades of studying this, that men
are suffering from their sense of dependency on
women, their sense that at any moment they could be
returned to that slavery and servitude they experienced under a woman's thumb, when they were a boy
in the shadow of the mother. I got this from studying
all world culture, and comparing and noticing how
often there were these patterns in many different cultures. Many things that erupt in rape or violence,
battery and so on, are happening when a woman is
pushing that button of fear and dependency.

I'm saying that sex is a surging power thing between the sexes. It's a sex war. You cannot solve it by
legislation. We can regulate the work environment.
We must have equal opportunity and sexual harassment guidelines, but you cannot legislate relationships. This is why I think the date-rape thing has
become propaganda and hysteria. We cannot legislate
what happens on a date. It's up to women to realize
it's dangerous. Sex is dangerous—it's a dangerous
sport.

As a Sixties liberal, I am saying we do not want
to overpolice life-style. And this demand that feminism
has that date rape be policed by campus grievance
committees, it's totalitarian. It's deeply Soviet. And
they don't realize the degree to which it is de-sexing
and de-individualizing women.

What I'm saying is that even in my era, we knew not to go to fraternity parties. We knew fraternity parties were about scoring! I say let's leave fraternity parties to be about scoring. That's what I want. Leave it. I am pro-sex. I am radically pro-sex. I think women should have a choice: go to the party or don't go to the party. I don't think that when you're there, you should be assaulted. On the other hand, if you drink a certain number of drinks and behave in a certain way and go to a man's room alone—I believe it's time to take the Sixties attitude toward that; that is, you are consenting to sex.

———

Interview with Sonya Friedman, *Sonya Live,* CNN Television, December 13, 1991.

Friedman: While some women around the country say they felt betrayed by the verdict in the William Kennedy Smith trial and see it as a setback for women, there are some who feel differently and say that women share the responsibility when it comes to sex. Camille Paglia is such a woman. Everyone's going to have to listen carefully because I know you have a different point of view. Your view of the outcome of the William Kennedy Smith trial?

Paglia: Well, I was delighted that Smith was acquitted, because I think this was a terrible case to base the rape cause on. I think there's been too much date-rape propaganda coming out of the feminist establishment in America in the last few years. I feel that—

Friedman: We can't go any further, now that you've said "date-rape propaganda." What in heaven's name does that mean?

Paglia: I think real rape is an outrage. And for me real rape would be either stranger rape or the intrusion of overt sex into a nonsexual situation. I feel that women should take full responsibility for the dating experience. This is one of the rights that my generation of the Sixties won. When we arrived in college in 1964, the dorms were all-women, and we were locked in at night. We are the ones who broke through the parietal codes and said to the authority figures, "Get out of our sex lives." Now one of the freedoms we won is the freedom to risk danger, the freedom to risk rape.

Friedman: But Camille, the idea that I agree to go out with a man does not mean that I agree to have sex with that man. Why in the world would you suggest that just putting myself in a proximity to him would really allow him to feel that that was the message that I'm giving?

Paglia: Well, Sonya, dating is a very recent phenomenon, historically speaking. It's confined principally to the industrialized democracies. You know, God did not come down on Mount Sinai and say to Moses, "There's going to be risk-free dating forever." It's not like that. I feel that the moment a date happens that it's a social encounter that is potentially a sexual encounter. And the question of sex needs to be negotiated from the first moment on.

Friedman: "Hello, I'm not here to have sex with you." Is this what the new law of consent is going to be?

Paglia: No, I think it should be in the air. I think it should be hovering above the date—that is, the question of what is being expected on both sides. I think a woman should not put herself under the control—

Friedman: So a pickup is out, as far as you're concerned?

Paglia: I think if you're going to pick up people—men do that with *men;* it's part of the gay life-style—if you're going to do that, you *have* to realize the risk involved. I think it's a very exciting kind of sex. But you have to realize you are risking injury and not just rape but *death.*

Friedman: So then what do I have to do, find out about a man's entire history, know him only through family, be introduced to him and then only see him in public? I mean, are we going back to the chaperoned date?

Paglia: We have to be aware of people like Ted Bundy, a very smooth and charming man, who could be a murderer!

Friedman: Do you see this as liberated feminism, Camille?

Paglia: I see a liberated feminism that takes full responsibility for the woman's part in the sexual encounter or the potentially sexual encounter. Yes, I do. You see, in the old days, you did have a system where fathers and brothers protected women, essentially. Men knew that if they devirginized a woman, they could end up dead within twenty-four hours. These controls have been removed.

Friedman: I'm so lost here, Camille. What I hear is not something that is either modern or egalitarian. What I hear is a woman going back into *veils,* in effect.

Paglia: No, no! I'm encouraging women: *accept* the adventure of sex, *accept* the danger!

Friedman: Do you see a difference between sex and rape?

Paglia: I think this is one of the biggest pieces of propaganda coming out of feminism, the idea that rape is a crime of violence but not of sex. *All* rape is erotic. *All* rape is sexual.

Friedman: Erotic for *whom?*

Paglia: Erotic for the man!

Friedman: Yes, but there are two people having sex. You don't just want it to be erotic for him, and you feel vulnerable as a result of it.

Paglia: From twenty-five years ago, the material that goes into my book is coming from my study of rape as demonstrated in the whole of human cultures, everywhere in literature and art. All ethical men, from the beginning of time on, have protested against rape. This is not just a recent feminist discovery.

Friedman: Okay, now you use an interesting term—"ethical men."

Paglia: All ethical men, yes.

Friedman: Do you agree that a man has some responsibility to have discipline for himself?

Paglia: Correct! Oh, *yes*!

Friedman: Is it that you feel that we are being the enchantress, that we are sending out messages that we deny that we're sending?

Paglia: First let me say that I think that rape cannot be discussed separate from ethics, that we have to consider it as part of *all* of human behavior. We must begin training people for ethical behavior from earliest childhood. You cannot suddenly focus in on the freshman year and expect to solve the rape problem!—if you have people who are raised without religion, without ethical codes, without morality. Throughout all of history, ethical men have not murdered, have not stolen, have not raped. Feminism's claim that it discovered rape is simply false. Now, yes, I do believe there is an element of provocative behavior. I do feel that women have to realize their sexual power over men. This is part of our power.

Friedman: Okay, let's get this out of the way. A woman wants to wear a see-through blouse, a very short skirt, walk out on the streets at any time of the day and night. She says, "I have a right to feel free to do this. I can dress or undress any way I choose, and a man doesn't have a right to touch me unless I *tell* him that he has that right." What's your position on this?

Paglia: Let me make a parallel, Sonya. We have the *right* to leave our purse on a park bench in Central Park and go play twenty-five feet away and hope the purse is going to be there when we return, okay? Now, this is just simply stupid behavior. If someone steals the purse, we pursue the thief, we put him in jail. We also say to you, "That was really *stupid*!" Now, the same thing here. You may have the *right* to leave your purse there, you may have the *right* to dress in that way, but you are running a *risk*!

Friedman: Isn't that really what the verdict says? I mean, he was found not guilty, he wasn't found innocent.

Paglia: Oh, I think that was an *appalling* case, because that girl had her own private agenda—

Friedman: How do you know that? What an assumption on your part—

Paglia: —trying to *glom* onto the Kennedy *glamour*! Puh-*leez!* Going back there in the middle of the night! She's a party girl!

Friedman: Let's see how some of our callers feel about this.

> [A woman, identifying herself as a feminist and a member of NOW, calls from Tennessee: "I completely disagree with what Camille Paglia says, and I think she's just rationalizing rape."]

Friedman: I think you're going to find a lot of women taking issue with what you say about date rape.

Paglia: Actually, I find that a tremendous number of women agree with me, especially working-class women. Women who are street-smart agree with me. It's the white middle-class women who have a problem with it. And also I find that foreigners, people from Europe, know that *I'm* the one who has the voice of realism in rape. I have to explain to them how absurd the feminist position is today on this question!

> [A woman from Massachusetts calls: "Her attitude is *condoning rape*!"]

Friedman: It does come across a little bit that way. I don't think you mean to condone rape—

Paglia: Certainly *not*!

Friedman: But you're really putting the responsibility on women—that if they go out with a man, that whatever happens, they have set themselves up for.

Paglia: I feel that sex is basically combat. I feel that the sexes are at war.

Friedman: Oh, my goodness.

Paglia: I do feel it. It's like going to Atlantic City and gambling, okay? Every date is a gamble. Now, when you lose, you cannot go running to Mommy and Daddy. Sometimes you win, and sometimes you lose. I am a sexual adventuress. I am a member of the Sixties generation. I *believe* in going out and taking these risks! But you have to realize you are risking injury and even death when you go home with a stranger and get into the car of someone you don't know and go into the apartment of someone you don't know. And until women wake up and face the reality of this, there are going to be *more* such rapes. There have been naïve and stupid women from the beginning of recorded time—we have chronicles of this going back. This is *not* something new. The tunnel vision about this, the focusing in on this date-rape thing in the last ten years, is an absolute madness. It's part of the parochialism and provincialism, naïveté, and sex *phobia* of American feminism!

Friedman: You know, Camille, you should really learn to speak up, to articulate your positions more clearly! [*laughter*] Well, it *is* different, and I'm glad to have had an opportunity to hear it and to be able to think about it.

CLEOPATRA

SOLD DOWN THE RIVER

LUCY HUGHES-HALLETT'S
CLEOPATRA: HISTORIES, DREAMS
AND DISTORTIONS

Cleopatra is one of the few women of world-class stature in political history. She enamored two strikingly different men: Julius Caesar, a cerebral master strategist, and Marc Antony, an impulsive, convivial warrior. She was pivotal in one of the great turning points in Western history, when the Roman Republic shifted into Empire. As sensualist and femme fatale, she became a half-mythological legend in literature and art.

   Lucy Hughes-Hallett, a British journalist, television critic, and former writer for *Vogue*, has assembled the rich materials for what could have been a

[*Washington Post Book World*, May 13, 1991]

definitive work. There are diverting and rewarding moments in this book, which has fifty sensational, well-chosen illustrations of the highest quality. However, the text has too many defects, absurdities, and pretensions.

One would think the 2,000-year saga of Cleopatra's oscillating reputation would be enough to occupy Hughes-Hallett's attention. But no, we must have facile and unsupported opinions trotted out on everything from rape, suicide, racism, homophobia, and historiography to "the fantastic penetration of the East by the West," the results of which, we are airily told, have been "generally deplorable." Never mind about Western medicine, transportation, communications technology, or agricultural reforms—mere trifles.

Hughes-Hallett confidently offers her book as an exercise in "deconstruction," but she is just dabbling in what she admits is the "intellectual fashion" of the moment. Her own vivid personality emerges only in fits and starts. A great curse and plague upon contemporary writing, seen in spades here, is the compulsive nervous genuflection to overpraised French theorists whose ideas have little relevance outside their own country and era. It is time to reassert the vitality and authority of the Anglo-American tradition. Hughes-Hallett, could she liberate herself from her deference to trendy ideologues, would be a constellation of splendid British virtues—sensible, pragmatic, energetic, lucid, and witty.

The first and primary fault of the book is its skewed presentation of the historical background of Cleopatra's reign. There is a long, listless, potted survey that, tunneling in on biography at the expense of political context, can only baffle and misguide the general reader and exasperate the informed one. The cursory scattered references to the Ptolemies are woefully inadequate as an account of Cleopatra's lineage and heritage.

Hughes-Hallett shows no comprehension whatever of Roman character, culture, and achievement. Augustus, one of the greatest men of history, is dismissed as if he were the strutting bullyboy of a banana republic. By trivializing and ignoring him, Hughes-Hallett seriously diminishes Cleopatra, his formidable

mortal enemy. Unjustly, she praises Cleopatra for her vision of
"universal concord" without noticing that it was Augustus, not
Cleopatra, who in fact achieved this: the Pax Romana gave birth
to Christianity and spread Mediterranean high culture throughout illiterate tribal Europe. Projecting a cartoon Bible-movie fantasy of nasty Rome trampling on noble, struggling native
populations, Hughes-Hallett shows no awareness of the epochal
cruelty, autocracy, and belligerence of the ancient Near Eastern
states. Furthermore, there are indications, as in her unnecessary
excursus into Dionysus, that her sense of the large periods of
classical antiquity is uncertain.

Hughes-Hallett is so busy digressing into esoteric minutiae
(like Lady Bankes heaving stones over battlements) or parading
ponderous, pointless, and incompletely understood quotations
from Hegel, Freud, and Lacan that her reflections on Cleopatra,
the ostensible subject, are too often rushed and truncated. For
example, the important paradox that the "fabled seductress" was
big-nosed and plain is mentioned but left utterly undeveloped.
A potentially illuminating comparison to Sarah Bernhardt, pic-
tured elsewhere in the book, does not occur to her.

The superficial discussion of Shakespeare's Cleopatra as
merely a "comic coquette" suggests that Hughes-Hallett has been
attending bad performances rather than patiently studying a
major play. No contemporary British actress is capable of this
complex role, which requires a grand operatic theatricality and
passionate tempestuous charisma of the Maria Callas kind. An
assessment of modern literary criticism on *Antony and Cleopatra*,
showing the radical transformation of attitudes toward its heroine
from the Victorian era to the feminist Seventies, belongs in this
book but isn't there.

The ferocious nineteenth-century Cleopatras, particularly
those of the French Decadence, offer Hughes-Hallett an opportunity to shine, but they are presented in a hasty, clotted jumble
with little regard for the evolving phases of literary and artistic
style. We never get a complete analysis of anything. H. Rider
Haggard's interesting Cleopatra, for example, keeps whizzing in
and out like an annoying mosquito. Alma-Tadema's magnificent

moody painting of Cleopatra on her barge, reproduced in glorious color on the cover, is only partially examined before the author breathlessly skips on to something else.

With the final chapter, "Cleopatra Winks," we come with relief to the movies. Hughes-Hallett's description of Elizabeth Taylor as Cleopatra entering Rome is superb and sharply observed. My favorite moment in the book is the devastating portrait of "good-girl" Debbie Reynolds, Liz's rival, in her pigtails and "nappy-pins." The detailed account of Hollywood Cleopatras is spirited and funny, although Hughes-Hallett, yielding too readily to received opinion, underestimates the considerable historical accuracy of the Mankiewicz *Cleopatra*. Her description of Richard Burton's Antony, "smouldering with boredom and irritation" as he dines with his pious wife and a loudly clicking clock, is very fine and shows what she can do. But even this chapter eventually collapses into the usual muddle of dizzy pirouettes and backtracking: we jump from Liz to Vivien Leigh to Liz to Theda Bara to Sophia Loren, back to Liz and Debbie, and so on.

This book was published prematurely. It needed more research and rigorous rewriting and restructuring. As is, it too often becomes yet another example of the sorry pattern of great women being exploited for private agendas.

ALICE IN MUSCLE LAND

SAMUEL WILSON FUSSELL'S

MUSCLE: CONFESSIONS OF AN

UNLIKELY BODYBUILDER

One day, Sam Fussell, the shy, bookish son of two English professors, was converted to bodybuilding. *Muscle* is the vivid, lively record of his four sweaty years in the strange underworld of gyms, trainers, dumbbells, and steroids. It's a kind of beefcake *Alice in Wonderland*.

Fussell's epic journey begins with a dark night of the soul in New York City, whose polluted, crimefilled streets terrify him. Fleeing from a menacing thief with a crowbar, he cowers in a bookstore, where he discovers the autobiography of Arnold Schwarzeneg-

[*Boston Globe*, January 27, 1991]

ger, Mr. Universe, "the Austrian Oak." Arnold's "great chunks
of tanned, taut muscle" seem to him "modern-day armor."

Embarking on his quest for knighthood, Fussell joins the Y
and creeps into his first weight room. It's a wild scene right out
of the Mad Tea-Party. The claustrophobic heat is like "a Saigon
summer." "Savage screams" fill the air. There are bars on the
windows and a jungle of infernal equipment. First off, Fussell is
kidney-punched by a double amputee, then humiliated by a hostile chorus chanting, "New meat! New meat!"

There are eager volunteers, some of them lecherous, to break
in the novice. Fussell welcomes the "beautiful simplicity" of
weight lifting, its program of ritual exercises that give order to
his emotionally chaotic life. His body rapidly gains strength and
mass. Soon he comes to the attention of old-timers who see his
raw talent and potential for the contest circuit.

A tough master plan of sequenced workouts is set out for
him. He is exhorted with stentorian mottos and mantras and put
on a gargantuan diet of five six-course meals per day. There are
six eggs for breakfast and a pound of hamburger for midmorning
brunch as well as at dinner. A gallon of milk washes down the
daily dose of 108 chewable multivitamin tablets. Often, he ends
up vomiting on the street or at the office, "to rid my guts of the
wretched surplus."

Fussell's parents and most of his friends are embarrassed
and horrified by his new life. It's "disgusting," "vulgar," "gross,"
"perverse." He becomes a freak and exile. As his body grows,
his personality also changes. His "cautious, passive" manner
disappears: "I went from answering the phone meekly to shrieking 'SPEAK!' into the receiver on the first ring." After he tosses
a copy editor through a doorway and onto his rump, Fussell's
white-collar job is finished.

The "iron" world takes over. "You *can* defy both nurture
and nature": determined to remake himself, Fussell turns his back
on his past. He is indifferent to his mother's tears. Women fade
from mind. He becomes obsessed with reps, pounds, muscle
shape, getting and staying "pumped."

Pursuing his dream, Fussell moves to California, where he
meets a hilarious array of cute, vacuous, surgically altered "gym

bunnies"; overmedicated female bodybuilders with deep voices, enlarged genitals, and beards "like Spanish moss"; and screeching, stinking, hulking weight lifters who smack each other in the face, wear diapers, and snack on baby food.

Now Fussell sees drugs used on a vast scale. Lifters drop their trousers to take syringes of steroid into their scarred and knotted buttocks. "Roid rage," the heightened state of violent aggression induced by excess testosterone, is everywhere. Chemical strength enhancers and growth hormones are relentlessly "shotgunned." Despite the long list of side effects, including death, Fussell begins taking steroids in a "Faustian bargain" for success: "I was my own alchemist."

The dramatic climax is two tense bodybuilding contests, a week apart. To improve his standing, Fussell consents to a radical crash diet to strip the last fat off his frame and give him better muscle "cuts," the "shredded" or "shrink-wrapped" look. Fainting and hallucinating, he barely survives. His body and ego shrivel together. Gaunt, haggard, skin blotchy and pitted and dripping orange-brown competition dye, he comes in second place. It's over. He can take no more.

Muscle ends with a brief coda, as Fussell returns to real life. He declares his cure from his "addiction" to the iron "disease." Friends and family rejoice. I was disappointed. I was rooting for Fussell's rebellion, his alienation from establishment values and mores.

This book may have been published prematurely. As reportage, it has a marvelous, entertaining, you-are-there quality. Fussell has a great eye for eccentric characters and a great ear for the crackling vernacular. But too little time has passed for him to have psychological perspective on his profoundly self-altering experience.

Fussell merely touches on, without developing, the crucial question of social class in his saga. Like the seekers of my Sixties generation who went to India, he is right to reject the shallow, stale WASP world of prep schools, English departments, fast-track careers, good manners, and "constructive" love relationships.

I'll take the stink of healthy sweat any day over the stink

of the authoritarian language of contemporary therapy, which is all over the finale of this book. A wider world perspective is necessary. Surprisingly, sumo wrestlers are mentioned only once in passing. For me, Fussell's punishing iron adventure belongs to the noble tradition of warriors, athletes, and ascetic monks and yogis.

Muscle has interesting possibilities as a text for classroom use. It would probably split the sexes and smoke out the rabid feminists and pious do-gooders, who would beat their breasts over Fussell's self-abuse. I myself found this an inspiring book, since I identify not with those who seek comfort and contentment but with those "who strained and starved for the saber," the "glorious" silver prize that eludes Fussell's grasp.

Again and again, this book confirmed my theories about masculinity and Western culture. A woman simply is, but a man must become. Masculinity is risky and elusive. It is achieved by a revolt from woman, and it is confirmed only by other men. Feminist fantasies about the ideal "sensitive" male have failed. Manhood coerced into sensitivity is no manhood at all.

Fussell reveals that bodybuilders, imitating onstage the Farnese *Hercules* and Michelangelo *David*, seek what they call "The Apollonian Ideal," a sharply visual, sculptural outline. I have elsewhere demonstrated at length that Western personality, like Greek athletics, law, logic, philosophy, architecture, and drama, is an Apollonian construction. In other words, it is a work of art, a protest against nature. The quest for masculinity recapitulates the birth of civilization and the history of high art.

Modern bodybuilding is ritual, religion, sport, art, and science, awash in Western chemistry and mathematics. Defying nature, it surpasses it. *Muscle,* sympathetically read as an archetypal hero saga of embattled masculinity, exposes the parochialism, preachiness, and bourgeois assumptions in contemporary academe, psychotherapy, and feminism.

THE CRITIC

AT GRACEFUL EASE

WENDY LESSER'S

HIS OTHER HALF: MEN LOOKING AT

WOMEN THROUGH ART

This is a wonderful book. Not since Mary Ellmann's *Thinking About Women* (1968) has there been a book about sex that is so lucid, cultivated, amiable, and free of feminist claptrap.

Wendy Lesser, editor and publisher of *The Threepenny Review*, is the author of *The Life Below the Ground*, a broad study of "the subterranean" in literature. *His Other Half*, her new book, is a model of the kind of flexible, interdisciplinary culture criticism that is desperately needed to bridge the gap between the general reader and the academic ghetto.

Lesser, moving with graceful ease from literature

[*Washington Post Book World*, March 10, 1991]

raphy and cinema, is concerned with the image
racted through male imagination. Though she
late degrees from King's College and Berkeley,
is delightfully nonacademic. We feel the largeness
oɪ ꓨ he university, the permanence of sexual differences,
and yet tne... ambiguous dissolution in art. Lesser's remarks on
love are rueful, knowledgeable, humane. There is no strident
resentment toward men, no hidden agenda. Meditating on universal human experience, Lesser shuns the trendy jargon and
sterile quarrels of the inbred academic conferences.

Many times while reading *His Other Half,* I smiled with
admiration at Lesser's supple phrasings, whose disarming simplicity conceals a true sophistication of psychological observation
and judgment. Several times, I actually shouted "Yay!" and
"Hurrah!" at her penetrating judgments about that rickety house
of cards, academic feminism.

As a critic, Wendy Lesser has sensibility and discernment,
things that cannot be taught. I place her in the Pater and Wilde
line, which requires strong personality in the critic and a posture
of receptive appreciation toward art and beauty. Hence her work
is a marked departure from today's prevailing academic style,
which sneers and condescends, rends and tramples, all in the
name of chic politics and cockamamie theory. Lesser's prose
shows criticism returning to the Anglo-American mainstream,
that clear, candid, pragmatic language descending from Dr. Johnson through Jane Austen, Hazlitt, Darwin, and Wilde to modern
British scholars like C. M. Bowra and W. F. Jackson Knight. It
is as fresh and lively as ever.

Lesser dislikes the cant, "rigid separatism," and "dearth of
historical perspective" of women's studies. She protests the "self-
defeating" feminist suspicion of and resistance to literature and
art by men, which is in fact our "artistic inheritance." She intends
to defend her male artists against the simplistic charge of "misogyny." Against feminist fashion, Lesser declares her "allegiance
to Freud," whom she hails as "a literary critic and a cultural
phenomenon." This is most welcome: in my opinion, American
feminism, spurning Freud, condemned itself to intellectual mediocrity. Lesser has more respect for Lacan than I do, though

she deftly exposes several of his major errors. She cites D. W. Winnicott as a third influence on her thinking.

Lesser's book is "developmental," charting "a progression" in men's view of woman, from mother to "woman alone," then from woman as sexual opponent to "woman as the artist's mirror." The first chapter deals with Charles Dickens (her favorite novelist), D. H. Lawrence, and, in Lesser's one quirk, Harold Brodkey, who is cited throughout the book but seems out of his depth.

In the second chapter, on Degas's nudes, Lesser shows her power. Blowing a dully conventional feminist misreading of Degas right out of the water, she conclusively demonstrates that feminists see only what they want to see. Lesser finds in Degas's women not "violence," "degradation," and "contortion" but their opposite—a muscular "natural physical grace." She forcefully disputes the stale cliché of "the male gaze," that tiresome assumption of feminist discourse.

Lesser's other literary chapters are on George Gissing, Henry James, and Randall Jarrell. I relished her scornful trouncing of an unbelievably inept misreading of James's *The Bostonians* by Sandra Gilbert and Susan Gubar. A witty chapter on Cecil Beaton unfortunately lets Susan Sontag derail its crisply Wildean line of thought. The Alfred Hitchcock chapter splendidly captures the fluidity, uncertainties, disturbances, and cruelties of sex—though I like Hitchcock's cool, brittle blondes better than Lesser does. A rich, fascinating chapter on Barbara Stanwyck vigorously defends the "honest vulgarity" of *Stella Dallas* against feminist snipers.

But Lesser's tour de force is the Marilyn Monroe chapter, which is hands down the best analysis I have ever seen of this much-discussed star. It makes Gloria Steinem's mawkish Monroe book look silly and cheap. Lesser's eerie interpretation, negotiating between persons and "ghostly images," is deeply informed in major Western principles of theater, art, and psyche. The discussion of *Some Like It Hot* is simply superb.

The 1990s, after the reign of terror of academic vandalism, will be a decade of restoration: restoration of meaning, value, beauty, pleasure, and emotion to art and restoration of art to its audience. Wendy Lesser has made an important contribution to this volatile American drama.

THE BIG UDDER

SUZANNE GORDON'S

PRISONERS OF MEN'S DREAMS

In *Prisoners of Men's Dreams,* Suzanne Gordon argues that American feminism has lost sight of its original goal of transforming the world into a kinder, gentler place. Gordon deplores the sort of feminism that has triumphed instead: cold, ruthless, "equal-opportunity" feminism, which aims for women's entrance into the masculine public world and their achievement by male standards of excellence.

The heart of the book consists of excerpts from a hundred interviews with career women, who do a lot of complaining about fatigue and disillusion. At

[*The Philadelphia Inquirer,* May 12, 1991]

the end, Gordon calls for a National Care Agenda that would make "caregiving" rather than competition the ultimate American value.

Suzanne Gordon is obviously an intelligent, sympathetic, and well-meaning person, but *Prisoners of Men's Dreams* is a good example of the kind of sentimental, unlearned effusion that has become a staple of contemporary feminism and that most men rightly ignore.

Like so many American feminists, Gordon is completely out of her depth as a social analyst. Awkward, unintegrated quotes from Adam Smith and Woodrow Wilson are waved around to disguise her lack of familiarity with economics, history, and political science.

We are presented with the usual three-handkerchief tearjerker scenario about Big, Bad, Ugly America—that corrupt, empty, greedy society which all those wonderful, warm, benevolent people around the world look at with disgust. This point of view is the essence of chic these days among know-nothing feminists and the preening pseudo-leftists who crowd our university faculties.

Well, let me tell you: as the child of Italian immigrants, I happen to think that America is the most open, dynamic, creative nation on God's green earth. As a scholar, I also know that it is capitalist America that produced the modern independent woman. Never in history have women had more freedom of choice in regard to dress, behavior, career, and sexual orientation.

Gordon's insistence on defining woman as nurturant and compassionate drove me up the wall. My entire rebellion as a child in the Fifties was against this unctuous, preachy stuff coming from the teachers, nuns, and Girl Scout leaders.

Gordon's caregiving "transformative feminism" is just as repressive and reactionary as the "patriarchy" it claims to attack. Minerva save us from the cloying syrup of coercive compassion! What feminism does not need, it seems to me, is an endless recycling of Doris Day Fifties clichés about noble womanhood.

I agree with Gordon in a number of areas. American workers should have more annual vacation time, in line with their European counterparts. Preschool children should not be forced into punishing premature lesson plans for the gratification of their ostentatious yuppie parents. Nurses, not doctors, run the hospitals and should be respected and remunerated accordingly.

But I dispute Gordon's classification of teachers as "caregivers." Her idea, now so common, that "self-esteem" is the purpose of education is one of the main reasons for the increasing scientific and intellectual mediocrity of American students. Education is not a branch of the social-welfare agencies. Mawkish social-welfare propaganda, which has reached epidemic proportions in Ivy League humanities departments, has got to be purged from academic discourse.

Gordon's portrait of frenetic, materialistic American careerism is marred by her nonexistent grasp of the complex development of institutions through Western history. Professionalism was not, as she thinks, invented by evil capitalism. Just to give one example: the efficient international administrative structure of the Roman Empire was adopted by the Catholic Church, to which we owe the very survival of literacy and culture in Europe in the early Middle Ages. Innocent of sociology, Gordon cheerfully fantasizes about comfy, woman-inspired "nonhierarchical" or egalitarian work environments, which would obviously lead to the total collapse of any large company.

Like most feminists, Gordon has a resentful, simplistic attitude toward patriarchy, which is perceived as tyrannical oppression. She never pauses to note the benefits, gifts, and privileges she takes for granted in the male-created world around her—the hot showers, flush toilets, automatic washers and dryers, electric lights, telephones, automobiles, the grocery stores overflowing with fresh, safe foods, the high-tech network of medicines and life-saving hospital equipment.

American feminism, which likes to make posturing gestures of solidarity with working-class or Third World women, is in fact trapped in a princess mentality of snippy entitlement. *Prisoners of Men's Dreams* is overconcerned with upper-middle-class white women and the demands of their prestigious, high-paying office jobs.

Yes, these women are frazzled and exhausted from trying to do two jobs at once—motherhood and a fascinating fast-track career. Gordon's answer to this dilemma is that "the system" has to change. Again and again, she exudes an envious malice toward the unmarried or childless women who, due to more time and energy, are able to outshine and outstrip those with household responsibilities.

But feminism was always wrong to pretend that women could "have it all." It is not male society but mother nature who lays the heaviest burden on woman. No husband or day-care center can ever adequately substitute for a mother's attention. My feminist models are the boldly independent and childless Amelia Earhart and Katharine Hepburn, who has been outspoken in her opposition to the delusion of "having it all."

Women must take personal responsibility for the path they choose and stop whining about the options they have thereby lost. There is nothing more important than motherhood—not because it is "caregiving" but because it is the primal source of all life and contains its own dark, ambiguous dualities.

The well-heeled yuppies who dump their newborns off at day care six weeks after delivery and streak back to the office with screeching tires don't have a clue about motherhood or anything else. I agree with Gordon that there must be a reordering of priorities in America. But I take the larger world perspective of the Sixties, with its cultural influences from Hinduism and Buddhism, which teach us about the necessity for an individual search for enlightened consciousness.

For all her criticism of materialism, Gordon is a narrowly secular thinker. Religion never seems to enter her mind or the minds of her interviewees. Nor, oddly enough, does sexuality impinge, except in some cavilling remarks about women having the right to wear whatever they like, no matter how provocative, to the office.

The feminist naïveté about life, history, and culture must end. We must eliminate social injustice where we can. But all "human needs" will never be fully met, except in a totalitarian regime of bloated centralized authority. Life will never be a utopian paradise of universal happiness, harmony, and good will. Life is combat, strife, limitations, obstacles met and overcome by self-discipline and self-criticism.

I vigorously support feminism in its quest for the complete political and legal equality of women. But I oppose it when it sanctimoniously asserts woman's moral superiority to men and when it suppresses recognition of the vast achievements of male civilization.

"Transformative feminism," which Suzanne Gordon nostalgically eulogizes, was always a naïve daydream. A feminism that canonizes itself as unconditional love just turns itself into a big udder for hating and hateful people.

Before it makes prescriptions for society, feminism must put its own house in order. Maps for the future can be drawn only by those who have deeply studied the past.

BRANDO FLASHING

RICHARD SCHICKEL'S

BRANDO: A LIFE IN OUR TIMES

Marlon Brando is one of the most brilliant and charismatic artists of the twentieth century. Like Elvis
Presley, he is a supreme sexual persona, an icon who
has entered our dreams and transformed the way we
see the world.

All contemporary American actors owe a debt to
Brando and are in some sense in his shadow. He took
the self-analytic and ensemble-based Stanislavskian
"Method" of the New York Actors' Studio to Hollywood and helped put an end, for good or ill, to the

[*The New York Times Book Review*, July 21, 1991]

old paternalistic studio system, with its corporate populism and army-like cadres of polished technicians.

Today's young white actors, emerging from comfortable, respectable homes and lacking access to the hardening experiences of factories, freighters, or battlefields, search for masculinity by aping Brando. Sean Penn, Richard Grieco, Ken Wahl, Mickey Rourke, Sylvester Stallone: the list of Brando imitators goes on and on.

Arrogant and manipulative, seething with raw sensitivities and burning rage, alternately harsh and kind, selfish and generous, Brando is a monumental personality of profound complexities and contradictions. He must be approached from the direction of other major Western artists suffering spiritual conflicts and thwarted ambitions: Byron, Keats, Caravaggio, Michelangelo.

Marlon Brando deserves a better biography than Richard Schickel has written. *Brando: A Life in Our Times* approaches vandalism in the dogged way that it strips everything dark, dangerous, and titanic from its subject. What we have here is Brando reborn as Richard Schickel, polite, bookish, and perpetually worried. One of the grandest and most disorderly personalities of our era has been reduced to a pedestrian narrative of terminal blandness.

Schickel, a movie critic for *Time* and the author of biographies of Cary Grant and James Cagney, unwisely prefaces *Brando* with a long, unctuous letter to the actor. A hand-wringing lamentation over "this wretched moment," when Brando's son Christian has been charged with the fatal shooting of his half-sister's lover, turns into a droning litany of all the wonderful similarities between the doting fathers Schickel and Brando. Schickel's suffocating, condescending compassion is a literary affectation forced onto a major performing artist, who operates in a totally different imaginative realm.

The book proper begins with a wandering account of The Group Theater and Stella Adler, Brando's New York acting teacher and mentor. Then we skip backward for a listless and patchy account of Brando's birth in 1924 and his upbringing in Nebraska and Illinois. The cultural origins of the family are ignored. Schickel latches onto one bright idea—"Brando was the child of alcoholics"—and runs it into the ground for the rest of the book. It explains nothing, for the world is full of children of alcoholics who did not become Marlon Brando.

Dropping out of military school, Brando moved to New York, where his sisters were living. Schickel, pushing the parallels between Brando and himself (both are shy; both played the drums), now rhapsodizes about their arrival, ten years apart and forever, alas, unknown to each other, in New York in its heyday. We follow Brando through his acting apprenticeship and first bit roles, leading to his Broadway appearances in *I Remember Mama* in 1944 and Maxwell Anderson's *Truckline Café,* directed by Harold Clurman, in 1946.

Sparks began to fly when Brando was cast opposite Tallulah Bankhead in Jean Cocteau's short-lived play *The Eagle Has Two Heads* (later nicknamed "The Turkey with Two Heads"). At their first meeting, Tallulah was soon making drunken sexual advances. When the play opened in Wilmington, Brando upstaged Tallulah by squirming, leering at the audience, and staring into the wings. He was fired before the play got to New York. Schickel, whose psychological insight seems nonexistent, is stumped at Brando's simmering aggression and benignly labels it "sheer youthful devilry" or noble "disgust with the status quo."

Brando's big break came in 1947 when he won the leading male role in Tennessee Williams's *A Streetcar Named Desire,* a part that the producer first thought of offering to John Garfield. Schickel, lazily assuming everyone alive knows all about this, flubs badly. Marlon Brando's raw, brute, comic performance as Stanley Kowalski, in the play and the 1951 film, was one of the most spectacular and explosive moments in modern art. It has come to symbolize American theater. Schickel just spreads a little schmaltz and hurries on.

Though he acknowledges that "rumors of homosexual behavior were rife" during Brando's early career, Schickel curtly dismisses them as pranks by the actor's roommate in New York, the comedian Wally Cox. There is also evidence of epic womanizing that Schickel mentions but loftily announces that he disdains to tell us about. Arriving in Hollywood with a wardrobe of T-shirts, blue jeans, and one ripped suit, Brando embarked on a movie career of extraordinary ups and humiliating downs. At one point, Schickel reports, the actor had "fourteen consecutive flops." But even in his worst, most eccentric, and self-parodic performances, he never lost the power to fascinate.

During the 1960s, Brando became progressively disenchanted with acting and began to choose his roles to make sometimes arcane political points. The culmination of this was his stagy refusal of his Oscar for *The Godfather* in 1972; as his proxy at the Academy Awards ceremonies, he sent a mysterious woman in lavish tribal dress, Sasheen Littlefeather ("real name, Maria Cruz," Schickel reports, "sometime occupation, Miss American Vampire of 1976"), to deliver a speech on the plight of the American Indians to an annoyed and restless Hollywood audience.

Schickel's treatment of Brando's public politicizing is indulgent, admiring, and one-dimensional. He never draws connections between Brando's grandstanding and his notorious problems with directors, his psychological turmoil with male authority—a social theme at the heart of our century. Similarly, Schickel is frustratingly inert in approaching major issues like Brando's gluttony, his romances with non-Caucasian women, and his Gauguin-like migration to the South Seas.

Plodding plot summaries of Brando's films are systematically studded with cheap shots at the movie critic Pauline Kael. There are also scattered slighting references to Roman Catholics, whom Schickel portrays as the conspiratorial, spoilsport, antimovie prudes of Fifties America, which was in fact firmly in the grip of a censorious WASP establishment.

Schickel, whom I have always respected for his intelligent, thoughtful movie reviews, is best here when he sticks to unpretentious reportage about the production history of specific films. There are many striking or piquant details. Brando was originally offered the lead in *Lawrence of Arabia*, the part that went to Peter O'Toole. Before Brando won the role of Don Corleone in *The Godfather*, the film's director, Francis Ford Coppola, "endured casting brainstorms" that ranged from Danny Thomas to Melvin Belli and Carlo Ponti.

For his death scene in *Mutiny on the Bounty*, Brando "bedded himself on 200 pounds of ice" to duplicate his own mother's death tremors. On the set of *One-Eyed Jacks*, the only film he directed, he dislocated his shoulder while showing Karl Malden how to use a bullwhip. In Paris to film *The Young Lions*, Brando was hospitalized with burns around the genitals when a waiter spilled a pot of scalding tea in his lap. Always a tart critic of his own films, Brando said of *The Night of the Following Day* that it makes as much sense as a rat copulating with a grapefruit.

When Schickel has to leave the rich, fact-based political dynamics of Hollywood deal-making for the mercurial psychological dynamics of biography, his book is a disaster. My idol, Keith Richards, virtuoso rhythm guitarist of the Rolling Stones, named his son Marlon. Why? You would never know from Schickel's book. Marlon Brando, the wild, sexy rebel, all mute, surly bad attitude, prefigured rock and roll, the great art form of my Sixties generation.

Marlon Brando, mumbling and muttering and flashing with bolts of barbaric energy, freed theatrical emotion from its enslavement by words. He brought American nature to American acting. And he brought American personality to the world. In this stuffy, maudlin, pious biography, Richard Schickel gives us not Marlon Brando but a Fifties lost soul, a man in a gray flannel suit.

WHAT A DRAG

MARJORIE GARBER'S

VESTED INTERESTS: CROSS-DRESSING

AND CULTURAL ANXIETY

The publication of a book on transvestism by a high-ranking woman professor of English at Harvard University should be the occasion for us to rejoice in the cultural changes in America over the last twenty-five years. Manifestations of sexuality once labeled immoral, deviant, or sick are now legitimate subjects of scholarly inquiry, even in the once conservative, ultra-WASP, and all-male bastions of the Ivy League.

But Marjorie Garber's *Vested Interests,* which examines real and fictive examples of cross-dressing from the Renaissance to the present, is too often a dem-

[*Boston Globe,* December 15, 1991]

onstration of what is wrong with academe rather than what is right. The book is appealingly packaged, with many handsome illustrations. Flipping through the pages, the reader is drawn to juicy, piquant sexual details about famous people or pop stars. But when one begins to take a closer look, it's downhill all the way.

Garber, the author of two books on Shakespeare, had an early interest in Freud at a time when it was not popular. Unfortunately, the only solid material in *Vested Interests,* which forges into a dozen trendy, new territories, remains Shakespeare and Freud.

The book is stunningly disorganized. It is basically a cut-and-paste job, a scrapbook of newspaper clippings, gay gossip, pedestrian plot summaries, undigested quotes from other books, and fulsome praise of prominent academics. We bounce giddily from medieval sumptuary laws to the death of Laurence Olivier, from Ted Kennedy in a blonde wig and falsies to Peter Pan, detective stories, black drag, Liberace, Valentino, and finally, Little Red Riding Hood.

This might sound like fun, but alas, it's a hard slog through lumpish patches of tedious Lacan jargon, which has infested Garber's formerly clear, plain prose, presumably through toxic contact at Harvard. There are the numbing buzz words of conference cant: "transgressive," "hegemonic," "taxonomies," "problematize." The tone oscillates wildly between droning academese and slick flippancy; headings read, with the kind of sophomoric whimsy that passes for wit these days in the Ivy League, "Toot-Toot-Tootsie Goodbye" and "The Chic of Araby."

The book's mishmash of meandering topics is framed by a grand "theory," meant to persuade us of a preconceived plan. The book has two large parts with vague, portentous names. The introduction promises, "*Transvestite Logics* explores the way that transvestism creates culture, and *Transvestite Effects,* the way that culture creates transvestites." But "culture" is never defined, and it becomes increasingly clear that Garber's grasp of intellectual history is weak. A preposterous sentence, trumpeted on the dust jacket, asserts, "There can be no culture without the transvestite." But Garber appears to know nothing about world culture before the medieval period or even, aside from a passage on Kabuki, world culture today. Except for two paragraphs on Sophocles and Virgil, she totally neglects Western antiquity, where there is a staggering amount of literary and anthropological material crucial to her subject.

Vested Interests is simply an English Department book that has lost interest in English literature or canonical art in general. It is symptomatic of the bankruptcy of the humanities, whose custodians now seek instant hipness and career cachet rather than deep knowledge and lasting scholarly achievement.

The book is unjust to its own subject, from which it constantly swerves away into arch word games and elephantine theoretical gimmicks. Despite its claimed liberalism, it too often coyly treats transvestites as freakishly amusing, or it tries to make them symbolic of something else, "category crisis," a challenge to false "binarisms" in other spheres.

Despite its dazzling, diverting variety, *Vested Interests* is inadequately researched. Garber knows little about the general history of fashion or the visual arts. Marcel Duchamp, Andy Warhol, and Robert Mapplethorpe appear not as artists but as transvestites, merely because of one playful experiment in drag. Warhol's far more important sponsorship of transvestite Superstars, still vastly influencing contemporary culture, is not mentioned. Josephine Baker becomes a transvestite because of an appearance as Marlene Dietrich in a tux.

Garber is carelessly reductive, with remarkably little feeling for psychological complexity or multiple personae. Reasoning is tabloid-sloppy. Rumors of homosexuality or sexual ambiguity of any kind become evidence of transvestism. Elvis Presley is grotesquely feminized and caricatured to support Garber's ridiculous idea that he was a "female impersonator." The same faulty logic is applied to poor T. E. Lawrence, who becomes, in a dully padded chapter, another female impersonator.

Garber makes no systematic distinctions among the archetypes of genders being impersonated or among the styles and moods of impersonation, from reverence to satire, which stream by chaotically. Nor does she relate the frequency of impersonation to specific periods and their sexual assumptions. She exaggerates the atypical and ignores cultural norms.

The cutesy treatment of clerical dress as drag, with Tallulah Bankhead cited as an authority, sets a new low for cheap vulgarity and exposes the spiritual emptiness of academe. Even a passing familiarity with anthropology or comparative religion would have helped here. But Garber's interdisciplinary skills are amateurish: one of her principal sources is Vern Bullough, a contemporary archivist and unreliable popularizer. She treats history like cake batter in a swirling Mixmaster. Romanticism, the birth of modern sexual identity, is never mentioned, even apropos of Byron.

The superficial treatment of current popular culture is grossly exploitative. There is a telling gap between Elvis and Little Richard (in Garber's adolescence) and the present. The remarks about Madonna, attributed to another academic, are fragmentary and distorted; the description of Michael Jackson doesn't move us beyond *Entertainment Tonight;* the passing sentences about Prince, about whom Garber clearly knows nothing, are quotes from published sources. The female illusionist Jim Bailey is barely mentioned, and the brilliant Jimmy James not at all.

Garber missed a golden opportunity. The time is right for a major scholarly book on transvestism that would speak in lucid, sensible language to a general audience. Since the psychedelic Sixties dissolved the rigid sex roles of the Fifties, we have been in a maelstrom of gender. Androgyny, the promise of the Seventies, has ceased to satisfy, as each sex searches for its lost identity. Homosexuality, more common as well as more visible, is part of this movement for sexual self-knowledge and self-definition.

The drag queen has emerged in America in the Nineties as a symbol of our sexual crisis. A pagan priest whose ancestry is in the ancient cults of the Great Mother (unmentioned by Garber), the drag queen defies victim-centered feminism by asserting the dominance of woman in the universe. With geisha-like sophistication of gesture and costume, sometimes elegant, sometimes comic or phantasmic, the drag queen re-creates the dreamlike artifice of culture that conceals the darker mysteries of biology.

Sexual history is cyclic, a point never seen by Garber. Are we in a decadence, like that of imperial Rome? The drag queen ritually acts out and exorcises our confusions and longings. But the shaman with secret knowledge is often vilified, outcast. Forever reducing transvestism to politics or vaudeville, Garber never catches its uncanniness, its dangerous magic.

The world's great libraries contain 200 years of fascinating erotica, some in special collections of pornographic private editions. Marjorie Garber's slack, cluttered book barely taps that quirky, anecdotal but often impressively learned and encyclopedic material. The irony is that *Vested Interests,* with its "cutting-edge" pretensions, has collapsed back into anecdotage. But coherence, objectivity, plausibility, and respect for history are gone.

SEXUAL PERSONAE:

THE CANCELLED PREFACE

Sexual Personae seeks to demonstrate the unity and continuity of Western culture, something that has inspired little belief since the period before World War One. Volume One surveys literature and art from antiquity to the end of the nineteenth century. Volume Two examines modern popular culture—cinema, television, sports, rock music.

Personality is at the heart of the West. Governing its representation in art are principles I call Apollonian and Dionysian, in a theory elaborated from passages in Plutarch, Nietzsche, and G. Wilson Knight. These ms were used by German scholarship in a sometimes vague or portentous way. I fine-tune them for practical criticism. I see the Apollonian and Dionysian as a cyclic pattern of expansion and retraction, of the shapeless and the definitive. Everything implicit in the *Iliad,* the first great Western book, returns in a historical wave in modern popular culture, which I view as an eruption of our buried paganism. Western man represents himself, on the political or psychological stage, in a spectacular world-theater. Our personality is innately cinematic, light-charged projections flickering on the screen of Western consciousness.

Sexual Personae shows how much morally disturbing material in literature and art has been overlooked or glossed over by scholars, and secondly how this material can be understood as a survival or re-creation of paganism. Many of my assumptions are quaintly premodernist. I believe that history has shape, order, and meaning; that exceptional men, as much as economic forces, produce change; and that passé abstractions like beauty, nobility, and greatness have a shifting but continuing validity. I want to restore the terms *art* and *culture* to their general nineteenth-century sense. But I also want to apply "art" to everything artificial or fabricated, including engineering projects like roads and bridges. Art for me means all works of imagination, from poetry to television commercials to pornography, with questions of quality still operative. I see the Western past as a story, episodic and cumulative. My reading of that story will show its symmetries, echoes, and internal development, its symbolization of thought and action in modes of personality I call personae.

Persona is the Latin word for the clay or wooden mask worn by actors in Greek and Roman theater. Its root is probably *personare,* "to sound through or resound": the mask was a kind of megaphone, projecting the voice to the farthest tiers of spectators. Over time, *persona* broadened in meaning to include the actor's role and then a social role or public function. Finally, it defined an individual under Roman law, as a citizen with rights and duties. We retain this sense in reverse in our "nonperson," a political victim. By late Latin, *persona* became a person as we now understand it, a human being apart from his social status. Vico economically fuses the early theatrical and later legal meanings of *persona* when he says of the Roman *paterfamilias,* "Unde person or mask of the father of the family were concealed all children and servants."[1]

Western personality thus originates in the idea of mask. Society is the place of masks, a ritual theater. Persona's artistic origins were recovered by modernism and the New Criticism, which stripped the text of biographical baggage. For the New Critics, a writer never speaks for himself but only through an assumed persona, a mask. Following World War Two, the class-room set piece was Jonathan Swift's *A Modest Proposal,* where a self-absorbed voice, airily proposing the cannibalistic farming of Irish infants, is the butt of the author's satire. Irony and game-playing are central to this view of literature and life. The New Critical persona was indebted to Jung, who sees a split between our inner and outer selves, an authentic psychic reality versus the mask conforming to social expectation. Popularized Jungianism, especially in its American feminist form, has become increas-ingly Rousseauist; that is, it tends to view society as automatically restrictive or oppressive instead of educative or civilizing.

My personae are not strategies of irony or social adaptation but cinematic visualizations, products of an archaic process of picture-thought. The brain is the neurological repository of the human past, and personae are the hidden masks of our ancestors and heirs. Man is not merely the sum of his masks. Behind the shifting face of personality is a hard nugget of self, a genetic gift. I believe only some master principle of heredity, defying liberal theories of environmentalism, can account for the profusion of human types, often manifested within a single family. The self is malleable but elastic, snapping back to its original shape like a rubber band. Mental illness is no myth, as some have claimed. It is a disturbance in our sense of possession of a stable inner self that survives its personae.

My title was inspired by a film, Ingmar Bergman's *Persona.* When I saw it at its American release (in January 1968), it seemed to crystallize the reflections of my college years, which led to the thesis of *Sexual Personae:* that the high development of personality in the West has produced a perverse sexual problematics unique in world culture. *Persona,* surely inspired by Strindberg's one-act play, *The Stronger,* is about power relationships and the use of personae in scenes of psychic combat. Nature's law here is cruelty, not pity. In a dreamy atmosphere of sexual ambiguity and through interludes of speech and silence, the film shows the resolution and dissolution of Western personae. Its stunning close-ups force us to contemplate the plasticity and yet stoniness of the human face. Bergman's style, alternately iconic and metamorphic, respects both Apollo and Dionysus. *Persona* is a case study of the themes of my book: fascination, entrancement, obsession, narcissism, vampirism, mesmerism, seduction, violation—all the still-uncharted psychodynamics of erotic, artistic, and theatrical cathexis.

Power struggles, dominance and submission: *Sexual Personae* often invokes the "great chain of being," the ancient idea of a pyramidal system uniting earth and heaven. One of my constant words is "hierarchical." "All things being equal. . . ." But things are never equal. The traumas of the Sixties persuaded me that my generation's egalitarianism was a sentimental error. Woodstock turned in four months into Altamont. After endless quarrels with authority, prankish disruptiveness, and impatience with management and procedure, I now see the hierarchical as both beautiful and necessary. Efficiency liberates; egalitarianism tangles, delays, blocks, deadens. I marvel, in fact, at the extraordinary orderliness of human life, which must be the instinctual brain-based recall of the individual to the group. Even the gods, the preeminent sexual personae of this book, are projections of our innate biological hierarchism. But while biology is our hidden Fate, it is art and artifice that I am in love with, and they are my subject.

As far back as I can remember, I saw a universal pecking order among persons. Every conversation or social event seemed to swirl and solidify, falling into hierarchic structures sharply visible to my child's eye. In school, I was struck by the mystery of authority and leadership. Some teachers, tall and solid, were hopelessly befuddled by classrooms of giggling, contemptuous teens. I particularly recall one hushed, painful moment when a weeping teacher was led down from study hall, where a student had somehow mashed chewing gum into her hair! Meanwhile, another teacher—often a tiny woman, mighty of heart, with a voice like the roar of a lion—could charge into a mob of brawling boys and instantly reduce them to trembling submission. An inborn force of personality, always present in great teachers, speakers, actors, and politicians, automatically marshals people into ordered groups around a focal point of power. In history, the human drive is toward monarchy. Western culture has produced the best system yet for organizing and taming those king-seeking energies: representative democracy, part of our pagan heritage. But our atavistic longings for hierarchy are satisfied by another pagan institution, Hollywood, with its charismatic, imperial stars.

My overview of politics comes from my early interest in classical antiquity and the ancient Near East, particularly Egypt. My understanding of motivation and behavior comes from my reading of Nietzsche and Freud, as well as Homer, Shakespeare, and the nineteenth-century novel. The will-to-power must be contained, but is not generated, by society. In my apartment building in New Haven lived an affectionate calico she-cat named Teabag who ferociously patrolled the sidewalk and fire escape, spontaneously attacking other cats and large dogs and driving all before her. The passion for dominance emanating from this scrawny little fluff, hurling herself hissing and snarling at window panes, was obviously nonacculturated, a prehistoric triumph of the will. My theory of nature follows Sade rather than Rousseau: aggression and violence are primarily not learned but instinctual, nature's promptings, bursts of primitive energy from the animal realm that man has never left. Civilization is an ethical stronghold, the Apollonian palace that reason has built.

Sadean nature, the dark hero of *Sexual Personae*, is the Dionysian or, as I prefer to call it, the chthonian—raw, brute earth-power. Geology is my favorite science. My vision is of a globe shaped like clay, its tectonic plates slipping and sliding over the vastness of time. Volcano, earthquake, stormy sea: nature is a catastrophist, the ultimate source of the Christian idea of apocalypse. Dionysus, trivialized by Sixties polemicists, is not pleasure but pleasure-pain, the gross continuum of nature, the subordination of all living things to biological necessity. I shall argue

orm, not even Greek tragedy in Athens's Theater of
ver gave full voice to the Dionysian until our own
ll, a raucous development of Romanticism.

ceptance of sadomasochism as an immanent principle
sharply separated me from the prior generation of literary scholars, who were largely, in my view, Rousseauist liberals. I considered their assumptions to be tenuous constructs of nineteenth-
century progressivism and Christianizing goodwill. Liberal pieties still hang heavy in the air of American universities. *Sexual
Personae,* so enamoured of personality, is nevertheless a book written against humanism, or rather, against the humanities in their
present academic dilution. My ambition is to rescue humanism
from Rousseau and return it to its first Renaissance audacities.
Understanding of literature and art, as well as current campus
policy, is woefully muddled by philanthropic good intentions.
The Greco-Roman Italian Renaissance, a period of strong personality and incandescent artistic genius, was fiercely competitive
and conspiratorial, showy and violent. Similarly, the neoclassic
eighteenth century, before the advent of Rousseauist tenderness,
was a spectacle of clashing wills, with its satirical broadsides,
public fisticuffs, and rocks flying through dining-room windows.
Aggression and culture were not yet divorced.

Rousseau's hypothesis of a benevolent nature and of humanity deformed by society eventually led to the collapse of confidence of the Age of Anxiety, typified by T. S. Eliot's *The Waste
Land* and Samuel Beckett's *Waiting for Godot.* Twentieth-century
history, with its nightmare-cycle of war, poverty, and organized
sadism, shocked the liberal sensibility into self-reflexive postures
of chic despair. In America, Rousseauism has turned Freud's
conflict-based psychoanalysis into weepy hand-holding. Contemporary liberalism is untruthful about cosmic realities. Therapy,
defining anger and hostility in merely personal terms, seeks to
cure what was never a problem before Rousseau. Mediterranean,
as well as African-American, culture has a lavish system of language and gesture to channel and express negative emotion.
Rousseauists who take the utopian view of personality are always
distressed or depressed over world outbreaks of violence and
anarchy. But because, as a Sadean, I believe history is in nature

and of it, I tend to be far more cheerful and optimi
liberal friends. Despite crime's omnipresence, thing
ciety, because biology compels it. Order eventually r
by psychic equilibrium. Films like *Seven Samurai* (1954) ana *Two
Women* (1961) accurately show the breakdown of social controls
as a regression to animal-like squalor.

Liberals, following Rousseau, believe man is free, but everywhere he is in biologic chains. I am partial to cyclic theories of
reality, as in Hinduism or astrology and the ever-turning Wheel
of Fortune. Nothing so astounds me as the delusion of rationalists
that human life is free of biophysical influences. It is irreligious
and hubristical to imagine that we are divorced from the continuum of living things, alone among plants and animals in our
imperviousness to lunar and seasonal rhythms. Science has barely
begun to chart the complexities of our multiple hormone systems,
which intricately interact and alter us physically and psycholog-
ically hour by hour. Hormones are our link to pagan nature.
Thought itself is a net of racing electric impulses, the energy that
unifies the cosmos, a music of atom's dance.

At midlife, I now accept that there are fundamental sex
differences based in hormones. As a fractious adolescent battling
the conformist Fifties (falsely romanticized today as milkshakes
and sock hops), I thought that men and women were the same
and that all sexual differences were nothing but convention. In
the theory of gender, I began from zero. There is no masculine
power or privilege I did not covet. But slowly, step by step, decade
by decade, I was forced to acknowledge that even a woman of
abnormal will cannot escape her hormonal identity. One of the
themes of this book, unpalatable to liberal well-wishers, is woman's limitation by the body. It might seem that a battle-scarred
veteran of the sex wars, born with a personality so ill-suited to
the prescribed sex role, would have the most grounds for com-
plaint against society. But the opposite is true: my noisy resistance
to primary socialization brought me full circle back to biology.
From my militant history comes a conviction of self-knowledge:
I can declare that what *is* female in me comes from nature and
not from nurture.

The terms *masculine* and *feminine*, which some wish to banish, are used in this book in their ordinary received sense. The traditional association of assertion and action with masculinity, and receptivity and passivity with femininity seems to me scientifically justified. As mammals, we are each an unstable, idiosyncratic mix of both male and female hormones, but human males have an average of eight to twenty times more testosterone than females. I have found the words *masculine* and *feminine* indispensable for my notations of appearance and behavior, but I apply them freely to both sexes, according to mood and situation.

Here are my conclusions, after a lifetime of observation and reflection. Maleness at its hormonal extreme is an angry, ruthless density of self, motivated by a principle of "attack" (cf. "roid rage," produced in male bodybuilders by anabolic steroids). Femaleness at its hormonal extreme is first an acute sensitivity of response, literally thin-skinned (a hormonal effect in women), and secondly a stability, composure, and self-containment, a slowness approaching the sultry. Biologically, the male is impelled toward restless movement; his moral danger is brutishness. Biologically, the female is impelled toward waiting, *expectancy;* her moral danger is stasis. Androgen agitates; estrogen tranquilizes— hence the drowsiness and "glow" of pregnancy. Most of us inhabit not polar extremes but a constantly shifting great middle. However, a preponderance of gray does not disprove the existence of black and white. Sexual geography, our body image, alters our perception of the world. Man is contoured for invasion, while woman remains *the hidden,* a cave of archaic darkness. No legislation or grievance committee can change these eternal facts.

Thus, despite my deviant and rebellious beginnings, I have been led by my studies to reaffirm the most archaic myths about male and female. I aim to recover the truth in sexual stereotypes. Was woman's ancient mystery really only a male mirage? As a woman, I am a mystery to myself. In this book, I accept and celebrate woman's fabled incarnation of mystery and glamour, which man cannot rival except in hierarchic intensifications of kingship and godhead. Woman is at the heart of my myth-system, as she is in Harold Bloom's. Bloom wrote on the manuscript of my dissertation: "Woman is born of woman. But man is born of woman and never recovers from that fact." Possibly because of my Italian heritage, I am partial to the mystical idea of the mother. Paternal or communal proxies can never supplant the magic unity of mother and child, begun in the nine-months' dialogue of the womb.

But woman's maternal fate, from which I made an Amazonian swerve, has a darker side. From puberty to menopause, women are hormonally mired in the liquid realm to which this book gives the peculiar name the "chthonian swamp," my symbol for unregenerate nature. Pregnant or premenstrual, the female body is slowed or even immobilized by edemic engorgement, a Dionysian dowry. Women with water signs prominent in their astrological charts know what I'm talking about. The chthonian swamp, my mythic equivalent to the dread Black Forest of Northern European fairy tales, is perhaps a racial memory of the malarial Pontine Marshes of central Italy, which were finally reclaimed by Mussolini. But ultimately it is the oceanic matrix, the primal soup from which evolution inched forward and into which woman plunges month by month, in the marine obscurity of her hormonal cycle.

Equality of opportunity, a crucial political ideal that all must support, should not be confused with sexual similitude, which remains a wishful fiction. Some past tests (never entirely reliable) suggested that female intelligence occupies the broad median of the spectrum and that women do not reach the heights and depths of men, who may be genius or moron. This rings true to me. I do not believe that the historical absence of great women composers, mathematicians, and philosophers is entirely due to social factors, that is, to woman's lack of access to education and mentoring. Note, for example, in this liberated age, the rarity of world-class female chess masters. Chess shops and parks all over the world are filled with men, not women. Obsessed computer hackers are mostly male. Even sex crimes and mass murders demonstrate the greater conceptualism of men, who have a monopoly on fetishism and perversion.

I suspect men are able to "think cold"; that is, they can detach logic from emotion, in ways that may be creative but also inhumane. However, though men may be deep, mentally they are slow. Compared to women, they are poor at the rapid absorption of verbal data. Narration of complex social incidents is hopelessly impeded by male auditors, who require backtracking, repetition, and endless clarification. Women, on the other hand, can communicate even by sentence fragments: "Did he know that she saw that he—?" "Yes, absolutely!" "Oh, no! And did they—?" "Yes, right then!" This giddy telegraphy is the daily demotic of female intuition, another myth I happily defend. Women finish each other's sentences in the same way that nuns, roommates, and sorority sisters end up menstruating together— a phenomenon that even Madonna, on the road with her backup singers, has complained of. Women are in league with each other, a secret conspiracy of hearts and pheromones.

My odd point of view from the disputed borderline between the sexes began in childhood. I was an early mummer of sexual personae. Halloween was my pagan high holy day. My ingenious parents sewed and constructed splendid costumes to my specifications. At four, I was Alice, in homage to Lewis Carroll's two books, my all-time favorites. After that, my personae were trans-sexual: at five, Robin Hood; at six, the toreador from *Carmen;* at seven, a Roman soldier; at eight, Napoleon; at nine, Hamlet. Long before the women's movement, I was making eccentric nonconformist gestures.

Jung says every man has a repressed female self, the anima, and every woman a repressed male self, the animus. In my case, it was the anima that took longer to emerge, for the animus was never repressed. I remember my fifth-grade teacher making me stay after school because of some shoving and wrangling—I was always fighting with boys to be first in line. Furious, she pushed a dictionary toward me and made me look up the word *aggressive,* which I did, hot tears of shame rolling down my cheeks. Colorful incidents abound, such as when, as a graduate student shopping in Liggett's drugstore at Yale, I broke my umbrella over the head of a rash molester. From childhood to the present day, I have considered it my task to challenge, by word and deed, the public standards for female behavior.

Marooned in the conformist, domestic Fifties, I felt little connection with the boy-chasing girls of my time. Instead, I was galvanized by late-night movies from the Thirties and Forties, which showed a quite different kind of woman, either bold *a* pioneering, like Katharine Hepburn in *Woman of the Year*, or elegant, sophisticated, and sexual, like Marlene Dietrich in *Dishonored*. Film became my door into a lost world. What I was glimpsing was the first phase of feminism, born from the push for the vote and then peaking in those rugged individualists, the brilliant career women of the prewar era, like Dorothy Parker, Dorothy Thompson, Anne Morrow Lindbergh, and Clare Booth Luce. I scoured secondhand bookstores for the works of Mary McCarthy, whose sharp, scathing wit retained, it seemed to me, a Thirties flair.

The ancestor of *Sexual Personae* is the book on Amelia Earhart that I began to write in high school. For three years, I gathered materials and wrote nearly 300 letters of inquiry. Earhart was a symbol to me of female freedom, thought, and movement. She is behind the Artemis myth of *Sexual Personae*. She provided a role model when there was none. Every Saturday, I buried myself in the bowels of the Syracuse public library and systematically rummaged through the magazines and newspapers of the Twenties and Thirties, throughout the course of Earhart's career. I was fascinated by the advertisements, the rotogravure sections, the picture profiles of celebrities at swank parties and lush estates. The prewar era, in the shadow of the Depression, was a period not only of female achievement but of beauty, glamour, and style, values that I found in ancient Egypt but nowhere in my own world, whose applecheeked dictator was Doris Day. My sense of identification with gay men, which began in college, came from this shared adoration of Hollywood and the sleek international high style. Because of these early experiences and tastes, I am out of sync with current feminism, which has lost its memory of prewar feminist history.

The Catholic Church in the Fifties was at its most dogmatic and censorious, and I struggled restlessly within its rules. As we were being drilled for Confirmation, I asked the nun in our catechism class, "If God is all-forgiving, will he ever forgive Satan?" This innocent and, it seems to me, interesting question produced a violent response. The nun turned beet-red and began screaming at me—odd, I thought, since we were sitting in the pews of the

n, needless to say, was not answered. That
w there was no place in the American Church of
or an inquiring mind.

On my sixteenth birthday (in 1963), a Belgian colleague of my father, Josphina van Hal McGinn, gave me Simone de Beauvoir's *The Second Sex*. It made a tremendous impact on me, and I date my intellectual independence from that moment. Beauvoir's imperious French voice, descending from cold, clear Enlightenment skepticism, is one source of the assertions and overassertions of *Sexual Personae*. *The Second Sex*, summing up my social complaints as a wild-eyed adolescent, released me from my passion of opposition to the Fifties. My Amelia Earhart project faded, as I began to imagine a vaster project, which would build on Beauvoir and go beyond her. *The Second Sex* remains for me the supreme work of modern feminism. Most contemporary feminists don't realize to what degree they are merely repeating, amplifying, or qualifying its individual sentences and paragraphs. Its deep learning and massive argument are unsurpassed.

Sexual Personae began to take shape in the essays I wrote in college (1964–68), where I explored questions of sexual ambiguity and aggression in literature, art, and history. The first version of the book, with the present title, was my dissertation at the Yale Graduate School. It was while I was in New Haven that the women's movement burst onto the national scene in 1969. My attempts to join the movement, then and later, ended in calamity. I was nearly tarred and feathered, for example, when I insisted that the Rolling Stones—condemned as "sexist" by a pack of screeching feminist Harpies—were the greatest rock band in the world.

At an early conference in New Haven, I had a chance to mingle with and to observe at close hand a number of the new feminist leaders, including Kate Millett and Rita Mae Brown. I was disturbed by their tunnel vision, their lack of hard political knowledge, their indifference to aesthetics, and the shrill reductiveness of their discourse. And I sensed that too many of these women had an underlying depressiveness or emotional imbalance caused not by the "patriarchy" but by a chaotic family history and their own personal misjudgments. The women's movement had many virtues, but it attracted totalitarian minds. Independent voices like mine were silenced or driven into the wilderness, from which it took me twenty years to return. There is something wrong with a movement that could not tolerate pioneers like me. In certain ways, this phase of feminism was a reactionary turn away from the authentic erotic and spiritual liberation of the Sixties. It has tried to redefine and control sex in order to change and control men. But perhaps we can only change ourselves. I contend that feminism has smugly attributed to itself many of the revolutionary social changes wrought earlier, in fact, by my generation, with its scrappy new individualism. From the moment the Beatles appeared on *The Ed Sullivan Show* in February 1964, our Sixties energy broke the spell of the Fifties.

The first focus of my formal sex studies was images of the androgyne, which I found throughout the history of art and cult. My aim was to give shape and order to the highly nebulous area of sexual ambiguity. I was searching for a language that would avoid the jargon and rigidity of postwar Freudianism as well as that of the new overpoliticized feminism, which rolls over art like a Soviet tank. *Sexual Personae* treats the work of art as a sexual force field disturbed by fluctuations of masculinity and femininity, eddies stirring the surface of a still psychic pond. I see fluidity, surges, reversals. Understanding of the creative process remains unsatisfactory. A huge gap remains between artist and work, which (like Harold Bloom) I am trying to fill. One thesis of *Sexual Personae* is that the inner dynamic of artistic creation consists of a fleeting union between male and female powers. Another is that no Western genre, even epic, is wholly free of self-projection by the author. In college I was already writing on a problem that had received little attention: cross-sexual identification, where a male author projects himself into a female character, and vice versa.

The method of *Sexual Personae* is psychoanalytic. I consider Freud one of the geniuses of literature. He invented modern sex-analysis, without which feminism would be helpless. The wholesale rejection of Freud—which began when Kate Millett declared him a sexist—was one of the gravest errors of contemporary feminism. Despite the sympathetic commentary of a few, and too often narrowly sociological or drearily Lacanian, feminists in

gland, and America, Freud is not directly or system-
udied in feminism. On the contrary, cheap, ignorant
him can be heard everywhere among women, in and
ou. cademe. It is the number one cause of my real-life head-
to-head clashes.

I esteem Freud for his deftness of psychological notation
and his power of speculation, his ability to frame long arguments.
Freudianism, with its ideological excesses, must be separated
from Freud, whose followers never approached his comprehensive
power. But I am a revisionist: I supplement Freud where necessary, sometimes with Jung, whose archetypes I like but whose
foggy prose I deplore. One of the biggest influences on me is Sir
James George Frazer's twelve-volume *The Golden Bough* (1890–
1915), which also influenced Jung but which is invisible in the
sanitized, upbeat Jungianism produced in America after World
War Two. I particularly loathe Joseph Campbell (a seminal
figure for many American feminists) for his mawkishness and
bad research.

My largest ambition is to fuse Frazer and Freud. In a sense,
I am also restoring Frazer to Jung. Some of my character typologies, which may seem Jungian, are coming from astrology,
that complex Babylonian system standardized during the Hellenistic era. I am indebted to the entire Cambridge School of
Anthropology but above all to Jane Harrison, whose *Prolegomena
to the Study of Greek Religion* (1903) I consider one of the books of
the century. I rank Jane Harrison among the greatest women
writers. Other works behind *Sexual Personae* include Spengler's
Decline of the West, D. H. Lawrence's *Women in Love,* and Ferenczi's
Thalassa. Following World War Two, besides the collected works
of G. Wilson Knight and Harold Bloom: Erich Neumann's *The
Great Mother* and *Origins and History of Consciousness* (Jungianism
at its learned best), Kenneth Clark's *The Nude,* Bachelard's *Poetics
of Space,* Norman O. Brown's *Life Against Death* and *Love's Body,*
and Leslie Fiedler's *Love and Death in the American Novel.*

Central to the psychologistic approach of *Sexual Personae* is
its concern with style, studies of which are surprisingly few. My
immediate experience of a literary work is in terms of style, for
which I have sought to develop a critical vocabulary. Unlike

French post-structuralists, I believe there is always
hind every text. Kenneth Burke says, " 'Style' is an
identification."[2] For me, style *is* persona. My interest .
comes from Walter Pater, whom I first stumbled on in high su
and whose notoriously purple prose-poem on the *Mona Lisa* is
the model for many of the art analyses in *Sexual Personae*. In 1974,
Harold Bloom said of Pater, then long out of fashion, that "[he]
has had little influence upon modern academic criticism, but one
can prophesy that such influence will yet come."[3] The first paper
I submitted in graduate school (on early Wallace Stevens as
Decadent) was returned with a comment dismissing it as an
"appreciation," an anti-Pater slight: *Appreciations* (1889), Pater's
book of literary essays, influenced Wilde, Yeats, Joyce, and Pound.

Pater inspired me with the desire to restore writing on art
to nineteenth-century belles-lettres. In college, I was exasperated
by the New Criticism's discouragement of psychological inquiry
and its suave pretense of objectivity. In Pater, and in British
scholarly writing of the first half of the twentieth century, I found
an urbane style, lucid and personal. Paterian subjectivity claims
for the essay the imaginative authority normally reserved for
poetry and fiction. Oscar Wilde says, following Pater, "The highest criticism is the record of one's own soul."[4] Today the traditional genres can no longer say enough. They have been crimped
and curtailed by history, which (one of my major theses) has
permanently diverted artistic energy and authenticity into popular culture.

My early attempts to write poetry were frustrating, since I
sensed that the learned style I was drawn to—Metaphysical or
Italian Mannerist—was misaligned with the times. If only there
were a poetry that could explain itself as it went along. Hence
my fixation on a Paterian poetic prose, which would marry intellect and inspiration. Contemporary poetry is largely lyric, but
many passages in *Sexual Personae*—such as those on Nefertiti or,
in Volume Two, Rita Hayworth—are really odes, in the sublime
Pindaric style, lofty, celebratory, and ritualistic. The emotional
heights of dance or opera, the ecstatic gestures of Baroque saints:
why was it not possible to get these intensities into the essay? In
Sexual Personae, I have tried to extend the emotional range of

English expository prose. To analyze while still leaving the magic
and the mystery. To elucidate and complicate, to explain and
mystify at the same time.

I pity the poet or novelist in this age of mass media, but
my envy is frank and unconcealed for *the musician,* who is able to
affect the audience with such emotional directness, a pre-rational
manipulation of the nerves. I long for a prose of Classic structure
yet Romantic fire, as in Monteverdi or Chopin. A prose with
both clarity and passion, eternal opposites of Apollo and Dionysus, a harmony of brain hemispheres. My domination by music
is total. *Sexual Personae* could be subtitled, after a 1972 Stevie
Wonder album, *Music of my Mind.* My "reading" of Western
civilization was directly inspired by the four Brahms symphonies,
which entranced me in college—in particular the third, which I
listened to hundreds of times while writing this book.

Pater made me intolerant of arid abstraction in discussions
of literature, bad in second-generation New Criticism but far
worse in the French invasion, with its coarse, clumsy construc-
tions. From the poet Milton Kessler, my college teacher, I learned
a respect for the sensory quality of literature, the primary level
that is too quickly overleaped by most criticism. I am a sensa-
tionalist, in all meanings of the word: I make my sensations into
ideas, and I reduce my ideas to sensations, so that thought and
feeling are simultaneous. My treatment of art works is a kind
of electrocution therapy, applying a live wire (that is, me) to
make them jump and light up with a neon glare. "Luridness"
is for me, as for admirers of the Mannerist El Greco, a compli-
mentary term.

Sexual Personae makes Paterian appreciation a rite of Italian
memoriousness. Jacob Burckhardt speaks of the "frightful viv-
idness" of Italian imagination, which led to the Renaissance ven-
detta but also to "the corresponding national virtue" of
gratitude.[5] As a part-time court interpreter in the Twenties, my
paternal grandfather expedited the acquittal of an Italian immigrant charged with murder. Forever after, when the two met
on the street, the man would fall to his knees and kiss my grandfather's hands. My appreciations of art are in the fervid, florid

Italian style. Melodrama means melodious dramaturgy, a musical theater. The greatest honor that can be paid to the art work, on its pedestal of ritual display, is to *describe* it with sensory completeness. We need a science of description. Too much criticism is dull as dishwater because the object has receded into the academic distance. I try not to allude to but to re-create, to reproduce the first, baffling experience of reading a text or seeing a painting or film. Criticism is ceremonial revivification, like the *nekuomanteia* of the *Odyssey*, the magic "evocation of the shades."

My hyped-up style is the route of *enthousiasmos,* making a big deal out of what was thought to be nothing, showing the divine in the common. The lavish ceremonialism of Italian culture is a Greco-Roman bequest. In English, "Let me show you out" originally meant not "Let me help you find the door" (though this was relevant in a large house) but "Let me make a show to accompany you out." Only Italians, it seems, still observe this protocol. Group departures are characterized by what I call "Milling and Shouting," as twenty people kiss each other in turn (a sum total of four hundred kisses). Next is mass evacuation onto the lawn, piling into autos, and frantic waving on both sides until everyone is out of sight. Art is a ceremony, and so is criticism. Appreciation, a commemorative magniloquence, is inflated psychoeconomic value. And description is a pagan offering, George Herbert's "wreathed garland of deserved praise."

My primary technique for revivifying interpretation is the metaphor. Bloom says the meaning of a poem can only be another poem.[6] My practice is to meet metaphor with metaphor, fire lighting fire to rekindle an art work smothered by overfamiliarity and received opinion. For all his genius, Freud was indifferent to music and at a loss with art criticism. His disciples served him poorly with reductionist diagnoses presenting the artist as patient and art as neurotic symptom. The metaphors of *Sexual Personae* mesh Freudian theory with the art work by providing a mediating link, a Janus-face looking two ways. The metaphors are notes toward a new art criticism, projecting tiny unsuspected movements into the still space between the lines of a text or between artist and work. The metaphors are subordinate dramas catching the artist midthought. My method is microscopic, showing an apparently smooth surface to be pitted by psychic abrasion, scourings of love and war.

Metaphor operates by simple analogy: this is that. My analogies may seem farfetched. They have indeed been fetched from afar, a Magian gift-bearing by a scholar with stars in her eyes. My fetching—or schlepping, as I like to call it—is meant to demonstrate likeness, unity, and coherence where there was division, disorder, or irrelevance. I subscribe to a Renaissance cosmology, a divine network of correspondences, where everything is in analogy to everything else. I see a world cluttered with portents, what Jung calls synchronicity. Emerson remarks, "Some people are made up of rhyme, coincidence, omen, periodicity, and presage."[7] To the despair of sensible friends, I am forever crying out things like, "Good God! That license plate is not only the street number of our restaurant but the birth date of that poet we heard read exactly ten years ago today!" As early as Pascal, we find a distinction drawn between "the mathematical and the intuitive mind."[8] My point of view is stubbornly pre-Enlightenment, allowing intellection to cohabit with intuition and superstition. Virginia Woolf says of the Renaissance poet Orlando's first encounter with his beloved, "He called her a melon, a pineapple, an olive tree, an emerald, and a fox in the snow all in the space of three seconds."[9] I follow the metamorphic logic of Renaissance metaphor, images rapid, abrupt, and incongruous. My metaphors are surreal visualizations or literalized clichés, concrete raids on the abstract. Clichés are for me a comic folk poetry.

I condemn as an intellectual error, parochial and time-bound, the modernist view of the "discontinuities" of experience and of a meaningless universe, typified by Samuel Beckett's flat, bare stage. Fragmentation is in the eye of the beholder. As a child of popular culture, teethed on the electronic media, I feel the neighborly nearness of nations, continents, planets. Wires, wires everywhere: our thoughts are beads on the endless chain of connectedness that is the cosmos. My metaphors are sports of a mysticism of *things*, a pagan crusade to "save the phenomena."

All objects, all phases of culture are alive. They have voices.

They speak of their history and interrelatedness. And they are all talking at once! The model of relationship in *Sexual Personae* is the vast, sprawling Italian extended family, where cousins are numbered unto the nth degree. Metaphors assert germaneness, literally "kinship." Throughout the book, anecdote, digression, and metaphor are used as bizarre juxtaposition or apposition, the surreal collage of dreamwork. High and popular culture freely intermingle, brought together by the Greco-Roman guest-host ethic, detoured through Lewis Carroll ("Alice—Mutton; Mutton—Alice. Pudding—Alice; Alice—Pudding"). *Sexual Personae* provides the formal introduction of Nefertiti and David Bowie, Michelangelo and Gracie Allen, who have never met before and thus not realized what they have in common. My syncretism is Alexandrian and anti-modern, herding into one compound the wandering strangers this century has made.

Women have never written epic, the longest and most military of literary forms, taking in the gods and heaven and hell. In its excessive scale and all-fencing inclusiveness, *Sexual Personae* is a Roman omnibus, a gazetteer of points of cultural transfer. Samuel Johnson said of *Paradise Lost*, "None ever wished it longer than it is." A reporter witnessed this exchange between the young Hayley Mills and the actress's middle-aged lover, producer Roy Boulting. *Mills:* "Mummy is writing her memoirs." *Boulting:* "Oh, really? Is she going to sell them by the pound? She always has so much to say." The two volumes of *Sexual Personae*, with the author as Amazon epic quester, may be the longest book yet written by a woman, exceeding in this respect even George Eliot's hefty *Middlemarch*. That book contains as its moral irritant a huge unrealized project, Casaubon's *Key to all Mythologies*, which I dutifully complete here.

There is no war between ancients and moderns. The cultural space so prematurely emptied by modernism must be replanted and reforested. I make metaphors as Italians make gardens, turning a tiny scrap of city soil into a row of tomatoes or geraniums. The will-to-adorn: my Baroque extravagance goes against the modern type of "the thinker." Susan Sontag, for example, a generation older, is tall, thin, and cerebral, in European terms a northerner as I am a southerner. Her gravity and austerity belong to the era of Sartrean nausea, of metaphysical dyspepsia, of "no" rather than "yes." I, on the other hand, with my Mediterranean mesomorphic bullishness and frenetic Joan Rivers comedy routines, am an overeater and overstater, a gourmandizer of the grand manner.

"Abbondanza!" proclaimed a television commercial for Mama Celeste's frozen pizza. Culture is nurturant, sustaining, inexhaustible. Language is fruit and meat, physical, sensual. My mental template was undoubtedly formed by the mammoth wedding receptions I witnessed as a child in the Sons of Italy hall in Endicott, festivals of a now-vanished tribalism. Four generations jammed into rollicking, supersaturated space. Ham sandwiches heaped in towering ziggurats on white-draped tables. But what ham, what bread!—the finest prosciutto in snowy rolls of crusty gold. Soda bottles swimming like fat trout in silver tubs of ice water, into which one gleefully plunged one's small arm. Lavishness, accessibility, capaciousness. It is no coincidence that the biggest kettles and bowls in cookware shops are for Italian pasta and salad. *Sexual Personae* is a *ragù* with a cast of thousands, an ode in an Italian pot.

The book's transhistorical ambition and interdisciplinary method are meant to cure the disease of the small afflicting American academe. Specialization has made mincemeat of the great body of knowledge. G. Wilson Knight says, "It is easier to communicate with spirits than for one university department to communicate with another."[10] The humanities are dismembered and scattered, with music, art, and literature residing far afield. Literature is chopped into national fiefdoms. English departments are split by recruitment "slots," a triumph of the minim, producing such atrocities as ads for "Opening in nondramatic literature, 1660–1740." What kind of scholar, what kind of teacher could satisfy this sad little mouse-view of culture? American universities are organized on the principle of the nuclear rather than the extended family. Graduate students are grimly trained to be technicians rather than connoisseurs. The old nineteenth-century German style of universal scholarship is gone.

Without specialization, I have been virtually unemployable

in this country, except in arts colleges. Yet surely on
can represent the humanities in this time of crisis, as ι.
generation is being swallowed up in materialism and technolog,
American academic life is further enfeebled by its genteel code
of professorial deportment. Our universities are the bland leading
the bland. Are academics born sedate, or is sedateness thrust
upon them? Promotion requires respectability, spirit-killing re-
straints. Eccentricities, for which the English are noted, are not
tolerated, except in the already famous. The WASP ethic of
American universities has given birth to a scholarship the mirror
image of itself, passionless and humorless. David Cecil says, "Artists seldom are the same sort of people as critics—that is why so
much criticism is inept."[11]

To be a scholar is the greatest of vocations: to compose a
devout commentary, a Talmud, on the created world. My tradition is far older than the WASP one. I feel in the direct line of
priests. My mother was born a few miles north of Monte Cassino,
the sixth-century Benedictine monastery where St. Thomas Aqui-
nas was educated. Her great-aunt Camilla was an abbess of the
Italian Sisters of Charity; her uncle was a sexton in the Vatican.
My paternal grandfather's uncle was Bishop of Avellino in Italy,
and his cousin was the first priest of St. Antony of Padua, my
baptismal church. My cousin is a nun of the American Pallottine
order. My father was a professor of Romance languages at a
Jesuit college.

The teachers to whom I owe the most, Harold Bloom and
Milton Kessler, are less professors than they are visionary rabbis.
The rabbinical paradigm also applies to other minds I admire:
Geoffrey Hartman, Alvin Feinman, Richard Tristman. In England, the origins of Oxford and Cambridge in medieval mon-
asticism produced the tendency of their faculties toward celibacy
or homosexuality. The urbane, witty, verbally aggressive English
professorial style strongly contrasts with the enforced standard
in America, where, until recently, the mild, upright family man
was most prized. Colin Still remarks, "The critic of imaginative
art is essentially an interpreter of dreams."[12] I claim descent from
mantics, augurs, scribes, alchemists, and heretics. The spiritual

...ities is compromised by their in-
...ism and cant. Of the scholar I say: the
...he monk, but never the bourgeois.

...ach to art is multipartite, a psychomedical work-
...palpation: I record the work's emotional and sensory
...cter, photographing it by faithful description. Second, genealogy: the work's psychohistory, its relation to the artist and
era. Third, X-ray: its skeleton or ritual deep structure. Fourth,
analogy: its resemblance to other things, past and future, high
and low. Because I came into literature from classics and archaeology, I tend to think of the text as a ruin or rune of desire
and of the critic's task as reconstruction of the vanished temple
of intention or possibility. Freud, an amateur collector, also uses
an archaeological metaphor to describe the unlayering of the
psyche in analysis. The ur-model for *Sexual Personae* as magnum
opus is undoubtedly the Metropolitan Museum of Art, which I
first saw as a small child: a towering citadel of chambers organized by period and hoarding every artifact, pristine or weathered, royal or domestic. *Sexual Personae* has a simultaneously
bird's-eye and worm's-eye view of culture, examining well-known
art works from curious angles. It rarely comes in the gallery door
in the usual, "common sense" way.

Bird and worm: Apollo and Dionysus, sky-cult and earth-
cult, illumination and mystery. I honor Apollo and Dionysus
equally, as the Sixties did not do. The key words in my theory
of the Dionysian or chthonian are "strange," "primitive," "uncanny"—linking me to Harold Bloom. It was the absence of a
sense of the daemonic that I found so alienating in New Criticism, with its sunny Christian courtesy. I can date very precisely
between the ages of three and six my first vision of the uncanny
and hieratic: the mummy cases and stone sphinxes of the Met's
Egyptian galleries; the stormy birth of the world in Walt Disney's *Fantasia;* the cruel, beautiful witch-queen of Disney's *Snow
White;* Yma Sumac's unearthly *Voice of the Xtabay* (1950), with
its album photo of the Peruvian-American singer in the spangled
costume and posture of a prophesying priestess, against a background of menacing sculpture and erupting volcano. The modernist universe of too little yields to the daemonic universe of

too much. For despair I substitute awe. For anxiety I substitute terror, Coleridge's "holy dread" of a universe choked with meaning.

To the Dionysian night-world I oppose the cold crystalforms of the Apollonian, with its haughty conceptualism. Chastity, as an aesthetic and psychological rather than moral ideal, is one of the Apollonian themes of *Sexual Personae*. Also Apollonian is my theory of high comedy, which I define as a hierarchic mode. The comedy of *Sexual Personae* separates it from Bloom's work, for whatever riches may be harvested from my distinguished mentor, it cannot be said that reading him is a barrel of laughs! My double view, taking in the primal with the artificial, is a rite of intellectual reconciliation. My appreciation of glamour and aristocratic style (anti-bourgeois *and* anti-liberal, as in Baudelaire and Wilde) is another point of divergence from Bloom. We belong to different Western traditions. Bloom, who prefers the Bible to Homer, is Judeo-Christian. His consciousness is completely literary, an orchestral dynasty of the Word. I am Greco-Roman, ruled by visual images and formal theatrics, in art, sport, politics, and war.

In the twentieth century, the West has had a bad conscience about itself. During the Sixties' tilt toward the Far East, I became fascinated by Asian music, religion, and, of course, cuisine. But the more I learned, the more I was convinced of the West's perverse greatness and of my own radically Western character. *Sexual Personae* accepts and reinterprets the canonical Western tradition. It does not construct a feminist countertradition—except with Sade and popular culture, which it pulls into the Western main line.

I proceed not by the cynical Stracheyan debunking of modern disillusion but by a *re*bunking. I am an Italian pagan mythomane. I am an American surrealist: this is a *Twilight Zone* book, born, like Rod Serling's eerie tales, in placid, pleasant upstate New York. *Cast a Cold Eye,* said Mary McCarthy in 1950, advocating postwar ironic detachment. To which I reply, cast a hot eye, amorously acquisitive and devotional. My personae are like the glossy saints' pictures on Catholic Mass cards, theatrical and outlandishly polychrome. In its psychedelic view of the West,

Sexual Personae is like Mantegna's *Procession of Caesar,* a crowded triumph bristling with strange symbols but observing classical order and form. History moves on, but art never forgets.

NOTES

1. *The New Science,* trans. Thomas Bergin and Max Fisch (Ithaca, 1970), p. 341.

2. *The Philosophy of Literary Form* (New York, 1957), p. 266.

3. *Selected Writings of Walter Pater,* ed. Harold Bloom (New York, 1974), p. xxviii.

4. "The Critic as Artist," in *Selected Writings,* ed. Richard Ellmann (London, 1961), p. 68.

5. *The Civilization of the Renaissance in Italy,* trans. S.G.C. Middlemore (New York, 1958), II, pp. 430, 432.

6. *The Anxiety of Influence* (New York, 1973), p. 70.

7. *Selections from Ralph Waldo Emerson,* ed. Stephen E. Whicher (Boston, 1957), p. 351.

8. *Pensées,* trans. A. J. Krailsheimer (Baltimore, 1966), p. 210.

9. *Orlando* (New York, 1928), p. 23.

10. *Neglected Powers* (London, 1971), p. 31.

11. *Poets and Story-Tellers* (London, 1949), p. 23.

12. *The Timeless Theme* (London, 1936), p. 13.

MILTON KESSLER:

A MEMOIR

Once in a lifetime, if you're lucky, you have a great teacher. Mine was Milton Kessler.

My book, *Sexual Personae,* was born in my experiences as a college student during the turbulent, florid Sixties at Harpur College (the State University of New York at Binghamton). Harpur, with its strong presence of avant-garde, intellectual Jewish students from New York City, was seething with raw creative energy. People called it Berkeley East.

During the Sixties, poetry and rock music were in sync. Long-haired, barefoot young men with guitars

[*Sulfur,* Spring 1991]

...s reading poetry books. Allen Ginsberg's bardic
...d Whitman's nature litanies, Hart Crane's urban
...and African-American jazz rhythms into Bob Dylan,
...rsh lyrics made rock an art form. Jim Morrison of
the ... rs was an omnivorous reader with a photographic memory. Poetry has gone out of fashion in today's rock world, and
the music has suffered. Rock has lost its spirituality and sense
of mission.

Poetry flourished at Harpur College. Books of Lorca,
Rimbaud, and Baudelaire were strewn among the latest Jimi
Hendrix and Jefferson Airplane albums. Poetry readings were
jammed. We saw dozens of important American poets in their
prime—Robert Creeley, Robert Duncan, Galway Kinnell, and
many others.

Milton Kessler is everywhere in my memories of that time.
He was at the readings and raucous receptions afterward at remote faculty houses. He was at the art exhibits, the performances
of the Guarneri Quartet (then in residence), the endless foreign
films, those spectacular, sophisticated hallucinations which so
formed my imagination.

Kessler embodies for me an ideal of the arts in dynamic
synthesis. I despise specialization, separation, narrowness, track-
ing. I despise academe as it is presently constituted. Kessler is
not so much a professor as a visionary rabbi—something that
can also be said of my graduate-school mentor, Harold Bloom.
Great teachers live their subject. The subject teaches itself
through them. It uses them and, in return, charges them with
elemental energy.

Purely by chance, I took "Introduction to Poetry" with
Milton Kessler. I have never been the same. Kessler's classes on
Theodore Roethke's *Words for the Wind* showed me what poetry
is and how it works on the body. As I flip through that book, I
see countless images and phrases that ended up, transformed by
my dream life, in *Sexual Personae*. There are the eerie spirit-
presences of nature, the oozy mire, mute beasts, and mystical
Muse-women.

Kessler teaching Roethke or Whitman's hypnotic "Out of
the Cradle Endlessly Rocking" stressed the body-rhythms and

organic pulses that underlie all poetry. Words are merely a veil through which we glimpse other, deeper realities. It was primarily because of my training by Kessler that I was later able to recognize Saussurean language-theory for the fraud that it is. A whole generation of academics my age destroyed themselves by chasing after Saussure and his Parisian disciples. Right now, at mid-career, they are waking up to the nullity of their work.

Reading poetry aloud, Kessler made great use of dynamics, another of the losses rock music has suffered since the Sixties. Like the blues shouters, Kessler could roar, then drop off to a rasp or whisper. Poetry was music-drama. I recently learned that Kessler studied voice and opera as a young man and had even been a spear carrier at the old Met. This explains much of his impact on me. Italians invented opera. It is our way of living in and reacting to the world. In opera, emotion fills the body. Italians experience emotion in sensory terms, as if it were something eaten, drunk, or poured over the flesh. Long ago on TV, Dick Cavett said he didn't like opera; he didn't "get it." As I looked at his small, thin body and large, smirky, Ivy League head, I said: yes.

Kessler made me the teacher I am. He believed in the dramatic moment. Everything that you were, everything that you had ever seen or experienced pressed upon the text in front of you. The class hour seemed to melt and expand. Memory is central to both the Jewish and Italian traditions. Reading a poem, Kessler strove to remember everything, to fill it even fuller than the poet had left it. With the improvisation of great Jewish comedians like Lenny Bruce, Kessler would weave in and out of the class his own passing thoughts, reminiscences, disasters. His classic formulation: "I think of. . . ." It echoes in my mind, I use it in my book. Listening to Kessler, you were understanding how the poetic mind works, how sensations and images flow, twist, and bond.

I remember bursting out with startled laughter when Kessler once said offhandedly in the middle of class, "So last week I was driving along and, in my usual trance, ran into the back of a truck." Master teachers, revealing themselves, show the continuum of life and thought. The physical and psychological realms coexist in a fifth dimension. Kessler interested me in the shocking segue, the disconcerting juxtaposition, an existential collage. Eight years ago, while I was teaching as a visitor at Yale (and dodging the preppy gases), a puzzled senior said to me, "Your teaching style is so unusual." Of course, it was Kessler's style. I think of a *New Yorker* cartoon from the 1930s: the dark, stocky figure of Fiorello La Guardia is shown entering towered City Hall, which, in subsequent frames, swells, puffs, wheezes, steams, explodes, then wearily sighs and subsides as the mayor leaves it at the end of the day. That's what Kessler's classes were like. Architecture seemed to dissolve and remold.

French post-structuralism, among its many stupidities, denies that a coherent self exists. Academic nebbishes love this notion. Anyone interested in the performing arts knows that personality is a vitalistic, uncontrollable phenomenon. Talented performers and teachers have an electric power of personality, a charismatic magnitude and density. Kessler was a burly, robust man with the inner emotionality of the melancholy Jewish tradition. He told of once, among strangers, marching heavily up to a table and a woman calling out, "Taurus!" Italians have always been grounded in practical material reality, from the sewers and aqueducts of Roman engineering to our control of today's concrete and stonecutting trades. Kessler's Taurine physicality and materialism appealed to me. His new book reveals that he once worked in the garment industry. I hate the airy, affected, rich-bitch dilettantism of the art world. The artist has more in common with the car mechanic, all sweat, grease, and ingenuity. Kessler was blunt, profane about pretension. Once the professors took the English majors to a poetry conference at another college, where a girl speaker welcomed us: "We the special ones, the sensitive ones. . . ." Afterward, Kessler said, "If she'd done that at Harpur, the students would have dragged up cow manure and hurled it at her!" He made comic gestures of manure-heaving.

In class, Kessler gave me my first warning about the deplorable condition of academic criticism. Second-generation New Criticism was then in decline. Kessler described the spirit-killing academic approach, which tried to "crack" the poem, smashing it like a nut. Worse things were to come, in the French fad of the

Seventies, which exalted mundane, jargon-sp

the artist. Kessler found graduate education in geı.

thought. He told of an incident where a graduate stuu

cilessly goaded by Roy Harvey Pearce, pulled a knife on ho

class. This story impressed me. I dislike the bland, WASƿᵧ,

business-as-usual style encouraged by American graduate

schools. It's Kraft cheese slices on the grand scale. Emotion is

suppressed and contorted. A criticism alienated from emotion is

false, doomed.

Kessler freely showed emotion. Once in class, he suddenly exploded with rage at some boys in the back row. He accused them of "peeking," of peeping Tomism: "Get out! It's *obscene!*" He meant, I assume, that they were sneering cynics, keeping themselves apart from the class. It's good for students to see honest emotion from their teachers. Around this time, I visited the classes of a friend at another university. Midway through a history lecture, the professor's briefcase slipped off the desk and fell with a huge clang into the wastebasket. No one in the jammed hall breathed. The professor blanched but, stone-faced, kept talking and at last, with difficulty, rescued the briefcase. Strange and dead. At Harpur, there would have been hilarity and Jewish shtick, the free play of humor and self-satire. I welcome all random incidents—from chairs tipping over to explosions in the street—and try to incorporate them into the class flow.

Returning from a trip to Europe, Kessler commented to us about the poor quality of American food, then in its Wonderbread and TV-dinner phase. He said, "If you ever asked for *an orange* in an American restaurant, the walls would fall and the staff go mad!" From Europe he excitedly brought us a personal discovery: Bachelard's *The Poetics of Space*. He said the moment he saw it he knew "this is *the* book" he'd always been looking for. I too now loved Bachelard, whose dignified yet fluid phenomenological descriptive method seemed to me ideal for art. I had been reading Bergson and Poulet. Bachelard was the last modern French writer I took seriously. Post-Sartrean French literature got more and more deranged, sudsy conceit-tempests in a Parisian teapot.

I remember Kessler in warm relation to the Harpur hippies and radicals, who were mainly from urban and suburban New

York City. One picture is especially vivid: a crowded, drunken reception for a visiting writer at the Kesslers' Binghamton house. It was a time when rebellious young men, letting their hair grow, had a soft, open look of poetic innocence. You can see it in news films of Sixties demonstrations and rock festivals. Afterward, in the Seventies, American faces got hard, snide. Too much had happened. Sprawled in the middle of the Kesslers' jammed living-room floor was a ring of hippies singing amid the din. The leader, sitting cross-legged, was laughing, exuberant. His bearded, beautiful face, lit by a ruddy lamp, was framed by a wild crown of glossy, jet-black hair. It was at such moments that one recognized the pure Romanticism of the Sixties. Kessler was deeply moved. Arms folded, he stood watching the animated boy and then, his eyes moist, remarked to another professor, "He is a young David." Overhearing this unobserved, I was overwhelmed by a sense of Jewish history, of cultural transmission from fathers to sons over time.

Another of my memories is less pleasant. As I attended or audited course after course of Kessler's, I came into conflict with another of the radicals, a brilliant, smouldering New Yorker with dark, lank hair, rough skin, and piercing blue eyes. He had an implacable Scorpio intensity. Studying was not fashionable in the psychedelic Sixties. This fellow, Jeffrey, found my busy in-class note-taking totally unhip and reactionary. Notations, at every hour of the day and night, are in fact the basis of my writing. At home, at work, in stores, in cars, I constantly record my fleeting impressions and mental flashes, which zip by like meteor showers turning quickly to ash. Jeff cut a glamourous figure on campus. Once while I was sitting in the cavernous snack bar, he and his coterie, with enormous éclat, came sweeping in, half-clothed, dripping from an impromptu dip in the plaza fountain. It was a radical gesture for a generation emerging from repressive Fifties convention. When I decided to go to Yale for graduate school, Jeff confronted and denounced me: Yale was not "where it's happening." I should go to Buffalo, then a hotbed of poetry and psychoanalytic criticism, my special interest. He upset me, and I sought advice from several teachers. In a way, he was prophetic: two years later, I was sitting in the office of the Director of

Graduate Studies at the Yale English Department, formally pro
testing the way "Freudian" and "psychoanalytic" were con-
temptuously used as dirty words by professors in class. That same
year, when Leslie Fiedler came to speak at Yale, not a single
English Department faculty member showed up.

Kessler was, I think, quite unaware of the bolts of hostility
passing between Jeff and me in class, particularly when we were
meeting in the round in living rooms or on the grass outside.
Once, as we were discussing a poem, I suggested there was (what
else is new?) an element of "onanism" in an image. Kessler, head
bowed and gravely scrutinizing the text, said the very idea was
"horrifying," "repellent"—here Jeff looked up and glared at me
in malicious triumph—but "there's no question it's absolutely
there"—now *I* glared back in triumph, as Jeff wilted. The whole
thing was absurd, but I cannot separate it from my memories of
Kessler's classes. I tell the story because of its extraordinary
conclusion. I never saw or heard of Jeff again after graduation.
Seven years later, while I was teaching at Bennington, I picked
up the local newspaper and saw, in headlines, that three miles
over the state border from my Vermont house there had been a
mysterious murder-suicide. A New York man of Jeff's name had
arrived with his girlfriend for a vacation weekend and had killed
her and then himself with a rifle. I called Harpur. The Washington Square–area street address was the same. I wrote immediately to Kessler, who was devastated. He wrote back that,
getting the news, he nearly "fell on the floor." It was one of the
most haunting things that ever happened to me. I do believe in
karma. This was a Sixties tragedy, a story of promising but un-
fulfilled talent, which in so many cases was shortcircuited by
drugs. Drugs first liberated and then destroyed. I never learned
anything more than what I have said here. It is an odd destiny
that it has been left to me, Jeff's unwilling enemy, to remember him.

At my commencement ceremony, it was announced from
the podium that I was the first known second-generation Harpur
student. (My father had entered when it was Triple Cities College
and had been in the first Harpur graduating class.) It was also
announced that I, as the valedictorian, had received "only one

of college. Meeting my parents afterward at the
said, laughing and making rueful bearlike mo-
ms, "When I heard that, I quaked in my seat!"
he B, which I wore proudly, then and now. It
ol to me of Kessler's original imagination, his
higher standard. What Kessler gave me is beyond the conventions
of academe. I saw so clearly in graduate school and afterward
that my early exposure to Kessler had miraculously spared me
the stultifying formulas of thought and decorum that afflicted
most of those who had gone to older, more established schools.
With Kessler, you begin literature and art fresh each time you
come to them.

In reply to a recent inquiry about artistic influences on his
work, Kessler listed Verdi, Puccini, Jussi Bjorling, and Giovanni
Martinelli in opera; Antonioni, Bergman, and DeSica in cinema;
Post-Impressionism and German Impressionism in painting;
Chekhov, Gogol, Babel, Sholem Aleichem, Camus, and Sartre
in fiction. He reveres Torah and classic Chinese poetry, and
names these as poets with whom he feels a special kinship: Blake,
Whitman, Thomas Hardy, Dylan Thomas, William Carlos Wil-
liams, John Crowe Ransom, Roethke, Elizabeth Bishop, A. R.
Ammons, John Logan, David Ignatow, Donald Hall, George
Oppen, Charles Reznikoff, Karl Rakosi, Jackson MacLow, Clay-
ton Eshleman, Jerome Rothenberg.

Kessler says of his fifth book, *The Grand Concourse* (1990),
that several of the poems were "written in hospitals." He speaks
of "the Ars Medica" of his work, of "illnesses determining body-
states." I remember him speaking in class of the psychological
"meaning" of asthma, of its power in a specific family romance.
It was the first time I had thought in this way, and I never forgot
it. I continue to interpret disease and anxiety in psychodramatic
terms and to see the art work as an emanation or displaced and
projected body of the artist. The cover photo of Kessler's new
book is a striking aerial view of an enormous strip of aging brick
apartment buildings along the Grand Concourse in the Bronx,
where he grew up. The name of this broad, sweeping avenue
makes me ponder the immigrant experience. My family, coming
from Italy, bypassed the city and settled in upstate New York,

where the Endicott-Johnson shoe factories needed the ancient leatherworking skills of our region in Lazio. Most European immigrants of the last century arrived here poor. But behind us stretches the grand concourse of the Western tradition. Teaching is another kind of grand concourse. Through it, you produce and set into motion spiritual progeny, those who Plato says are under the protection of the higher or Uranian Aphrodite.

Kessler's poems are filled with visual images. Interestingly, he once worked as an optician. This is another parallel between his sensibility and mine. My earliest memories are of staring, transfixed, at objects, clouds, colors, light. As a writer, I strive to save the gorgeous world of appearances. I have always been conscious (here comes my scorn for Saussure and Lacan) of the prodigious labor of transferring or translating sensory impressions, the flux of life, into language. Inscribing his new book to me, Kessler paid me the great compliment of calling *Sexual Personae* an "optical masterpiece." Kessler's poetry seizes my attention by its fidelity to both visual and emotional truth, a rare combination. Kessler negotiates between the outer and inner worlds; he records the day-to-day moments of truce won by our ever-shifting consciousness. Even when he alludes to "Nietzsche, Wagner, Furtwangler" ("Everyone Loves Children"), there is nothing academic about it. His style is stripped down, abrupt, emphatic, concrete. The rhythms are spoken, flexible. All the poems in *The Grand Concourse* have a different "look." The lines, the shapes vary, like our own moods.

One of my favorite poems here is "The Machine of Sundown": an "orange-rot Liberty hull freighter," "welded with gull-dung and war slime," has, like "the vanished gas tanks at Coney Island,/ fallen to blue-torch scrap-truck" and "slides on slabs of orange river slag." These explosive aggressive rhythms reproduce the impact and surprise of visual signals hitting the optic nerve. They carry with them the bruising workdays of steelworkers and longshoremen. The gritty, decaying riverscape-details write history around us, an unsentimental elegy still vibrating with the energy of the industrial past. The poem has the ugly/beautiful surrealism of the modern city. Its choppy alliterations remind me of effects I tried to achieve in my passage on the Venus of

Willendorf, and its chain-link of lurid, atomized images resembles my associative anatomy of Emily Dickinson's fierce metaphors.

"Women Seen" is a series of cinematic glimpses of archetypal woman in her many modes, changing yet always, like Pater's Mona Lisa, the same. She fixes her sandal with a gesture seen in Greek sculpture. She is the pregnant teenager, the cocktail waitress, the little girl on her parent's lap, the woman trying on dresses in front of the multiple mirror of her and our eyes. In one vivid moment of special meaning to me, she is seen "hanging up laundry barefoot like a dancer / on a windy day, clothespins in her mouth." In our age of laundromats and automatic dryers, children have lost this old experience, detectable as early as Homer's Nausikaa episode, in which woman is fused with wind and sun, in a public ritual of ablution and renewal. It is a visual memory with its own gusty sounds and crisp fresh smell.

Kessler is sensitive to interpenetrations of nature and culture. Empty ships float "like big tulips" amid the rushing ice under the Verrazano Bridge. At dawn in the snow country, "every fencepost wears a cap." "Hilltop cemetery mosses" bloom with blueberries. A lakeside spider threads its web "from red board to red board." We see "stumbling mossy boots in rusty brambles" and "the salt-white Yankee barn and house / under ice-starry barbs." In "Trills," nature plays many instruments: we hear "the shiver of wheat," "the chatter of birch," the "seething" of "the taller stiffer maples." Kessler's sharp phrases catch the motion, textures, and strange, beautiful voices of a physical world we live in but never fully know.

The Grand Concourse is filled with robust, if isolated, beings. In "Zero," with its horsehead silhouette, the war horses of Chinese, Greek, and Muslim adventure end in "the pinup stallions of gold college girls." In "Bleeding Through," "slaughterhouse cattle," bound for Chicago, groom each other. In other poems, a country cat, shooed out, "flies into the sizzling surprise" of winter, or a small city dog barks warily "right and left before stepping out." In "Going, Going," a ranting man with "white beard and black balls," roars, falls, and dies in the next hospital room, as a nurse screams. Elsewhere, a teenager, expelled from a counseling group because he does not, after all, have a brain tumor, sadly shuns home and joins the army, where he paints barracks. A queenly lady, in "pink robe charming and mandarin," waits and sleeps, "her shaved head crayoned purple for the X-ray." The most powerful figure in the book, besides the poet himself, is Kessler's father, frail but bossy, raising "his spotted smoky fist" against his large, bulky but still daunted son.

Many poems, like "A World of Men" and "South Bronx Chekhov," document the somber manners, enclosed space, and tattered souvenirs of the elderly Jews in America. There is a sense of a massive cultural era winding to its close. "God's Cigar" is a grave, resonant litany, a catalog of family objects destroyed in an apartment-house fire. The poem, moving from elegy to epic, reprises the wanderings, triumphs, and disasters of Jewish history, from Egypt and ancient Jerusalem to Russia and New York. This smaller, personal Holocaust seems to be yet another dream of a remote, musing God.

The Grand Concourse shows Milton Kessler's range and vigor, his acute responsiveness, and his operatic ability, so obvious in class, to capture the anguish and comedy of life.

EAST AND WEST:

AN EXPERIMENT

IN MULTICULTURALISM

In the spring of 1991, an experimental, interdisciplinary humanities course called "East and West" was co-taught at the University of the Arts in Philadelphia by me and Lily Yeh, Professor of Painting and Art History. The development of our project had been supported the prior year by a grant from the University Inter-Arts Council.

"East and West" originated in my conversations with Lily Yeh about the pressing need of American students for a broader international understanding, of the kind my Sixties generation had informally gotten from Hinduism and from the lingering Zen Buddhism of Fifties Beatniks. Yeh and I also expressed our dissatisfactions, as professional women, with present feminist ideology, which is too tied to white, upper-middle-class concerns.

In "East and West" we were looking for new and subtler ways to talk about gender, class, and world culture. We sought a simple, humanistic, arts-based discourse that would lead the student to quiet illumination and insight. Both of us were repelled by the strident politics, the wearisome preaching, the poses of moral superiority that currently afflict the multicultural movement in education. Both of us rejected the idea that history is only a record of oppression. In art, in temples, in the ruins of vanished civilizations, the wisdom of the past waits to be discovered by the students of the world.

Lily Yeh, like me, respects American freedoms because she too emerged from the immigrant experience. She was born in Kueizhou, China, and grew up in Taiwan. Her ancestral home was Hainan province. Yeh began painting when she was fifteen. For seven years she studied traditional Chinese painting with various masters in Taiwan. She had her first major exhibitions after her graduation from National Taiwan University. In 1963 she came to Philadelphia to study painting on the graduate level at the University of Pennsylvania, from which she received a Master of Fine Arts degree in 1966.

During her first fifteen years in the United States, Yeh recalls, she "struggled hard to become a contemporary painter and yet retain my Oriental heritage." Often she found herself "caught in clashes between Eastern and Western social values and views of time, the individual, and the world." She says, "What I cherished most in Chinese art was that 'dustless place' that is so clearly depicted in many Chinese landscape paintings. That place is pristine and tranquil, of this world, yet beyond the disturbance of worldly passion and desires." Yeh began exhibiting nationally in 1976 but regards her environmental installation work, starting in 1980, as her attempt "to reestablish that 'place' in my new home in America."

In 1986, Yeh, with the help of neighborhood residents, especially children, began to convert an empty lot in North Phil-

adelphia into a community park. It took five summers of hard
work. Today, Ile-Ife Park has bright, mosaic-studded sculptures
and a dramatic ninety-by-thirty-five-foot mural in a pleasant setting of trees, bushes, lawns, flowers, and a vegetable garden.

Yeh says, "North Philadelphia has all the problems of very
poor inner-city districts: drugs, prostitution, welfare dependency,
and violence. Yet, despite these problems, North Philadelphia
speaks so resoundingly of what it is to be human that it overwhelms an outsider's capacity to understand. It is a place of great
pain and great healing. In the darkness of our social landscape,
art and creative imagination are our guiding lights. They give us
hope, strength, and they invite others to join in."

Yeh wanted "to put to use what other people did not want:
empty lots, broken buildings, leftover construction materials, and
especially untapped human energy." She says, "Seeing that our
art world is primarily controlled by the powerful and the rich,
that it serves a small, prestigious population, and that artists and
their work tend to become commodities, I decided that I wanted
to make art that had no transactional value. I wanted to make
art that brought people's hearts together."

From 1980 to 1989 Yeh visited China regularly, giving lectures and exhibiting her work. Her lecture tours took her to major
cities in China as well as Tibet and Xinjiang (Chinese Turke-
stan). In 1987 she spent three months in the countryside in the
Yellow River region to research the origin and styles of Chinese
folk art. In May 1989, while exhibiting in Beijing and Tianjin,
she witnessed firsthand the student-inspired Democracy Movement, and she was part of the procession accompanying the statue
of the Goddess of Democracy into Tiananmen Square.

Yeh says of the "exhilarating but tragic" episode in Beijing,
"I realized that the gripping power of this event lay in students'
decision to do the right thing. In doing the right thing, they put
themselves on the line. They were ready to die for their cause.
They fought their battle, and so I have to fight mine. No use to
establish many statues of Democracy all over the world. That
would not help humanity. One must fight for justice in one's own
life, by doing the right thing and by not sparing oneself."

Yeh is currently executive director of the Village of Arts

and Humanities at 2544 Germantown Avenue. Its purpose is to create visual, literary, and performance art that, in Yeh's words, "does justice to the humanity of North Philadelphia and to the social conditions in which we live." The Village publishes *The North Philadelphian,* a community-based fine-arts and literary magazine. One of Yeh's best-known recent art works in Philadelphia is a two-story-high ceramic mural in Chinatown, at 9th and Race streets, completed in 1988. In 1992, she was awarded a Pew Fellowship in the Arts.

"East and West" was originally organized around the idea of "points of contact" between the Eastern and Western worlds. We had planned, for example, to study specific moments in the culture of Byzantium and Moorish Spain and to trace the influence of Japan and China upon Western art from the sixteenth and seventeenth centuries. But after the first week, the course evolved much more strongly toward Far Eastern sacred art.

Our aim was always to sketch out possibilities, to find threads of connection. We imagined the course as a mutual exploration. Yeh brought her history as a Taoist to our encounter, and I brought mine as a Roman Catholic. In class, we questioned each other and compared cultural assumptions and terms. Our students were all apprentice artists. We tried to provide them with themes and motifs that would bear fruit later in their creative lives. And we freely departed from the class plan in response to the students' questions and interests.

Lily Yeh and I both sense a spiritual thirst among the young. Comparative religion and world art offer a way to develop and expand students' imagination without coerciveness or partisanship. Though it rebelled against the institutional church, my generation was very religious in its own way, something that has been overlooked. Religion is a metaphysic, a philosophical view of the universe. Its panoramic perspective gives one an enlightened detachment from human suffering and desire.

"East and West" became a search for the missing spirituality in contemporary academe. I reproduce here my in-class notes for the semester. They are not a complete record of our activities. They simply represent points I personally found especially interesting or inspiring. In publishing them as is, in

...ts, I am imitating and paying homage to one of
...ous and influential books of my college years, Nor-
...rown's *Love's Body.*

...uary 18–22, 1991. Paglia discusses the first appearances of the
East versus West dichotomy in legends of the Trojan War. Paris
and Aeneas, princes of Troy, as effeminate, sybaritic in the eyes
of Greek warriors and Roman moralists. Minoan-Mycenaean
age: cosmopolitan, goddess-centered Crete versus masculine warrior culture of mainland Mycenaean citadels. Cults of the Great
Mother in Anatolia (Asia Minor); the Ionian coast and Lesbos
as artistic centers where women had a higher social status. Dorian
versus Lydian modes in music; Doric versus Ionic orders in architecture: plainness and male vigor versus emotion, femininity,
elegance, grace. The Persian Wars and the triumph of Athens.
Euripides' *Bacchae:* transvestite, woman-identified Dionysus as
an Eastern invader. Rome: Dido and Aeneas, Antony and Cleopatra. The decadent emperor Elagabalus: Eastern pleasure, lux-
ury, and androgyny versus old Roman duty, frugality, and
manhood.

January 25. Yeh discusses the two great river systems of India,
the Ganges in the east and the Indus in the west. India has two
seasons. Everything gets parched and dry from September to
May. Clouds come in late May. Rain extremely important, the
source of life. In literature and architecture, rain symbolized by
the elephant, who must be in the king's stable. Rain is torrential,
an inundation, waist-high. Even in its weather, India has two
opposed principles. In the West, there must be *one* religion, the
only truth. In the East, there is no absolute truth in the Western
sense. Rather, the absolute is all-encompassing.

Yeh draws parallels between Indus Valley culture (2500–
1500 B.C.) and the Minoan-Mycenaean age. The original inhab-
itants of India were of Dravidian stock, dark-skinned. The Aryans
were noblemen from the high plateaus and mountains in central
Asia. (Iran = "Land of the Aryans.") They were horsemen,
hence no architecture. Their gods were mostly sky deities; hence
offerings poured into the fire, to be carried upward. The Aryans

invaded the Indus valley and drove the Dravidians south. So Indus culture was abandoned and forgotten. The Indus valley is now a desert but was once heavily forested, with underground drainage system.

The Aryans wrote the Vedas (Veda = "revealed knowledge," divine, not from men. *Vid* = "to see"). The Vedic period in literature (1500–800 B.C.) is one of great epics: *Mahabharata, Ramayana.* Dravidians worshipped deities manifested through earth-centered forms like mother-goddesses, fertility gods, or bulls. The Aryans worshipped sky-dwelling deities. Yeh: Aryan ideas still evident in today's rockets and skyscrapers: the mystery is *out there,* upward. But in yoga, already present in the Indus Valley, the essence (*Atman*) is in us. Brahman is the source of life, the supreme power and knowledge. It has no form. You know Brahman only by knowing Atman.

January 29. Yeh: India has been frequently invaded. For example, Alexander's invasion in the fourth century B.C.; tenth-century Islamic army. British and Islamic influences are still only superficial in India. Northwest corner of India: evidence of invasion of Alexander the Great in strong Greco-Roman influence in representations of Buddha. Yeh recommends Kenneth Clark's *The Nude* for its chapters on Apollo and Venus but disagrees with him about Alexander's other influences on Indian art. Yeh thinks the female yakshi figure kicking the archetypal tree far predates Greek influence.

Shivaism, worship of Shiva. Lingam = phallic symbol of Shiva. Yoni = vulva. Snakes, caverns were worshipped in early cultures. Western perspective is based on the Apollonian eye, an external ascent. In Eastern art, the meditating yogi looks downward, an inward descent. In Mahayana Buddhism from the sixth century onward, Buddha, the historical figure, gradually becomes a metaphysical reality, weightless and made of pure mind-stuff. Figure becomes more fluid, because no substance of the gross body. Form and space are opposite in Renaissance painting, but not in Buddhism: "Form is emptiness, emptiness is form."

Yeh shows comparative slides of Greek kouros and headless male yaksha and asks the class to comment. The Greek body is simplified into linear and geometrical shapes; great clarity. The swollen abdomen of the Hindu figure is full of air, like a balloon. Subtle curves, complex. Transitions more intuitive, more felt. The kouros is moving forward, while the yaksha is solidly planted. The kouros is aggressive, confident, athletically defined; flaunting, an awareness of the viewer and of his own beauty. The yaksha is static, fixed, bulky, weighty. Its stare is totally impersonal. It is a force of nature, a tree spirit in columnar form. The breath in the expanded belly is virtue, power. The male wears a dhoti, a skirt or loincloth, one long piece of cloth tied and draped. He wears as little as possible in the Indian heat.

Next slide: small, beautiful, headless, armless male statue from India (2000 B.C.). Organic. We are less aware of bone structure and geometry. There is more flow, fleshier. Gentle curving convex belly. Looks female from the rear. Buttocks of kouros are clenched tight like a fist, but more relaxed in the yaksha. Kouros is stiff between back and pelvis, but yaksha has a flexed waist. Yeh says modern men's suits are architectural, just like the kouros. Western male body in a well-fitted suit looks like a plank. Other racial types with different body shape do not look good in Western suits. A student in the performing arts costume class comments that men's suits are the most fiendishly difficult of all designs to bring off; bad suits lose their shape in the wash. Paglia contrasts narrow shoulders of yaksha to the huge shoulders in American football, signifying Western masculinity. She compares stiff waist of kouros to the first white Americans trying to do the Twist, which Eldridge Cleaver called a black revolution, freeing the dead white pelvis. Yeh cites Paglia's theory of the overdevelopment of head and eye in the West and says, "So you go to the *shrink*!"

February 1. Yeh continues with juxtaposed slides. Cretan snake priestess sculptures: full breasts compared to those of the yaksha. Uplifted arms = power. Erotic but formidable, unapproachable. Compressed shape, severity, symmetry. Unflinching expression, staring eyes, ignoring limitations of human world. Minoan palaces built like labyrinths in a valley, the lap of mother earth. Sacred space aligned toward mountain in distance. Giant stones

in Mycenaean fortress palaces. *Tholos* beehive tombs to com-
memorate heroes. Mycenaean citadels built on hills: transition
point toward Greek architecture. Yeh compares Delphi to Mount
Fuji in Japan. Sculptures of Shiva as Mahesvara ("the Great
Lord") and as Nataraja ("The Lord of Dance") from Elephanta,
sacred site on island off Bombay.

Greek kore sculpture is compared to a statue of ancient
Indian goddess, skirt, chest bare, early turban; yakshi figure from
first century B.C., elaborately decorated but body is bare. Kore's
clothing, in contrast, conceals the body. The yakshi's ornate
wraps are designed to bring out the sensuality of the body, but
not to titillate in the Western sense. No sharp lines in the yakshi.
She is a ripe fruit full of juice, the life force pushing outward, the
nursing breasts. In no other culture is the worship of the great
goddess as big and significant as it is in India. But Indian women
are very suppressed in real life.

February 5. Yeh, in response to Paglia's questions, discusses the
yin/yang symbol. There are two equal parts, interlocking, opposite and complementary. The curved line is organic, implying
motion in the world. A straight line dividing the circle would kill
it. It is the circle of return. It is full of nothing, a paradox. Its
tranquillity is from inner tension, a charged dynamic. This serene
dynamic tranquillity is also the state of the Olympian gods. Yin/
yang is not dualistic, like Zoroastrianism; one *becomes* the other.

Yeh continues with Far Eastern religion. Chinese thought
is a combination of Taoism and Confucianism. *Tao* = being and
nonbeing. Words cannot define the Tao. Monism: Brahman is
the universal creative force, a universal power. Words, art can
only dimly suggest that presence. All Islamic mosques face
Mecca, the symbolic center of existence. The repetition of geometrical and arabesque forms expresses a sense of time and space
different than the Western one, which is focused on *this* world.
Quality of light. In Gothic cathedral: light coming through
stained-glass windows illustrates the concept of being and becoming in Catholic terms. Concentric rings of praying Muslims
around the world: primal center of Mecca. *Jihad:* originally and
primarily a spiritual battle.

In India yogis wrap selves in wet, cold blankets and dry them by *tapas,* inner heat. In China *ch'i* = breath, inner vital energy and source of life. Paglia asks about acupuncture and acupressure, based on the *chakras,* special points of energy on the map of the body. Yeh contrasts Western to Eastern medicine. In the West: medical specialties and specialists; cutting the body through surgery; pills, potent synthetic medicines, to heal instantaneously. Eastern medicine: slow; natural medicines, herbs to restore "heat," life energy, not necessarily temperature. Ginseng: fruit that looks like human child; it means "the essence of human *being.*" Taoist tradition teaches return to the state of the infant, before the sense of good and evil. Nondiscriminatory, total acceptance. Yeh compares the sublime in Chinese landscape painting to the luminist tradition in American painting. In Hindu art, symbol of union is *mithunas,* male and female lovers, always heterosexual. Michelangelo's Adam in Sistine Chapel: awaiting *ch'i,* the divine spark: he's impotent without God.

February 8. Yeh says we lack rituals of initiation in our culture. Paglia reads list of specialized how-to classes on sadomasochism now being offered in San Francisco and compares them to yogic self-lacerations. Yeh says, "The whole world is going West," but the result is "more freedom, justice, humanity." On the other hand, there is "a more materialistic, mundane, and fragmented way of life that leads to the disintegration of society and individuals." She says, "In Chinese history, you must submit to power or be killed, and your family too. The basic concept of human rights is a Western idea, although Confucius' teaching is also about humanity and compassion. In China, you are guilty until proven innocent. The East is a bigger mess! There is pollution, poverty, and the population explosion." Personal love is not a concern in China; marriage is to produce children. There is a marriage arrangement between families. What is evil, in Eastern and Western terms? In India, karma is cause and effect; you reap what you sow. It's like the law of inertia; it keeps going until everything is exhausted. The Indian goddess Durga, the Destroyer, has dark, tight, youthful skin. She is the mental emanation of eighteen gods; Yeh compares her to Athena. She has eighteen arms; each one holds a symbol of a male deity. There are no pupils in the eyes of Buddha figures. The eyes have a general openness, not focused at one thing. State of general awareness. Desire, attachment, passion = pollution of the mind.

February 12. Varna: the caste system of India. Lingering heritage of the Aryan invasion. Indigenous Dravidians were dark-skinned, thick-lipped, rounder of figure. The medieval caste system was very rigid, at first organized by profession. Four main classes and one subcaste. (1) Brahmin: priesthood, in charge of the mantras and rituals. Symbol: the head. (2) Kshatriya: warriors. The Aryans who reached the Ganges. Originally the highest class. Symbol: the body. (3) Vaisya: the working class. Artisans, farmers, merchants. Dravidian. Symbol: the legs. (4) Sudra: serfs. Lived on the land. Dravidian. Symbol: dirt. (5) Untouchables: pariahs. Indigenous mountain people. Untouchables said to have gotten there because of their karma, the universal law, absolutely just; bad acts never erased.

Hinduism believes in reincarnation. Buddhism is a religion with no god, no self, no soul. Nothing to be resurrected. In Buddhism there is no caste system, just a *sangha,* a brotherhood. Buddhism believes that a person is composed of five changing states of being (*skandhas*): the body, perception, feeling, intuition, reasoning. *Nirvana* is the world of full enlightenment. *Samsara* is the world of illusion. In Mahayana Buddhism, nirvana *is* samsara. Hinduism symbolizes the world of illusion as the veil of the goddess Maya. Hindu deities are in a dream world. The unveiled Reality is the all-encompassing and luminous void.

February 15. Yeh describes the Chinese tradition of foot-binding, which began as a court fashion in the Sung dynasty among the noble families and then filtered down through the various social strata to the peasants. It was an absolute rule, except for the lowest class, from the eleventh to the twentieth centuries. Yeh's grandmother underwent this and suffered great pain from the mutilation. All women had their feet bound from the age of five or six to restrict growth and keep the foot small. At night the bandage was released; pain was worst then, when the blood rushed to the foot. Result was stump feet. The ideal was the three-inch-long "Golden Lotus" foot; poetry was written to it. You couldn't find a husband without it. Women often had to crawl to get around. It was "obscene" for a woman to have a large, round foot. In 1912, after the establishment of the Republic of China, foot-binding was banned by law. Women's feet were to be set free. This also proved to be painful. Without the support they had gotten used to, it was hard for them to walk. They hobbled along. There was breast-binding also, under the bulky, body-concealing mandarin robes. Breasts never an erotic focus in China or Japan, in contrast to the West. Breasts associated only with reproduction: hence a Chinese grandmother is called "Breast-breast" and a son's wife "Young-breast."

Paglia relates foot-binding to Western erotic practices: stiletto heels, which shorten the calf muscle; the binding and mutilation of the *en pointe* style in classical ballet; both heterosexual and homosexual foot fetishism. She shows a fetishists' shoe catalog, with outlandish futuristic creations, red and lavender vinyl and suede women's shoes with eight-inch heels. She compares a picture of a woman's arm in a full-length, above-the-elbow leather glove to the slide of a Cretan priestess with snakes entwining her arms. She asks if there are other ways to see foot-binding besides the usual feminist one: shouldn't we also relate it to sadomasochistic eroticism? Yeh speaks of the "impersonal face" of the Chinese lady. In Japan, one strip of the geisha's face was left bare, without cosmetics, near the hairline; considered highly erotic. Since the geisha's costume had long sleeves, the exposed hand was very erotic. During the Heian period, there were ten or twelve layers to the kimono at times. In the West, women's legs are eroticized, but not in the East.

Paglia mentions that Freud has had no impact in Japan because his analysis is primarily of Western culture. Yeh agrees: "Freud makes no sense in Japan, because he deals with personal consciousness. Jung makes sense there." Personal happiness not important in Far Eastern thought; it's about "letting go." From the start, the East sees being-becoming as merely a mirage. In Hinduism, *moksha* = utter release from the endless cycle of birth and death, of pains and longings. Yeh says, "It's not about solving

the problem but about looking at things from a new viewpoint."
Paglia says that contemporary sadomasochism—which she has
studied as a scholar, not a practitioner—is all about relinquishing
of self, giving over control to another. An issue of trust, faith.
Yeh quotes Suzuki: Christ has to die on the cross due to Western
ego. Buddha doesn't have to die like that; he can just pass on.

February 19. Yeh describes China's political history, its many dynasties beginning in third century B.C with the Ch'in dynasty,
which gave the nation its name. Chinese "democracy" was established in 1912, but feudalism remains. Beijing still retains the
pyramidal structure created in 221 B.C. Mentally, the layout of
the city is a pyramid; things still work from top down in China.
In the rigid imperialistic political system, the examination system
offers something democratic in spirit. The British brought imperial rule and the example of democracy to India, but the caste
system still operates. Western human rights developed from the
greater Western concept of and emphasis upon the individual.
    Yeh and Paglia return to the question of evil in Western
and Far Eastern thought. Yin/yang symbol shows opposed forces
in harmony. At the start is being, without good or evil. Good
always implies the shadow of evil: the sunny side of the mountain
is called yang; the shady side, yin. They are complementary and
co-existing. In Judeo-Christian theodicy, there is polarity and
hierarchy: good is ranked *over* evil. In the West, God is perfect
and nature is corrupt; so you always must improve things. In
Buddhism, good and evil not so ethical; it's not about changing
the world but about *seeing*. Eternity is outside the rim of time and
so cannot be measured. Salvation is attained by seeing reality
totally differently. The idea of evolution or progress is Western:
better justice, better conveniences, better enjoyment. In Hinduism there are endless cycles; it doesn't get better. The Hindu
seeks release from these cycles. The West believes in free will, a
personal power of decision-making. Yet the individual decision
of Lucifer was already predestined.
    Buddha: a miraculous birth like Jesus's. He was born from
the right side of his mother, Queen Maya. Cf. Adonis. He would
walk and talk from the moment he was born. Buddha's feet didn't

touch the ground. He stood on lotus buds, which stemmed up from the earth to support him. He took seven steps northward (cf. the seven layers of planets) and faced south to proclaim, "I am the oldest. I am the wisest." His renunciation of property and social status was like that of St. Francis, who was also born wealthy. Asceticism is true freedom. The Taoist also seeks humble, simple living within your means. Gandhi renounced possessions and adapted Hindu nonviolence, which inspired Martin Luther King. Medieval suttee, the self-immolation of widows on the funeral pyres of their husbands, was also motivated by renunciation. The word comes from Hindu myth: Sati (pronounced Suttee), the consort of Shiva, destroyed herself out of love and devotion to her husband; became model of perfect Indian wife. Cremation is the norm in India. In Tibet, people practiced sky burial instead: bodies are dissected and left in the open in specific places for vultures to eat.

February 22. Holy harlots of Hinduism and the ancient eastern Mediterranean goddess cults. Temple prostitutes: to fulfill her vow to the great mother goddess, a woman, once in her lifetime, offers herself in the temple. Strangers were gods disguised in human form. No money is involved; it is an offering, not a business. Christian myth of the Virgin Birth and the Whore of Babylon. "Virgin" once meant unmarried or without a husband. The two Marys: Madonna/whore split in the Christian view of woman. Isis, the Egyptian mother goddess. Hindu holy harlots: *apsaras,* female celestial beings, and *gandharvas,* male ones. Carnal love and spiritual love are united in Hinduism. Nondiscrimination is the underlying feature of Oriental wisdom. The Sixties motto, "God is love," means God is all-embracing. Kali, the Hindu dark goddess, wears garland of human skulls and dances on graves. Is terror the right response? Buddha was tested before full enlightenment by (1) desire for life (carnal love) (2) desire for power and (3) fear of death, but he didn't flinch because no ego left. Ego is the source of fear, because of the desire for self-preservation. *Garbha griha,* "womb-chamber," is the word for the innermost sanctuary of a Hindu temple. Cathedrals are built like a fortress, to protect against the world. Were indeed originally

fortresses in early Middle Ages. Early persecutions made it necessary. Same with early Islam: strong outer walls needed, but
later changed.

March 1. Japan's Ise shrine: the most important site in Shintoism.
Temples based on the structure of a simple forest hut, the granary,
the center of an agricultural society. The raised floor was to
protect the grain from moisture and rats. The form of the Ise
shrine was fixed in the third century B.C. By imperial order, it is
torn down and re-created every twenty years; it is forever new
and forever old, built of perishable materials. Contrast with the
Parthenon: built of stone for eternity. Overwhelming presence of
nature at Ise. Its three hundred shrines are deep in the forest.
Its temple is hidden, protected. Shintoism has profound respect
for nature. Thatched roof extends far from walls, so very mysterious, and pillars needed to support it. Japan is Land of the
Sun; emperor is direct descendant of the sun goddess, Amaterasu.
Japanese noble families are of very ancient lineage. Imperial
family never overthrown in Japan, while in China there was
constant toppling of royal dynasties and creation of new ones.
     Shintoism: simple, physical cleanliness. Not a metaphysical
code. Purification by water. Cleanliness is very important in
Japan; sin is a spoiling of physical cleanliness. Same ritual as in
the tea ceremony: very common, not extraordinary things. The
torii: a threshold, the stately gates of the sacred compound. Un-
painted, natural wood, deliberately imperfect: knots, no nails.
The *torii* is clarity, structure, logic pushing against the dark
and untamed.
     Japanese *bushido:* the warrior way of life. Eighty percent of
China is still agrarian: the Chinese value endurance, survival;
hence they move smoothly and unobtrusively. But the Japanese
have a tradition of glory: compressed voices, absolute obedience
to the warrior code. Cherry blossoms are Japanese national
flower: huge, glamourous masses, two weeks only, then gone =
evanescence of human life. The morning glory is loved in Japan
because evanescent. Chinese national flower is *meihua* (plum
flower), which blooms in February, sparsely, often snow still on
the ground. Classical Japanese film: clarity, order, readiness to

submit, but also wild, rebellious, untamed. Suicide = statement of protest and dissent. Cf. Buddhist monks in Saigon.

Kami: "the gods," eight million of them in Shintoism; also the rice paper hung on ropes to honor the sacred spirits and show their presence in the breeze. Everything modest, simple. Japanese architecture: sense of emptiness, importance of the plane, horizontal and flat. Japanese architects don't think three-dimensionally, in terms of volume, as do Baroque architects. Ryoan-ji, Kyoto: prototype of the Zen rock garden. China has rock gardens also, but a different concept. Chinese rocks are unusual, extraordinary shapes, often dug up from the bottom of a lake. Japanese gardens: ordinary rocks made extraordinary. Zen Buddhism = seeing the extraordinary in the ordinary. Mystery and charged tranquillity of the Zen shrine. Modest, no flowers, mud walls. Coarse sand, raked. Done like Rothko paintings, says Yeh. Small, clear openings of man-made environment with thick, dense trees behind it. Yeh: "People say the Japanese garden is natural, but it's most *un*natural." Tense silence.

Japanese tea ceremony: no new garments or bright colors. You must drop any paraphernalia of rank or status in the world. It is a spiritual service. A central rugged post is necessary for the teahouse, hard wood, often crooked. Rice-papered windows and doors, instead of glass windows, filter the light. The teahouse and the utensils contain the five elements—metal, wood, water, fire, earth—of which the world is composed. Pebbles in the tea kettle = distant thunder. Steam = mist of nature. Little boil = "necklace." Big boil = "rolling water." Aesthetic values are very powerful in Japan. Japanese house has shrine-like alcove (*tokonoma*) to display a family treasure, honored like a work of art. The visitor goes immediately there to admire it. It is rude not to do so.

Zen master's riddles (*koan*) are unanswerable, but must try to answer, since the riddle breaks down our mental categories. Buddhist meditation often involves description of images: e.g., the thousands of rays around the Buddha and the thousands of Buddhas on thousands of rays. Must visualize it, so as to break through the restrictions of our minds. No logic, cannot understand Zen Buddhism with rational understanding. Enlightened concepts cannot be understood in linear, analytic way, the Western Apollonian style that Paglia traces in *Sexual Personae*. Zen masters use enigmatic language that does contain a logic, but different from the norm. Yeh says it's like the "dream logic" first described by Freud but made more useful to artists, in her view, by Jung. Not judging, not screening. Yeh says all spiritual traditions are about *giving up*. There are two ways to control wealth: (1) accumulation and (2) giving it away. Yeh: "Abundance is like a fountain. You are poor if you keep needing more."

March 19. Yeh: Buddhism is one fifth of the population of the world but was meant to be select. Buddhism is international, while Hinduism stays ethnic, regional. The Tibetan school of Buddhism is spreading everywhere. Self, soul, God: normally in religion, but Buddhism is without these things! *Sunyata* = the Void. In Oriental philosophy, it's about the all-encompassing and luminous space. Western landscape is about measured space perceived by man's eye. Oriental landscape is a landscape of the mind. Illuminated from within, it is not disturbed by darkened shadows or sharp, foreshortened views. The unenlightened mind sees things in terms of form, but the enlightened mind sees the Void. Paglia: cf. the Apollonian versus Dionysian dichotomy in the West.

Buddha says, There is no I. Feeling, consciousness, volition, perception, and body are all parts of the self, but when they disintegrate in death, there is no self. What is reality? The space that holds all that happens. The ultimate reality is *sunyata*, voidness. You try to attain nirvana, but Buddha is rarely spoken of: he is not God. And *sutra* (sacred texts) can't take you there. Nirvana is *in* our imperfect and suffering state. We are all sick (diseased = "ill-at-ease"), says Buddhism. The world is perfect; it's the way we see it that is wrong, imperfect. Buddhist sermons are about suffering and pain and how we can escape from them. There is little dialectic or analytic language.

"Buddha is the perfect psychiatrist," says Yeh. He understands human nature and human suffering. He is the Enlightened or Awakened One; "Buddha" is not a personal name. Buddha means the enlightened one—and all who have reached enlightenment. The common mind is asleep. We live in darkness and ignorance. There is no sense of original sin or guilt in Buddhism. Sin is ignorance. Ignorance = not seeing better, due to egohood and being taught wrong concepts by society, parents, self. Attachment, passion, yearning = pollution, dust. The *stupa*, originally a burial mound, becomes the symbol of Buddha's enlightenment. In Nepal or Tibet, stupas often have pairs of eyes on them to signify all-seeing, the coming of light, awareness, Buddhahood. *Samsara* = world of illusion, passion, attachment, duality, differentiation, multiple forms and phenomena. The samsaric world—this one, ours—is the dream world, the nonsubstantial world. Yeh compares this to Plato's parable of the cave: there is a brilliant light outside it, but if you talk of it, no one believes it; you are thought mad. *Nirvana* = total extinction of egohood, no thinking, no desire, the fire burned out. Desire = fire, energy that drives us to a goal, makes us blind to other things. Thinking is a linear movement. It distinguishes, discriminates, and separates. Parinirvana is like a candle burned out or like burned wood, with no traces left.

Yeh: Oriental painting rarely shows boys. Paglia contrasts this to the beautiful youths everywhere in Greek and Italian Renaissance art. Yeh: In Asian art, boys are too frail, inexperienced, not interesting. Only weathered old men are worth looking at; they have gained wisdom through age. No passion or flash; like old wood. Old men are the everlasting truth of nature, deep understanding; they contain it all. Paglia exclaims at the parallel to Wordsworth's poetry, where old, battered men are sanctified by nature. Yeh: In Chinese folklore, worth is disguised as a beggar; power always lies hidden. Whereas on our television, the best is all out front. In Oriental culture, in Taoism, you disguise your brilliance, your talents. In the West, men who are respected are called gentlemen. Paglia has written about this English male persona descending from the Italian Renaissance. Gentleness = the quality of the feminine. Cf. Indian sculpture: never about muscles; the stone is soft, treated as the matrix. Ego: "I want." Nature: "Thou shalt." Result: disharmony, pain, suffering. Wisdom of the old Chinese man: passion, yearning, desire dead. Diminishing of the individual leads to harmony.

Hinduism seeks *moksha*, release, but there are four stages to life: (1) student; (2) householder (married, satisfies passions); (3) hermit living in forest, after giving up possessions; (4) mendicant. Hinduism allows us to live in society, but Buddhism from the start is about disengagement, letting go. Buddha: meditation, not miracles and saving the world. The most Buddha does is standing. He sometimes stands but mostly sits. It is the most passive of world religions: it is knowing the world through inward reflectiveness. Siddhartha Gautama: his name before he attained Buddhahood. Born in small tribe in foothills of Himalayas in north India, near Nepal. Also called Sakyamuni, the Silent One of his tribe, the Sakya. His mother was Queen Maya, who dreamed she was brought to the highest Himalayan mountain, where a white elephant entered her womb—a miraculous conception.

When young, Siddhartha saw that everything was transient: how can we be joyful when surrounded by sickness and death? Then he saw a serene and radiant monk, and was convinced. Siddhartha got married but was sickened by the transient, worldly joy of the festivities. His father said, "You have a duty to me and society"; be a monk later: this is the Hindu way. But Siddhartha could not bear it and left the night after his son was born to become a monk. Siddhartha almost died after six years of severe methods of self-mortification, so he renurtured his body. He attained enlightenment under a bodhi tree, where he simply relaxed and achieved a total receptiveness and openness. That is, when he had finally given up the desire to attain enlightenment, he gained it. You have to let go. He was too attached to his desire for enlightenment. Buddha is often shown under this bodhi tree, just as Christ is shown on the tree of the cross.

One day Buddha came to a sermon with just a flower and smiled. Only one disciple understood. Zen traces its origins to this. The mind is like a pond, still and quiet. When the wind (= our thoughts) blows, the pond is ruffled, so images are distorted, not perfectly reflected. The enlightened mind is mirrorlike. Hence breathing exercises: concentration on the tip of the nose to yoke the mind and tame its energy. You listen to your breath in the here and now, immediate and spontaneous. The simplest thing is the most complicated to achieve. Taoist: achieve a child-like state, go back to the innocence of the child. Paglia comments on parallels to this in the New Testament—Jesus says, "You must become as a little child to enter the kingdom of heaven"—and the myth of the child in Rousseau, Blake, and Wordsworth.

Buddha, like Christ, underwent a series of temptations. He was tempted three times by the Kama-mara, the nature spirit representing carnal love and fear of death, desires and fires in all of us. He sent his three voluptuous daughters to evoke Buddha's lust. They failed because there was no one there to be tempted. In Buddhism you must get past the cycles of the body, the time-clock. The hand gestures of Buddha, like those of Christ, are always open, never closed into fists. Yeh speaks of the explicit sex scenes of Tantric Buddhism, which she says are ritualistic and not like our pornography since there are "no grasping hands." Paglia draws a parallel to Dante's imagery of fists and clawlike, grasping hands among the damned of the *Inferno*.

The moment before Buddha attained full enlightenment, he made a gesture of touching the earth. It is a symbol of reconcil-iation with the past. Yeh: You must come to terms with the past in order to move forward; otherwise, hang-ups. The past must be unblocked in order for energy to move forward; it is like stones in a stream, disturbing the flow. Paglia says this resembles Freud's "talking cure," in which the past is reentered, then dis-carded. Yeh: Christ and Gandhi gave up, yet gained enormously; huge influence. *Bodhisattva* = "a being whose essence is enlight-enment," a future Buddha. We are all potential Buddhas. We must do it on our own. Buddha cannot help us.

Intellectual knowledge is external; can be gained and can be explained. Realization comes from within; cannot be ex-plained. After Buddha attained enlightenment, he stayed in the sacred grove for forty-nine days. He pondered how he could teach the unteachable (his realization) to the others who were no longer the others. The mirror-like mind has no image of itself. The image it reflects and receives becomes its own image. Yet in the state of total openness, one feels compassion for all suffering beings. Buddha left the sacred grove and began teaching. He taught forty years before he attained *parinirvana*, the total extinction of body and self. In our ignorance we see ourselves as separate from others. Our mind is polluted by passion and desire. Each of us is like a drop of polluted water, separate and alone. When purified, the drop of water returns to the primeval ocean. The drop of water is and is not there. The primeval ocean is the ocean of emptiness.

Jung speaks of "synchronicity": there are no accidents in nature; nature follows strict laws. Yeh and Paglia recommend Jung's book of that name. Paglia laments absence of the *I Ching* in contemporary student life: it was everywhere in the Sixties. Yeh says *I Ching,* "The Book of Changes," is a book of profound wisdom but not a sacred text in the Western sense. It is a compilation of ancient practices of divination, originally with bones and now with coins. Wilhelm compares its system, based on chance and change, to that of Leibnitz. Yeh says commentators have compared it to computer language. Yeh and Paglia praise the poetic imagery of the hexagrams: the positive and negative forces, the lake, wind, and mountain, all aspects of nature.

March 26. During the Yuan Dynasty (Mongol) of the fourteenth century, a new kind of landscape appeared. It was pristine, frozen, and silent. It pointed to a transcendent world which the Chinese called "the dustless world." Dust here represents the mental pollution of attachment, desire, fear, and aggression of the human world. Out of the pain of defeat and humiliation, Yuan painters created a spiritual landscape of utter silence and stillness.

Tranquility has to be regained repeatedly through the descent into the depth of living. Unfortunately, painters of the later period copied the Yuan landscapes without the insight and the poetic vision of the Yuan painters. The result was the gradual decline and dessication of Chinese landscape painting. Yeh says she suffered from the "smothering tradition" of Chinese art of learning through copying masters' work. There was very little room for individual experimentation or expression. She considers the thousand years of foot-binding a metaphor for all the bindings, all kinds of conformity in China. Marriage in China is a social obligation; it is not a matter of personal love, which is a

Western idea. Similiarly, perspective is abnormal in non-Western traditions of art. Perspective assumes that the human eye is the measure of the world.

Yeh shows slide of Diana of Ephesus, with multiple breasts and mummy-like wrapped abdomen and legs: the bindings of procreative woman. Slide of Lilith, Adam's ferocious first wife, standing on beasts. Slide of eighteenth-century Tantric image of Kali cutting off heads. Yeh says it reminds her of having been frightened in childhood by a Chinese folk tale of an old woman who took off her head to comb her hair. The lion and tiger are associated with Kali, as with the Anatolian mother goddess Cybele. Kali has fangs and a long, doglike tongue, like the Greek Gorgon. She is holding a bisected skull of blood; she wears a skirt of severed arms, and bracelets and ankle-bangles of human heads. The hands are stigmata-like. There are four headless bodies on the ground. Yeh says it is both horrific and sublime at the same time: "She looks deranged. But the insane and the sane are *not* divided." Paglia says it shows how little we need Foucault—as usual.

Yeh shows a slide from modern Chinese folk art, a paper cut-out of a goddess turning into a tree, with womb exposed. Paglia compares it to Bernini's statue of Daphne, pursued by Apollo and turning into a laurel tree. Yeh juxtaposes the Chinese image with a sculpture of Sheila-na-jig, the mother goddess and cosmic womb of Celtic myth. It at first seems ugly, grotesque. She is all head and vulva, no breast, no body fat. A delta shape, symbol of fertility. She is contorted acrobatically on herself, dilated to give birth. Her pupils are empty; her smile is like the crescent moon. It is a divine epiphany. Paglia remarks on ritual exhibitionism, the sacred exposure of genitals, from prehistoric art to the Roman period. She believes the most explicit modern pornography, condemned by so many feminists, contains elements of this ancient tradition.

March 29. Yeh continues slide comparison. She shows an abstract goddess sculpture from Mesopotamia, 400 B.C. It is nothing but two eyes on spindles, like television antennas, above an armless, legless, blocklike body. The class discusses mystic vision, including modern ESP. Yeh is troubled by dabbling in the occult, which resurfaced in the Sixties. She and Paglia agree that consciousness is like an iceberg, with only the tip visible. Below is a forbidden, dangerous realm. Yeh says clairvoyance and occult phenomena automatically occur when the yogic masters either descend to the lower realm or attain high elevation of consciousness.

Yeh juxtaposes a slide of a Tibetan *Bodhisattva* figure, a goddess of compassion with hundreds of heads and a thousand hands as solar rays. It is covered with dots and seems to be all eyes: no grasping, all-seeing. It occurs in cosmic time. The Bodhisattva in early Buddhism is a being on the way to enlightenment, before reaching the level of Buddhahood. Bodhisattvas originally could not be female; they had to be reborn as a male. But in Mahayana and Tantric Buddhism the Bodhisattva is the embodiment of compassion. *He* eventually becomes *she*. Buddhist meditation has different guardians, gentle ones and fierce, dark ones.

The outer eye is scientific; the inner eye is intuitive. Deepest truths cannot be proved scientifically. The circle or red dot on the forehead in India = the third eye of Buddha, the lost point between emptiness and form. Beings radiating light are like the Tibetan sun-wheel, a symbol of infinite time and space. Buddhism is about inward contemplation, achieving a state of perception without the limit and distortion of egohood or identity in the Western sense. Bodhisattva is "the Lord Who Sits on High." His spiritual achievement brought him to a lofty place. He saw the suffering of sentient beings and felt compassion for them all. He is like a mirror, egoless: he receives and reflects the sorrow of the world.

Next: a stone head of Buddha. It is not a portrait. It's no one in particular. The head is tilted, listening, eyes looking downward, not focused, not looking at anything, a tinge of sorrow. Total enlightenment is total abandonment, total darkness, a dire and devastating state. We must be guided there gradually. Yeh: The Buddhist world contains myriad universes. The most delightful one is the western paradise of Amidha Buddha. It is full

‚rance, beautiful trees, buildings, and sensual beings. But paradise is not the ultimate place for the migrating souls. ‟‪ is only a space station!"

Slide of a portrait of Fu-hsi, a Chinese saint with three pairs of eyes. Yeh compares it to Man Ray's surreal photograph of a woman with three pairs of eyes. Fu-hsi invented the trigram, the foundation of the hexagrams used in I Ching. Next a statue of the Chinese patroness of childbirth. Mysteries beyond rational comprehension. Further examples of the many dark, ferocious deities of Tibet. Terrible, explosive power. Tantric yoga is about embracing and transforming negative energies (neurotic, destructive, demonic) into the various luminous qualities of Buddha wisdom.

April 2. Yeh recommends book, *The Tao of Physics* by Fritjof Capra. Western science is no longer the Newtonian system it was three hundred years ago. Physics is very Buddhist now, approaching a view of the world like that of the mystics of East and West. Modern sculpture uses space, holes: cf. the Buddhist "Void." Yeh compares Jackson Pollock paintings to the atom: the void and matter in energy field. Parallels between the Japanese tea ceremony and the wine of the Christian Communion service. Miraculous powers of the Buddhist masters are generated naturally. Buddha warns us not to get caught up in the quest for miracles: too much ego; don't get sidetracked. People donated pieces of fabric to monks. Scraps were sewn together to become the patchwork robe of Buddhist monk. Monks were once considered parasites. Begging is still the tradition; no eye contact, they silently wait, no coercion or emotional appeal.

Ancient history of Buddhism. *Theravada* = "the ways of the elders," written in Pali, ancient Ceylon script. Later called *Hinayana* by Indian Buddhists: "the Lesser Vehicle." Afterward, *Mahayana*, "the Greater Vehicle," a more developed and elaborate religious system. Zen Buddhism: intense meditative school. From *Ch'an*, "single heart"; contains ideas of "meditation" plus "alone." Tantric Buddhism: esoteric, uses mantras, visual images (yantras), mandalas (magic circles). Cf. Jung, *The Symbolism of the Mandala.* Jung got patients to draw, to show how drawing is

a portrait of the soul and reflects the mental state. In a disinte-
grated state, circles are in disarray. Gradual integration shown
by drawings. Like shamans' sand paintings: healing powers.

Yana = vehicles to get you to places. When you get there,
to the land of *nirvana* or Buddhahood, you'll find out that you
have not gone anywhere. You were originally there. *Tat tvam asi*
(Sanskrit): "This is that." There is neither "neither" nor "or."
Here is there, there is here. The language of paradox is shared
by Eastern and Western mysticism. Paglia: How widespread
these Eastern phrases and concepts were in the American Sixties
and how tragic that today's students have no access to them.
Yeh: Buddhism releases the categories of fixed time and space,
the physical eye; the world is not stable but always in flux.

The *Bodhisattva*'s aura looks solid but isn't; it's all energy.
Dissolution of objects expanding into multicolored rays of light.
What is reality? Buddhism and modern physics agree: all is in
constant motion. *Upanishads:* one of the late Vedas, esoteric Hindu
teaching. The word means "to sit near your teacher": not formal,
not a lecture, very reflective. Essence cannot be seen. Yeh: "All
mystical traditions are similar. Each culture puts its stamp on
it." *Tao* = "the way." Hard to define. An empty vessel that can
be drawn from without needing to be filled. Bottomless. A deep
pool that never dries. *Sunyata,* the Void, is not absence of anything
but the full presence of it all, like clear sun, white light. Paglia:
Western philosophy calls it the *plenum*. The Pre-Socratics were
concerned with the primary forces and elements of existence; then
philosophy split off from physics.

Yeh quotes a Buddhist master: "The mind moon is solitary
and perfect. The light swallows the 10,000 things." The fifth
Ch'an patriarch was looking for a successor. He asked each of
his students to compose a poem to express his understanding of
Zen Buddhism. The leading student monk, Shen-hsui, wrote:
"The body is like the bodhi tree. The mind is like the mirror
bright. So it must be constantly wiped to prevent dust from
collecting on it." The next day, another poem appeared next to
it: "The body is not like the bodhi tree, the mind is not like the
mirror bright. From the beginning there is nothing. From where
would the dust collect?" The poem was composed by Hui-neng,

an illiterate manual laborer in the monastery. Hui-neng was chosen to become the sixth Ch'an patriarch.

Chinese *koan* = public cases on file. Well-established questions that are obviously unanswerable: for example, "What is the sound of one hand clapping?" *Zen Flesh, Zen Bones:* good collection of *koan.* Yeh says it's like American est: "The same experience. You're abused, like the Marines." The *koan* literally break down your rational structure. We think linearly, logically, horizontally, vertically. Expository writing is completely linear.

Zen masters sometimes hit their students or kick their behinds. Yeh: "You don't take him to court. It's the right kick at the right time!" Paglia loves this and feels it's very Italian. Zen masters are always laughing. It's their profound realization. The slapstick knocks out the student's mental constructs or verbalizations. Chinese language is more compact, direct. "Suchness," "isness" = pure being, total awareness of presence. Language is rigid and rational, so mantra, music, slaps are better to get to truth. Yeh: "Our commercials gabble, gabble, gabble. Religion looks for the unexplainable." In Ming dynasty of 16th century, the Chinese fleet first explored to Africa, then China closed in and forbade ships to be used; no colonization. It was Dutch trading and exploration that made them leap forward. Zen Buddhism is a breaking through of all closed categories and cultural assumptions.

Yeh shows slide of the Sanchi *stupa* in central India, the oldest existing Buddhist architecture. The core dates from third century B.C., but it was enlarged and restored in the first and second centuries B.C. The *stupa* is a burial mound, used since ancient times in India. The Sanchi *stupa* contains a portion of the relics of Buddha after cremation and is a symbol of his full enlightenment. *Stupa* = the world and the axis and the center. It is like a sacred mountain (one in Borobudur, Java, is so big that it can be recognized only from an airplane). The *stupa* is in the center of a circle; cf. the mandala, a perfect, magic circle. A bar or fence at entry; at Sanchi *stupa* a swastika shape (swastika = ancient symbol of life, the passage of the sun). You must turn around; you can't go straight. Pilgrims perform circumambulation, making a circle to retrace Buddha's path, then ascend stairs,

which symbolizes transcending the physical world. Like lotus
flower rooted in muddy water of our world: the flower rises up
perfect and clear.

Slides taken by Yeh in Tibet. Numerous prayer-flags in
Lhasa, clustering like antennas on city roofs. Yeh says much
contemporary Western art re-creates rituals drawn from tradition
or invented new now. Many ancient rituals inflicted pain on the
body, as in the mortifications and self-flagellation in medieval
monasteries. Yeh: "The hard labor of the monastic life is good.
The mind is free." Physical work channels the mind's thoughts
into the right paths. Circumambulation, a common Buddhist
practice around *stupas* or images, is used around Lhasa, the city
of the Dalai Lama in Tibet. The right shoulder always faces the
monument. Islamic worshippers perform circumambulation by
the thousands around the Kaaba, the sacred shrine in Mecca.

April 5. Yeh and Paglia make an extended comparison of Buddha
and Jesus. Yeh agrees that Jesus' sayings are "simple and com-
pelling"; his speech has "the power of cutting through." Paglia
says that Jesus' parables and brilliant one-liners probably existed
for some time in list form; the biography was added later, as a
compilation of the oral tradition. Yeh comments on mythological
parallels: the births of Buddha and Jesus involve a miraculous
conception; Buddha has an evil cousin, just as Jesus has Judas.
Jesus was lowborn in a carpenter's family, but Buddha was born
a prince. Yeh says of the conflict between Rome and Christianity:
"The conquered becomes the conqueror. As with all empires."

Yeh says she resented Confucianism due to being indoctri-
nated in it. As an adult, she rediscovered it and now sees Confucius as a profound and compassionate man. Paglia says the
same thing about her experience with Christianity: it's so drilled
into you that you begin to hate it. As an adult, she too was able
to look at it afresh. Jesus is not God to her, but she now recognizes
his deep spiritual insight, his genius as a poet and performance
artist, with an amazing instinct for improvisation in dramatic or
dangerous situations. Yeh feels all religions come from the same
fountain or godhead; you use different cups to get it. Then we
become attached to the form and fight with each other. Love and

on are the essence of all religions. Paglia says, as an
ɔman, she has had the most trouble with that aspect of
anity, which wasn't part of Greco-Roman paganism; her
book searches for the aggression missing from Christian theology.
Yeh comments on the irony that Christianity, a pacifist faith,
ended up in centuries of violence in its internal struggles and
missionary adventures. The violent deaths of the martyrs are
glorified and lead to canonization. The crucifix is an exhibition
of pain and torture, so unlike the tranquil death of Buddha, who
just passed away. Paglia says these ironies show the unresolved
issues in Christianity.

April 9. Yeh: "If Jesus were alive today, he would not be recognized. He would be a street person. He would live with the
poor and suffering." She quotes Confucius: "Living is like walking
on thin ice." You must keep constant vigilance, attentiveness.
Most people want comfort, approval, authority: "Hence the Pope
has all that regalia." Paglia thinks the pomp and ceremony of
Roman Catholicism are pagan remnants; she loves it. In the last
twenty years, the American Catholic Church has downplayed all
that. Paglia agrees it's now more authentically Christian but
mourns the loss, in aesthetic terms.

Freedom for women? Yeh says we're preconditioned to interests, talents, and love from childhood: "What kind of freedom
is that?" Yeh often wondered about the disparity between the
great goddess Kali and the actual lack of rights of women in
India. An Indian woman whom she asked about this replied,
"Indian women *are* free!" That is, human existence is always
conditioned, contingent. Freedom begins for an individual the
moment he or she chooses to do the right thing without calculating the consequences. Yeh senses a Eurocentrism in current
feminism. Paglia agrees: feminism is overconcerned with social
status, the social realm, when the first lesson of Christianity,
Hinduism, and Buddhism is the transience and unreality of one's
social identity. We need to achieve social justice and equality,
but that alone will not bring enlightenment or make us happy.
We are much greater than our social selves. Paglia thinks feminism has lost philosophical perspective on life.

Yeh says Chinese households were ruled by
foot-binding. The grandmothers ruled. Paglia says .
experience of Italian culture; hence her book is dedic
two grandmothers, majestic personalities who dominat
body, even at a distance. Yeh: "Learning has nothing to o
college. You must be open, receptive, and it occurs at any tin ."
Architect Louis Kahn said: "One must not impose one's will on
a space. One listens."

April 12. The *Vedas* are more about ritual contract, as in Greek
religion. The *Upanishads* are more like ancient mystery religions
and Christianity. There is only one Christ, but there are many
Buddhas, an infinite number of the past and future. In Christianity, the sole cosmic event is the birth of Christ; he's unique.
There is only one True Cross. But the bodhi tree can be different
trees. In early Buddhist art, an empty throne beneath the tree
signifies the presence of Buddha, the presence of a person devoid
of ego. He is there and not there at the same time. Buddha is
only incidental in the chain of many Buddhas of many universes.
Christianity leads up to the big bang of the Second Coming, the
end of time and the beginning of eternity. But Indian mythology
sees the next universe as being exactly the same as this one. Yeh
sees the Western concept of progress even in our economics:
"Business gets bigger and bigger here, to prove it's doing well.
Greed is always wanting more. It's like cancer."

Different attitudes toward nature. Judeo-Christianity sees
nature as a fallen realm, God as transcendent, in supernature.
Genesis, the first book of the Bible, gives man dominion over the
animal kingdom. But in India humanity is in no sense superior
to animals. You could be a monkey in your next life. Elephants
are brothers of humans, not lower family of existence. Elephant
is the equivalent of the Western horse. Buddha had been an
elephant with six tusks.

Yeh shows slide of spectacular female yakshi figure. She is
leaning, almost as if drunk, half hanging from a tree. She has
huge nursing breasts. Her genitals are exposed, framed, with
sharp vulval cleavage. She is the fertile essence of the tree. She
kicks it to make it flower. Shows the unity of the sexual and the

sacred in Hinduism. Nothing shameful about the genitals; quite the contrary.

Next, a sun-wheel with the lotus flower in the center. The wheel = Buddha's teaching, like a sun dispelling darkness. Lotus is the equivalent of the rose in the West, a flower of transcendence: cf. the rose window of the great cathedrals. Lotus = the female genitals of the yakshi. Lush Hindu breasts are never found in Chinese or Japanese art, where there are no big bosoms, only complex layering of kimonos. In China and Japan, as in Islam, a woman's body is a mystery, and you make it profane by showing to the eyes with the wrong motives. Female beauty is not in her physicality but in the way she moves her body, her feminine gestures, and her veils of mystery.

Slide of St. Apollonaris Church, Ravenna, sixth century A.D. Yeh compares the interior to that of the Buddhist "cathedral" at Karla, second century A.D. The central aisle and rows of heavy pillars are the same. But Karla is carved out of living rock in a mountain. The light is entirely artificial, for purposes of the photo. The best-lit part of a Catholic cathedral is the altar. The opposite is true in Hindu temples. Yeh compares repetition of Byzantine saints at Ravenna to the repetition of Buddha figures. Cf. composer Philip Glass, influenced by Indian music: repeated modules versus the theme and variation style of Western music. In the twentieth century, it's the field of sound, rather than a melody; if melody is repeated over and over again, it's lost.

Cathedrals are strictly symmetrical; Chartres is unusual, with its mismatched towers. Some of the temples in India develop over centuries; they get more and more primitive toward their center, with fancy gigantic gates expanding outward—for example, Arunacal-eshvara Temple, Tirurannamalsi, Madras. Sometimes the only opening is at the front. Cathedral is in a cross shape; Gothic spires go up toward God. Ethereal effects of light, air, evaporation. But Indian temples get darker and darker, more entombed and enwombed as one moves toward the innermost chamber. Paglia: Pivotal moment in E. M. Forster's *A Passage to India* occurs in a pitch-dark, womblike Hindu rock shrine, where an Englishwoman panics; she misinterprets the assault on her Western consciousness as rape, and an Indian is falsely accused.

Sculpture of Buddha in the Gandhara style, sitting rather awkwardly in Indian position of geometrical balance. It looks Roman. Gandhara is a province in the northwest corner of India that belonged to Persia for centuries, so Greek influence was strong there in the Hellenistic period, thanks to Alexander. High-ridge Greek nose in Gandhara statues; head relatively big compared to the body, as in Roman provincial art. The draping of the Buddhist monastic robe, still used today, comes from the Roman toga. The open-palmed gesture of blessing made by Buddha, as well as Christ, comes from Roman art. Paglia: A good example of this is the Prima Porta statue of Augustus Caesar, one of her favorite works of art in high school.

Slide of the birth of Buddha: shows his body being pulled, leaping, from his mother's side. Early images of Buddha are like early ones of Christ as humble shepherd and good teacher: humanness stressed; he is one of us. Later on, Christ has a beard, signifying maturity, wisdom, power, and in Byzantine art he is enthroned as a king of heaven, full of dignity and stern authority. Buddha has thirty-two magic marks: one is a protuberance on the head, disguised under his wavy hairdo. A tuft of hair between the eyes = insight. Hands are webbed; flat feet—no arches. Enormously long ear lobes: men too wear earrings in India, so it's a symbol of noble birth to have very long ear lobes from heavy gold earrings. When Yeh's brother was born, her grandmother said it was auspicious that he had big lobes. In India, to be beautiful is to be highly decorated.

April 16. Yeh: "A lot of contemporary art tries to create ritual-like forms and icon-like images, because we don't have any religion. So happenings and performance art become rituals for people to participate in." Paglia: "So art has returned to its prehistoric origins in ritual and magic." Yeh shows slides of the mounds of offerings of carved stones in Tibet and Nepal: everyone who passes by helps to create the monument, which is accumulated over time. It's a sacred, collective public art. Paglia comments on inability of American media to understand intensely religious feeling in non-Western cultures; for example, Islamic fundamentalists are called "fanatical" or "medieval." Yeh: "Islamic law (*Shari'ah*) cannot change, because it is sacred. The real, the true never changes. It is the human realm that changes." Cf. papal infallibility, a doctrine that emerged long after the Church drifted from early Christian teachings. Yeh speaks of the development of the human mind. She compares rockets, with their "simplicity and beauty" to the spires of Gothic cathedrals; she thinks they represent an epitome of the human imagination. The *Voyager* spacecraft is out there right now and will disappear into distant space, "where mechanics and logic verge on the mysterious." Western space travel is "a quest to know the unknown"; "all that is finite is brought together to reach the infinite."

April 19. Yeh: Icons merely suggest the presence of Buddha rather than indicate his actual presence. Paglia: The same is true of Christianity, though there is a powerful element of iconoclasm in Islam, Judaism, and Protestantism. Yeh: Because there are many different Buddhas instead of one, there is a different sense of time: cyclical in the East, linear and developmental in the West. She says our musical forms differ markedly: the Western sonata (ABA form) and the symphony versus Oriental music, where there often is no sense of beginning or end. Paglia: The Indian raga goes on for many hours; Indian music, now vanished from the scene, had a profound impact on Sixties rock musicians. Yeh: Linearity of Western melody also evident in Western architecture: in a cathedral, you know where to go; you're led along. But in a mosque, the same architectural unit is repeated again and again. The space anywhere in a mosque feels the same. One loses a sense of time and space here. The only reminder of direction is a niche in the wall facing Mecca, toward which all Muslims pray.

Yeh speaks of powwows of the Northwest Coast, Native American drumming that summons and binds the community together, just one drum being beaten without end. Then singing and dancing, with room for everyone, young girls in capes, young male fancy dancers in full regalia, old men and women moving

slowly, even the crazy can join in. Capes allow you
no matter what your figure. Today's tight male sui\
regimentation of efficiency." Tribal life is gone; so\
come more complex, more affluent. "But whenever y
also lose something."

Yeh says she loves Western music and opera, with its full
voice and breath-carried melody. The class discusses the quite
different sound of the female voice in Far Eastern music: compressed, shrill, forced up from the chest. It seems thin, irritating,
monotonous to unschooled Western ears. Paglia wonders if its
lack of resonance indicates an avoidance of overt sensuality, as
with the thick kimono. Yeh describes Tibetan music, with its
slow chanting, a long continuous stream, sounding as if it is rising
from the bowels of the earth. There is a twenty- to forty-foot-
long horn, not a human sound but the voice of the earth itself.
Then cymbals to suddenly shatter the serenity.

April 23. Sri Lanka (Ceylon) is still a stronghold of Theravada
or early Buddhism. Yeh shows two gigantic images of Buddha
in Sri Lanka. One is standing on the earth, not on a dais or
platform separated from the earth. Back is straight, chin pulled
back, eyes staring. Implies self-effort, vigilance; a strong-willed
determined position. More slides: Yeh compares Grünewald's
painting of the resurrection of Jesus, rising, floating, legs dangling, to a fourth century Gupta stone Buddha from Mathura,
rising, floating, legs dangling. Heinrich Zimmer calls the latter
a "phantasmagoric" figure. It just appears; ease, effortlessness.
Tathagata: "Thus come" [Buddha]. This is the reality of the mind.
"Suchness": the immediate here and now, not intellect, emotion,
hopes. Yeh says lovers die in the Western tradition because they
cannot be fulfilled in life. Paglia: This intertwining of sex and
death is the subject of Denis de Rougemont's excellent book, *Love
in the Western World* (1940), totally ignored by current women's
studies, which is infatuated with itself.

Yeh gives as a superb example of ritual in contemporary
art Maya Lin's Vietnam Veterans Memorial in Washington,
D.C. It is an earthworks, like a ritual walk with offerings left.
"It is really a work of religious art. As in Tibet, people come as

pilgrims to bear homage." The objects left by the families and friends of the dead are collected and fill a government archive. Paglia: There were many protests when Maya Lin's winning design was first publicized. It was called "a gash of shame" in the earth. But it has become one of Washington's most popular monuments. People are emotionally overwhelmed when they visit it. It is very simple and powerful, both abstract and archaic in design. It represents an important contribution to American art by an Asian-American woman.

Bodhidarma, the founder of Zen, came from India to China at the end of the fifth century A.D. By the Sung dynasty of the tenth to the thirteenth centuries, Zen pervaded every aspect of the culture. Zen was established in Japan shortly after 1200. It has profoundly influenced Japanese culture. Japanese art and writing are also derived from China. But Chinese is based on the single syllable, while Japanese is multisyllabic. Yeh speaks of the Ainu, long- and curly-haired Caucasian remnants of the original people of Japan, who were persecuted and driven north by the later Mongolian immigrants. There are only a few left in north Hokkaido now. They have been oppressed and discriminated against by the Japanese through the centuries to the present day. This is a good example of how racism is a universal principle of injustice and not just the invention of white males torturing "people of color."

Ch'an (Zen) is a Chinese understanding of Buddhism. The metaphysic is very different from that of India. The Chinese approach is direct, intuitive, and meditative, where the Indian approach is elaborate, complex, and highly sophisticated. Buddhism came to China in the first century A.D.; around the third century Chinese politics were in disarray. Confucianism hadn't helped, so the people turned to the west to Buddhism, which gradually, with Taoism added, turned into Zen. In Hinayana and Mahayana Buddhism, you attain enlightenment by working through your life cycles. But in Zen and Tantric Buddhism, you attain enlightenment in *this* life cycle; hence it is very difficult. In Tantrism, you conjure up all kinds of power; it's dangerous. One must be guided by a guru, a spiritual teacher for the path to enlightenment. The guru exists primarily in Hinduism. The

Zen master may goad you, but ultimately in Bud responsible for your own enlightenment.

April 26. Sukiya, the Japanese word for teahouse, m abode of emptiness." It uses rugged, hard, deliberately ___ar wood, rubbed by hand. Irregularity of this kind is so un-Western. Paglia: Yes, sharp edges, steely surfaces, and mathematical perfection are Apollonian. Yeh says the mud walls of the teahouse are treated like a Rothko painting: every inch matters.

Oriental painters use silk, thin paper, water-based colors and ink, very fragile materials. Western painters prefer canvas, oil paints to assure permanence and lifelike accuracy in their images. Zen paintings were often executed in splash-ink style. Absorbent paper is used, so you must keep moving or the ink will turn into a big blob. There must be an urgency of expression. Speed and determination are crucial. The artist's intention is to depict the spirit and not the form of the subject. D. T. Suzuki says, "Every stroke of his brush is the work of creation, and it cannot be retraced because it never permits a repetition."

Yeh shows slides of contemporary art works by Duane Michals and compares them to Zen art: enigmatic, unexplainable, mysterious qualities. She juxtaposes a portrait of Andy Warhol by Michals, a blurry, silk-screened multiple photo, with a twelfth-century Japanese image of a monk's face in apparent duplicate, splitting down the middle as a *Bodhisattva* bursts through. The two works are startling in their interpretation of human portraiture.

Yeh and Paglia agree: world art and world religion have eternal themes that appear again and again, separated by continents or centuries. Man's nature has never changed. Positive and negative forces are at war within us. The distant past holds the key to the present and future. It is up to each person to seek knowledge, not just from books but from ordinary life, from common things. Enlightenment may never be fully achieved, but we must all journey toward it. It is the task of a lifetime.

JUNK BONDS AND

CORPORATE RAIDERS:

ACADEME IN THE

HOUR OF THE WOLF

I

On the back of David M. Halperin's *One Hundred Years of Homosexuality,* a series of American academics tells us that this book "shakes what has long been considered the foundations of Western culture." Halperin "takes giant strides" after Foucault; his book is "an intellectual feast," characterized by "remarkable elegance of style." It is "a major contribution" that will "leave an indelible mark." It shows "the breadth and

[*Arion,* Spring 1991. A description of the origins and history of this essay can be found in the Appendix (pp. 301–302).]

daring" that have made Halperin
gay studies."

As I read these passages, I ask myself,
I in? What are its values? What forces are at wo
that would produce such quotes for so shoddy a bo
article I will review two closely associated new books and
analyze the sorry state of literary criticism that has produce
them. Finally, I will make proposals for educational and professional reform.

One Hundred Years of Homosexuality is a short collection of
essays that seems to have only one coherent aim: the nomination
and promotion of David Halperin as a major theorist of sex. But
Halperin, like most of the American academics who have wandered into sex studies, lacks the most elementary understanding
of the basic disciplines of history, anthropology, and psychology
necessary for such work. The exposition of these essays is tortured, bloated, meandering, pretentious, confused. Halperin's
first book, *Before Pastoral: Theocritus and the Ancient History of Bucolic
Poetry* (1983), is quite different. Whether its precision and clarity
of argument—not to mention skill in simple paragraphing—are
due to the editors of Yale University Press or to a helpful dissertation director, it is evident that in *One Hundred Years* we are
getting Halperin *lui-même*.

Let me begin with the sensitive matter of the political pack-
aging of the two books under review. On the back of each, as in
the preface, is stated, to follow the wording of John J. Winkler's
The Constraints of Desire, "A portion of the profits from the sale of
this book will benefit the San Francisco AIDS Foundation."
Winkler, Halperin confides, offered his help while "learning to
meet and to master the challenge of living with AIDS." AIDS,
like all catastrophic diseases, is a tragedy to those who suffer it
and to those who must watch others suffer it. But what is its
relevance to two books on ancient Greece? Why is this private
medical information here, and why are donations to charity now
being advertised on book covers? A scholar's theory of homosexuality is not made truer by his death from AIDS—the fate also,
Halperin gratuitously notes, of Michel Foucault in 1984. Several
parables of the New Testament make vividly clear, to believers

...iseeism of public
...s is a new fad in
...these two cases, with
...affects us all, it is subtly
...these books a bad review, or
...ore people to die. That Halperin

...proceeds also mixes up his personal
...y in a way that should concern anyone
...s of the profession. This trend, if continued,
...athors suffering debilitating or terminal diseases,
...Hawking to Walker Percy and Reynolds Price, to
annou... their afflictions and their charities on the dust jackets
of their books. Scholarship must not become the tool of social-
welfare causes, however appealingly humanitarian. Oscar Wilde,
that gay genius, was rightly militant in his defense of art and
thought against the tyrannical liberal philanthropies of his day.

Let us turn now to Halperin's preface, which states that his
work reflects a new "shift in emphasis" from regarding "Greek
love" as "an isolated, and therefore 'queer,' institution" to an
acknowledgment that it is "merely one strand in a larger and
more intricate web of erotic and social practices in ancient
Greece." This is a false claim to novelty. Greek love may have
been celebrated in glorious isolation by late Victorian and Ed-
wardian poets or by nonacademic enthusiasts producing fancy
limited editions with X-rated illustrations, but the great tradition
of classical scholarship coming down to us from Winckelmann
has virtually always, when it dares or deigns to deal with homosexuality directly, regarded it as inextricable from the complex
social and educational structures of classical Athens. What con-
stitutes "erotic and social practices" for Halperin is, I will show,
a reductive view of culture that turns Athens into a bleak political cartoon.

Next the preface lists "the three most important intellectual
influences" on Halperin's work, "without which this book could
not have been written." The first is K. J. Dover's *Greek Homosexuality* (1978). In what respect can Dover's fine book, for all its
common-sense, plain-talk virtues, be considered an "intellectual"
influence? There is nothing intellectual about it. It brought a

brisk, no-nonsense, nonjudgmental approach to discussing the mechanics of Greek pederastic intercourse. But it contains few surprises—aside from its eye-opening account of "intercrural" sex. To anyone familiar with the rich scholarly record of the past two hundred years, Dover's book was a welcome clearing of cobwebs, but it was no revolution. Perhaps to someone thinking only in literary terms about the world, the sociological Dover seemed liberating. Halperin is determined in his book to date the modern Enlightenment from Dover and Foucault, whose *The Use of Pleasure* (1984) is the second of his claimed intellectual influences. In other words, the benighted world was struggling along, and we all woke up amidst a mighty thunderclap when Halperin, thanks to Dover and Foucault, lurched from his literary haze. I'm not kidding: the introduction later overtly states, "A new era in the study of the history of sexuality began in 1978." The most outrageous aspect of *One Hundred Years* is its contemporary parochialism, its strident hypothesis, pushed through hundreds of arbitrary footnotes citing trivial hot-off-the-press articles by eager-beaver greenhorn academics, that the entire foundation of classical learning, notably in classical anthropology, is now irrelevant. Modern thought did not begin in 1977, when David Halperin finally emerged with his M.A.

Halperin's third intellectual influence is Winkler's *The Constraints of Desire,* our other book under review. Straining to lift Winkler to Foucault's rank, Halperin lauds this "collection of essays whose combination of philological mastery, critical tact, methodological sophistication, intellectual range, and human engagement sets a new standard for the interpretation of ancient cultures." We will get to *Constraints* shortly, but the only items in this encomium that are remotely true would be "philological mastery"—which, remembering the eminent German philologists, I would amend to "expertise"—and the revealing phrase "critical tact." Winkler's sole modest distinction is that he is among the first classicists to try to start systematically applying the New Criticism to classical texts, a phase long overdue. Sad to say, Halperin, infatuated with the latest trendy thing and therefore believing the New Criticism long dead, does not recognize the small, solid virtues of his own mentor and injures him by forcing him into dizzy intellectual company, where he is painfully outclassed.

Moving now to the introduction, we must deal with Foucault, whose real field, as Halperin admits, was modern history. The truth is that Foucault knew very little about anything before the seventeenth century and, in the modern world, outside France. His familiarity with the literature and art of any period was negligible. His hostility to psychology made him incompetent to deal with sexuality, his own or anybody else's. The elevation of Foucault to guru status by American and British academics is a tale that belongs to the history of cults. It illustrates the Big Daddy syndrome, a searching for authority by supposedly free, liberal, secular thinkers. Foucault's biggest fans are not among the majority of philosophers, historians, and sociologists, who usually perceive his glaring inadequacies of knowledge and argument, but among well-meaning but foggy humanists, who virtually never have the intellectual and scholarly preparation to critique Foucault competently. The more you know, the less you are impressed by Foucault.

We will return to Foucault, but first let us deal with the account in the introduction of his alleged originality. Halperin, exposing his own deficiencies, gives us the shiny P.R. version: "Foucault did for 'sexuality' what feminist critics had done for 'gender.' That is, Foucault detached 'sexuality' from the physical and biological sciences. . . . He divorced 'sexuality' from 'nature' and interpreted it, instead, as a cultural production." Tipping his political hand, Halperin lauds the "extremely profitable alliance" Foucault thereby made between "radical elements in philosophy and anthropology." The idea that theories of sex and gender before Foucault and feminism were exclusively biologistic is ludicrous. Halperin lacks even a superficial undergraduate-level familiarity with the major schools of psychology, several of them American, that have ruled from the Thirties to the present, virtually all of which stress the socialization of identity. These movements were a turn away from the earlier medical orientation of psychoanalysis, as it was established by Freud, who emerged from European hard science of the late nineteenth century. In this respect Foucault was a follower, not a leader. The nature versus nurture controversy, furthermore, is a century old. Foucault did not make the first bold break from the nature hypothesis, and it is dishonest to imply that he did. His is simply one voice (and an incompletely informed one) in a long, stormy, ongoing debate about all aspects of human personality and behavior. Nevertheless, Halperin labels disagreements with his idol "Foucault-bashing," which since Foucault's death has become "the favorite indoor sport of a host of lesser intellectuals on both sides of the Atlantic." There are two unsavory implications here: that criticism of Foucault is inspired by petty jealousy and, secondly, that it is really gay-bashing and therefore secretly homophobic.

Halperin gets into constant trouble throughout the book with his fumbling newfangled usages of "sexuality" and "sex," which, imitating Foucault, he tries to force into English. It won't work. It makes no sense to try to redefine and therefore to distort, for the sake of one Parisian ideologue, the standard meanings of common English words. Sometimes in the Foucault school "sexuality" means the scientific study and categorization of sexual behavior, which all competent students of the history of ideas have known perfectly well began in the late nineteenth century. But sometimes "sexuality" for the Foucaldians becomes what in American psychology is more usefully called sexual identity—that is, our consciousness of and commentary upon our own sexuality, mediated through social conventions and norms. Again, despite the screechy claims that Foucault was the genius who told us this, scholars have known for more than fifty years that sexual identity in this sense is a product of the creation of the modern individual through and after Rousseau and Romanticism. "Sex" the Foucaldians use as a dumpster for everything else—all the tacky physical stuff, like anatomical dimorphism and sexual intercourse. Now, this kind of strained dichotomy between "sexuality" and "sex" cannot be sustained. The two words naturally flow into each other. A viable sex theory cannot be constructed out of a handful of sanitized, Sovietized terms kidnapped from the common realm of discourse. "Sexuality" under the red flag of Foucault describes something like the fate of cookie dough stamped by the cutter; yet oddly enough, the dough can speak and is in fact bizarrely alleged not to exist at all except through speech. Halperin synopsizes Foucault's aim: "to trace the evolution of the régimes of power and knowledge that constituted human beings as the conscious subject of their 'sexuality.' " There is an awful lot of ugly huffing and puffing here to do something very simple and already obtainable by a skillful application of conventional techniques of historiography, biography, and Anglo-American literary criticism, enhanced by Freudian analysis.

Next the introduction sketches an apocalyptic panorama of contemporary history: since 1978, "much of western Europe and America seems to have sunk into a reactionary torpor, embracing with a hollow and cynical enthusiasm the comforts of conventional pieties," but the universities, "under the impetus provided by Foucault" and feminism, have been in an "intellectual ferment," still "accelerating," with research making "great strides" and tremendous progress. In this amazing picture, like a grandiose tableau commissioned by the Czars from a sycophant court painter, the weak, silly world sinks into a new Dark Ages, while the torch of freedom and intellect is held bravely aloft by liberal academics in their dazzlingly creative enclaves. I will shortly give a quite different view of the recent academic past. One of the purposes of this book, says Halperin, building on his shaky progressivist premise, is "to tell the scholarly world the good news"— to reveal to us "the enormous scope and variety" of the "highly sophisticated and enlightening" work done since 1978 in the field of sexuality. Hence the packed footnotes, which indiscriminately suck up, in no useful order, everything that twitched in the last decade. If Halperin's motives were truly scholarly, he would have produced a real annotated bibliography, with honest acknowledgment of the important and still relevant work on sexuality done throughout this century. But that would require real research, and it would cancel out his first commandment—that the divine Foucault breathed life into our dead brain matter. The real source of Halperin's evangelical "eagerness" seems clear enough: the strategy of obliterating distinguished past scholarship and flooding us with minor works by callow nonentities allows him to emerge in the post-Foucault landscape as king of the pygmies.

Now for the essays. The first one, from which the book takes its title, begins by awkwardly conflating the upcoming 500th anniversary of Columbus's discovery of America (which will be celebrated by "the patriots among us"—snidely implying there are some among us, presumably leftists, who will not be celebrating it) with the 100th anniversary of the alleged invention of the word *homosexuality* by Charles Gilbert Chaddock, a major factual error. Straightaway, in this first sentence, Halperin makes one of his characteristic slushy slides, identifying a word with what it describes: he claims Chaddock invented homosexuality itself. This is the constant monotonous point, flogged to death but never persuasively argued or proved, in Halperin's book: that homosexuals did not exist before the word was invented which, according to the French fad, brought them into being. This is just absurd: it's like Antarctic explorers coming upon penguins for the first time and informing them, "I'm sorry, you did not exist before we named you." There is enough evidence to suggest that in most metropolitan centers of the Hellenistic and Roman worlds, as later in Renaissance Florence, Paris, and London and Baroque Rome, there were men whose persistent behavior was seen (and usually condemned) by others as what we would call homosexual. That people before Romanticism did not deeply reflect on and agonize over their sexuality or psychology is a completely separate issue, related to the breakdown of religious and spiritual authority after the Enlightenment. That heterosexuality and homosexuality as rigidly opposed categories emerged into medical discourse in the late nineteenth century is indisputable and has always been known to scholars of intellectual history. What is now being worked out is the relationship of these terms to the changing and diminishing family structure under nineteenth- and twentieth-century industrial capitalism, which has been extraordinarily beneficial in permitting both men and women for the first time in history to choose unmarried, self-supporting, and self-fulfilling lives. Halperin makes a lot of empty, important-sounding pronouncements, but he does not even clearly see, much less help in, the intellectual task before us. He favors crutch phrases like "modern bourgeois Westerners," big sloppy generalities, unqualified by place or time period, that indicate his naïveté and inexperience as a political analyst. I heard far sharper political talk in the all-night bull sessions that were the crucible out of which my generation of the Sixties forged its rebellion.

This first essay is verbose and incoherent, with interesting points raised and then buried under sludge. It's like the mashed-potato mountain obsessively fiddled with by Richard Dreyfuss in *Close Encounters of the Third Kind*. The essay steadily degenerates into a blizzard of footnoted addenda, contradicting and reversing points made on the same page. The reason for this can be detected in the essay's genealogy: we are told it appeared in three earlier versions and was presented at thirteen different conferences or universities; twenty-four people are listed and thanked for their help, advice, and suggestions. Now we know what Halperin has been doing with his time, which should have been spent alone in the library. I will address the question of the conference circuit, which I think one of the primary causes of the corruption of the profession in the last twenty years. Instead of taking personal responsibility for his research, Halperin (like a host of others, notably among feminists) relies on the audience, the co-conferees, and a swollen cadre of "expert" advisors to spoonfeed him additional examples or new leads and to correct his scholarly errors. This research-by-committee method produces the kind of work we get here—jerky, leaden, fragmented, backtracking. Things are added on at random—a dib, a dab, a dollop. The end result is as tangled up, matted, and unappealing as a cat's wet hairball. Rumination should be a private, not a public, process.

Halperin declares that he has found while "lecturing to different audiences around the United States" that the thesis of his title essay elicits "skepticism and resistance." You see the folly of this approach. Halperin has an exaggerated sense of his originality because he has mistaken the more mixed, volatile, and freewheeling lecture and conference audience for the larger, deeper, slower, more informed scholarly audience that judges you by and holds you accountable for every sentence of your publications. Many, perhaps most, very learned people prefer the company of their books to sitting in a crowd listening to history and art being mangled; furthermore, it is unlikely that venerable scholars will stand up afterward to declare, "This lecture was a

load of crap." The more profound a professor's dist₂
proceedings, the more likely he is to melt away at
the talk.

The actual dynamic behind Halperin's book seen
sprung from conference disputes with John Boswell and his followers in gay studies. Halperin, riding on Foucault's coattails,
evidently hopes to slip into first place past Boswell, who is a real,
professionally trained historian. Skirmishes and turf wars within
a new and not yet established field should not masquerade as
world-shaking issues. In point of fact, Boswell's reasoning about
"gay people" in the Middle Ages has been far from universally
accepted. I myself have minor objections to his jumbled survey
of antiquity and major objections to his treatment of medieval
culture, in particular his inadequate grasp or presentation of the
intellectually and socially ordering power of Catholic theology
and bureaucracy. The low point of Boswell's book is probably
his demagogic use of usury as an example at the finale.[1] Gay
studies will doom itself if it allows ideology to dictate to scholarship. Fortunately, we have the more rigorous example of James
M. Saslow: the crystal-clear notes of his *Ganymede in the Renaissance*
(1986), crisply covering the same ancient ground as Boswell's
murky first chapters, are of the highest scholarly quality and
integrity. Nevertheless, despite his wobbly moments, Boswell remains a serious scholar who knows how to range through and
interpret the historical record, a talent Halperin mimes but con-
spicuously lacks.

Space does not allow a line-by-line commentary on the innumerable problems of Halperin's first essay, but here are a few
of the outstanding ones. A laborious plot summary of Aristophanes' myth in Plato's *Symposium* leads to the assertion that Aristophanes' conclusions "help to illustrate the lengths to which
classical Athenians were willing to go in order to avoid concep-
tualizing sexual behaviors according to a binary opposition between different- and same-sex sexual contacts." Is there any
oxygen in the house? Note the way grade-school assumptions
about the relation between art and life are concealed under a
rock pile of pseudo-technical verbiage. Aristophanes is a literary
character and not the real-life man on which he was based, and

therefore one cannot judge from him what "classical Athenians"
thought, particularly since Plato was writing in melancholy retrospect, after the high-classic period was over. Halperin is simply
awful with chronology. He has no sense of how the historical
milieu changes from decade to decade, much less from century
to century. Typically, we bounce 600 years in the blink of an eye
from Plato to the second century A.D. and get a soggy reference
to what "the ancients" believed about this or that. The last time
I heard "the ancients" used in such a vague, sentimental, and
all-embracing sense was probably in high school. This is bush-
league stuff.

Halperin's ignorance of the language and insights of the
major schools of modern psychology is obvious at moments like
this, where he is hawking the Foucault line that "sexuality is a
modern invention" and therefore has no real permanent existence: "the very concept of homosexuality implies that there is
a specifically sexual dimension to the human personality, a char-
acterological seat within the individual of sexual acts, desires,
and pleasures." Note the mix-up between personality and character and also between body and psyche. Halperin has been taken
in, without really understanding it, by the notion of the decentered subject, one of the fattest pieces of rotten French cheese
swallowed whole by American academics. Foucault's simplistic
sex theory is self-entombed in a mouse hole because of its inability
to perceive, analyze, or describe the historical variety of human
personality types and the complexity, multiplicity, and daily flux
of thought, desire, dream, fantasy, mood, sensation, and action.
For thirty years, the sexual territory between biology and psychology has been far more successfully and sensibly explored on
American soil, at the Johns Hopkins University School of Medicine, by John J. Money, whose many pioneering books on sex
and gender identity Halperin does not mention and obviously
has not absorbed. He is too busy canonizing mini-works, like so-
and-so's twenty-page article in *Radical History Review,* which is
dubbed "a classic essay."

Halperin's loopiest moment is his disastrous disquisition on
food. Sexual preference is as meaningless as food preferences, he
says; no one would ever characterize or categorize people psy-

chologically or culturally on the basis of what they eat. Here's a sample sentence of blowzy Halperin doublespeak:

> Just as we tend to assume that human beings are not individuated at the level of dietary preference and that we all, despite many pronounced and frankly acknowledged differences from one another in dietary habits, share the same fundamental set of alimentary appetites and hence the same "dieticity" or "edility," so most pre-modern and non-Western cultures, despite an awareness of the range of possible variations in human sexual behavior, refuse to individuate human beings at the level of sexual preference and assume, instead, that we all share the same fundamental set of sexual appetites, the same "sexuality."

Halperin's ignorance of the literature of anthropology is almost shocking. He has to add a long, desperately backpedaling footnote (without bothering to revise his text) confessing what other people have now told him—that "a growing mass of historical data suggests that dietary categories have indeed provided, in certain times and places, a viable basis on which to construct typologies of human beings." But the propaganda continues here: "a growing mass" implies that this is, as usual, something new and innovative. On the contrary, observations about the consumption of or abstention from certain foods as an identifying mark of clans and tribes date from and are basic to the origins of anthropology in the nineteenth century. Unmentioned, incredibly, by Halperin is the most obvious one of them all: the Jewish prohibition against eating pork, biblically defined, with shellfish, as unclean. An interesting poem one might expect Halperin to know—it's called the *Odyssey*—makes ethical classifications of Mediterranean peoples and individuals on the basis of what they eat and how they prepare it. In the 1950s, America's massive production and consumption of milk was connected by wine-based European observers to our naïve optimism and family mythos. Since the 1960s, there has been an avalanche of dietary psychology: eating meat makes you aggressive; eating sugar makes you hyper; people who crave salt and fat are the active, bossy, top-heavy adrenal type; people who crave sweets are the slower, pear-shaped pituitary type, etc. Those who prefer a stable routine of bland "brown" food tend to be cautious and conservative; those who seek out spicy, ethnic taste sensations tend to be adventurous, liberal, even extravagant. I myself have contributed a raw-clam theory to this debate. And one could easily speculate about the relation between the preference for bloody-rare or well-done steak and one's attitude toward body fluids and menstruation, or about the relation between eroticism and a taste for messy, luscious, get-down-in-it finger foods like barbecued ribs.

How does all of this relate to classical culture?—the one area where Halperin should be at home. Anyone familiar with Greek and Roman love poetry knows that many men found both women and boys desirable but that boys' sexual attractiveness ended when they sprouted a beard and body hair. It should be perfectly obvious that there is an aesthetic issue here, vividly documented from Archaic monody through Roman satire, in praise of the girlish rosiness, smoothness, and glow of boys' flesh. But Halperin, following Foucault, can never admit that aesthetics exists; the only permissible criterion of judgment in art or life is the ideology of power. So we get ugly clunkers like this: Halperin says of the apparent bisexuality of Greek men, "I think it would be advisable not to speak of it as a sexuality at all but to describe it, rather, as a more generalized ethos of penetration and domination, a socio-sexual discourse structured by the presence or absence of its central term: the phallus." This display of old-maidish puritanism is scholarship reduced to *Mad* magazine parody, which at least knows it's funny. All those Greeks banging away had no idea they were having sex without sexuality. They were merely discoursing on power, you see. Halperin's explanation for the equal desirability of women and boys: both "were considered sexually inert." In other words, women and boys were just sperm spittoons. And sometimes a penis is not a penis. A phallus, in Francobabble, is just a power tool. But since only men have such tools, we have to somehow circle back and admit it *is* a penis after all. It's a case of Aaron's rod as the incredible shrinking dildo.

For the sake of the new god, Foucault, Halperin is willing to send classical Athens through a meat grinder of hack-work gibberish. Like Foucault, he is incapable of holding in his mind the brilliant but conflicted fusion of art, drama, philosophy, religion, and politics that was Athens at its brief high point. Nor do Foucault and Halperin give us even a competent political critique of Athens, which would need to trace internal and external political processes beginning 200 years earlier and then move outward through the destabilization of the late fifth century and the emergence of international *Realpolitik* in the mercantile Hellenistic era, with its rivalrous strongmen. Because he thinks in big, flat political stereotypes, Halperin is lost when he has to deal with specific constellations of government structure and their evolution over time, as economic conditions change. The most glaring fault of his midget clockwork view of Athenian sexuality is the way he censors out the central iconography of male nude sculpture, which began in the Archaic period, reached its peak at high classicism, and then spread throughout the Mediterranean in a tradition revived at the Italian Renaissance and still alive today. Beautiful boys were honored and idolized. Their transient physical gifts seemed sacred, god-given. This splendor of homoeroticism, never more dignified, moving, and transcendent, Halperin strips away to serve the myopic Foucault. With friends like these, gay studies doesn't need enemies.

The American Francophiles get themselves into a pickle partly by their ignorance of art history. They are spectacularly inept at reading visual materials, which they constantly reduce to *a priori* verbal formulas. A particularly atrocious example is Eva C. Keuls's *The Reign of the Phallus: Sexual Politics in Ancient Athens* (1985), where juicy orgy scenes from Greek pottery are clumsily misinterpreted in the most literalistic, burning-resentment Kate Millett style. To talk about ancient pornography, you'd better know something about modern pornography, but that's a no-no in feminist covens. Simplistically reading porn as if it were a photographic record of real life, Keuls misses its sprightly artistic conventions and its coarse iconoclastic humor. Halperin too makes elementary errors with the visual material, making little distinction between treatments of lower-class female prostitutes and upper-class wives, or between boy prostitutes and the upper-class beloved boy or protégé, whose supposed sexual inertness may more profitably be understood in aesthetic or spiritual terms as a formulaic decorum of stillness and perfection, beyond the agitation of need.

Before escaping from the muddle of Halperin's first essay, we should pause to note two tourist attractions at the end: first, the climactic quote from Adrienne Rich, who has 24 entries in the three-page index (poor unimportant Freud gets only ten). I guess Rich is a biggie in the with-it circles Halperin moves in. My opinion is that any scholarly book that relies on Adrienne Rich deserves to sink like a stone. But the *pièce de résistance* is a nearly page-length quote from—Jack Abbott! Yes, Norman Mailer's pet criminal appears here as a philosopher of sex. Not since the Black Panthers sailed into their Upper East Side tea party has there been so daffy an exercise in radical chic. One must chuckle at the irony that Abbott, cited here for his insight into homosexuality, has recently been televised from prison as, sporting a yarmulke and clutching the hand of his fiancée, he announced his engagement and his conversion to Judaism—where he will presumably learn about abstaining from pork.

Essay number two is, strangely enough, an interview with Halperin himself. Since when do scholars publish interviews with themselves? Especially since the text has admittedly been "revised" afterward. Here we see the brazen new commercialism of academe. How do you get people to think of you as important? Why, by showing yourself being interviewed by people flocking to sit at the feet of the sage. It's like having yourself paged in the lobby of a fancy hotel. George Hamilton's ploy upon arrival in Hollywood: though flat broke, he hired a limousine to stage a grand entrance. In features on stock and real-estate scandals, *60 Minutes* has shown us again and again how enterprising con men without a dime to their name fleece rich and poor alike by public paradings of fabricated wealth and power. It's called the "pyramid" scam. The next inevitable step for ambitious academics: a video disc packaged with the book, so we can see, with appropriate triumphal or pensive music, the author brooding at his desk or, à la Warhol, profoundly sleeping.

pertinence. This is special pleading with a vengeance. The fact is that the entire plot of the *Iliad* devolves from Agamemnon's seizing of one of those concubines, Briseis, and Achilles' angry withdrawal from the war, from which flow all subsequent disasters, including the death of Patroclus. In this essay, which gives us the usual blobby generalities ("most Western cultures"), Halperin muffs his one chance to show some original political imagination when he passes quickly over the question of kingship and priesthood in the David and Jonathan story. What *is* monarchy in political history? What does it represent in institutional terms, against the background of economic development and the evolution of national identity? Halperin plays at being a leftist, but his political consciousness is torpid and rudimentary. A final word on the title: I find "Heroes and Their Pals" vaguely queasy-making because its coy academic whimsy is actually a cheap shot at masculine men. There are no heroes; all those jocks who shoved the bookworms aside on the way to the locker room are really getting it on with each other but don't know it. This is rampant Stretherism, the wimp-centered view of the world that blights so much of the new academic discourse on sex.

Halperin's sloppiness with chronology makes a botch of the next essay, "The Democratic Body: Prostitution and Citizenship in Classical Athens." It is clear he has never pondered the most basic questions of historicizing about Athens, which requires minute attention to enormously rapid cultural changes occurring over a century. Compare, for example, the anxiety-provoking transformations in Renaissance Italy from 1500 to 1525, in Shakespeare's England from 1590 to 1610, and in America from 1915 to 1925 or from 1960 to 1967. Halperin jumps around amateurishly from the fifth century (whose many phases he does not see) to the middle or late fourth century, back to the fifth, then to the early sixth, then to the late fourth or early third, and back to the late sixth, all of which is funneled, like gravel pouring off a truck, into conclusions about "classical" Athenian attitudes. The unsurprising fact that male prostitutes were denied political privileges—exactly who *would* this surprise?—is trundled onto the carpet and worked over like a punching bag. Blinding lightning bolts of theoretical deduction are drawn from a common-sense detail that wouldn't raise the eyebrows of my old-school Italian grandfather. Being a prostitute or an ex-prostitute has carried a stigma virtually everywhere.

I am very interested in prostitution and welcome all scholarly work on it, but I have doubts about the strict social-constructionist approach, which tends to equate negativity toward prostitutes with the simple bias of other kinds of intolerance, like religious or racial discrimination. By excluding nature, biology, and psychology from its considerations, the school of Foucault is incapable of dealing with the emotional instabilities and irrational daemonic fears that may be inherent to sexuality and that may require prostitution as a ritual arena for their exploration outside the pale. Halperin tells us he boldly gives us the prices charged by prostitutes "to counteract a prevailing tendency on the part of classical scholars to overlook such 'sordid' matters." Which scholars? Where? When? A footnote admits what should more honestly be in the text itself: that these prices have already been "fully collected" by German scholars (in 1913 and 1960) and that Halperin is just reproducing their material.

There's a lot of phallus-tossing in this essay, but its nadir is undoubtedly Halperin's abuse of the herms, which have become the whipping boys of purblind feminists of the Keuls kind. The Attic ithyphallic herms are now treated like penis totem poles before which the Athenians prostrated themselves. It's like a Claes Oldenburg fantasy of monumental erections on the Acropolis, spotted by all ships at sea. This modern mutilation of the herms is one of the worst outrages of recent scholarship on sex. Since the new theorists are largely unread in the great tradition of classical anthropology dating from Frazer and the Cambridge school, they never acknowledge the agricultural roots of the herms and their significance as symbols of fertility. There are never any references to religious belief or to ritual and cult—only to politics. There is no sense of the larger social and civic meanings of boundary lines and their markers throughout the world. There is no reference to art-historical evidence that contradicts the notion of Athenian phallicism—for example, the brilliant Erechtheum caryatids, Ionic columns in the shape of voluptuous women; or, in the hand of the colossal Parthenon statue of Athena, the female winged Nike, supported by a pedestal. Halperin equates the "bearded face" of the herms with the new "masculine self-assertion" of classical Athens. More ignorance of religion and art history: the beard was an archaizing motif, referring to the distant past. Major sculptural artifacts, as scholars noted a century ago, show Hermes had lost his beard by the classical period. The cultic meaning of the herms as uncanny chthonian symbols of a lost rural past guarded by native daemons is overlooked in this latest mob hysteria that treats them as sexist billy clubs batting women down. The sepulchral herms were in league with the old powers of mother earth.

Halperin's final essay, "Why is Diotima a Woman?," has inspired the title of my article. Here we have one of the great junk bonds of the fast-track academic era, whose unbridled greed for fame and power was intimately in sync with parallel developments on Wall Street. This is yuppie entrepreneurship at its height. It's scholarship skating on a gold credit card, sweeping up everything in its path and dropping it unsorted and uncomprehended in a heap in the boutique window. Its inner bonds too are junk: the logic is specious and its claims counterfeit. The idea for the essay is attributed to a former student; eight conferences and twenty-one advisors are listed as its history. It illustrates how the French school sold a bill of goods to and then bankrupted a whole generation of American critics. A few interesting ideas are put to the rack and tortured until they give up the ghost. Nothing is thought through or developed in a sensible, plausible way. All energy goes toward show, pretense, posing. Twenty years ago, I hoped for a bright future for interdisciplinary studies. Now I see that the space that has opened up between disciplines is outside the law, a wasteland where wolves run free.

Halperin's technique in this essay is the sales practice called "bait and switch." Falsely complex explanations of simple problems are set before us, draped with red herrings, then whisked from view without resolution. Meanwhile, solid proposals by earlier scholars about Diotima's identity—that she is, for example, "an ironic mask" for Socrates—are buried deep in the 229 footnotes. Despite the ten headlines that divide it, the essay is almost unbelievably incoherent, crying out for the patient red pen of a freshman English instructor. It is a grotesquely convoluted response to the shapely symmetries of the *Symposium*. Plato is not Robbe-Grillet or Borges. Like Foucault, Halperin is persistently indifferent to drama, the central cultural expression of classical Athens. That cripples him here, where he has to evaluate a dramatic character created by another dramatic character at a dramatic moment in a dramatic dialogue.

It is amazing that Diotima could be discussed for nearly 40 pages without Delphi being mentioned once. Socrates took his maxim, "Know thyself," from the pronaos of the Temple of Apollo, where the oracle sat. Surely this should be the first hypothesis in tracing Diotima's origins. But no, in the school of Foucault, the obvious must be avoided at all costs. Oracles and prophetesses get mentioned late and in passing until the end, when they are unconvincingly argued away. Aspasia, whose facility in rhetoric has nothing whatever to do with Diotima's higher knowledge, is trotted out midway for a pointless song-and-dance routine. We also get some puffy interludes of Derrida but naturally no use of Jung, whose theory of the anima fits Diotima perfectly. We have the usual blanket indictment of "sexologists, psychoanalysts, gynaecologists," those puppets of scientific ideology. A promising passage on the couvade is abruptly terminated when it starts to lead toward thinking about biological sex differences. After leagues of heavy going, we end with a bout of fashionable flag-waving: a silly conflation of Virginia Woolf and male chauvinist Freud, the subject, we are vaguely told, of "the brilliant commentary of Luce Irigaray"—another empty, overpraised French export. The last sentences of the book engineer a typical Halperin quick escape. After six essays demonstrating his ignorance of psychology, biology, and sociology, we are firmly informed: "Gender—no less than sexuality—is an irreducible fiction. And so to ask why Diotima is a woman is to pose a question that ultimately has no answer." How chic, how hollow.

Never in my career have I seen a scholarly book of such naked worldly ambition, such lack of scruple about its methods or its claims to knowledge. It is exquisitely emblematic of its time. It is the perfect book of the hour of the wolf.

II

With *The Constraints of Desire,* we have something quite different. John Winkler, unlike Halperin, is a real scholar who can think and write well. Unfortunately, he has wandered away from his base of solid knowledge and produced a work whose legitimate contributions are too often overshadowed by false claims and coarse politicizing. The French trendies are wrong: there is a real person behind every text. This book dramatically shows both the gifts and the failings of its author. Winkler, neither an intellectual nor a political analyst, has been lured by the school of Foucault into overreaching, and so has marred his legacy. As I read this book, I could not get out of my mind the image of Mann's pensive Gustave von Aschenbach, sitting alone on the Lido and tarted up at the end by other people's idea of fashion.

    Constraints begins with a dedication to "the two people who made it happen": a "feminist anthropologist" sister whose "academic activism sets an example that I would like to be able to live up to," and David Halperin, who convinced Winkler that his essays were "unified by a common methodology" and therefore "unified enough to be a book." Halperin's work "has deeply influenced the shape and quality of this project." From these personal misjudgments by Winkler have come the book's serious deficiencies: the forcing of small individual insights into a jerry-built artificial structure, the specious generalizations, the posturing from a political platform where Winkler looks as out of place as the professor on the cabaret stage in *The Blue Angel.*

    The introduction takes us straight to the noisy agora into which Winkler so fatefully descended, to the detriment of his scholarly objectivity. We are told of his first visit to Greece in 1982 (rather late for a classicist?), whose signal memory for him is not the Acropolis, Mycenae, Delphi, or Epidaurus but the Gay Pride Day demonstration in Athens. The public behavior of the participants becomes Winkler's great revelation of how different those fascinating "Mediterranean people" are from *us.* As the child of Mediterranean immigrants, with close ties to a vast family still in Italy, I must say I was appalled and offended by this clumsy display of cultural naïveté masquerading as liberal understanding. At the demonstration, Winkler meets and befriends "Michael," who seems to have strolled in from a Jackie Collins novel. We learn of an episode at Michael's apartment, where he commented on a female cousin's sexual behavior by making a "ferocious" and "slashing gesture towards his own groin." Whatever compelling interest Michael and his groin may have had for Winkler, I submit that their necessary presence in a scholarly book has not been fully established.

"Sex and gender are the focus of these essays," says Winkler, but he has neither the training nor the temperament for speculations in this area. His references to sex theory are embarrassingly and narrowly contemporary. It is obvious throughout the book that Winkler has studied neither Freud nor Jung, much less their numerous successors. He has a sunny, simplistic pre-Freudian view of human psychology and motivation and a sentimental idea of noble womanhood that went out with World War One. The sugary picture of rococo femininity projected in this book is surreally overpainted by great red swatches of feminist acrylic, which have clearly been foisted on Winkler from elsewhere. *Constraints* is methodologically incoherent, even schizophrenic. It works so hard to be hip. Winkler repeatedly interrupts his natural smooth, low-key, coasting style for a galumphing revving of political engines and a deafening screech of tires. The don is determined to drag race with the Teddy boys.

Now for the many problems presented by the introduction. The primary error of *Constraints* is its repeated foolish parallelism between ancient and modern Greece, a misstep one expects in *Reader's Digest* but not in a scholarly book. The historical obstacles to such a comparison are never raised or examined. One would never know not only that two millennia have passed but that something rather large called the Ottoman Empire (all 600 years of it) has intervened in the middle. The heavy Turkish and Near Eastern influence on modern Greece—visible in the food, music, and national costumes—is never considered or even mentioned. Because Winkler has done no broad research into history and anthropology, he fails to realize that what he is simplistically

identifying in the modern Mediterranean as a su
ancient Mediterranean is instead a survival of are
generally, as it existed around the world. Again an
calls a motif typically Mediterranean when, had h   ...cu
to read even Frazer, he would have recognized it as also typical of preliterate British, Gallic, or Germanic Northern European societies.

Back to the introduction: modern interpretation of ancient
Greek eroticism, as Winkler depicts it, has only two forms important enough to be worth noting: "hedonistic liberation—sa-
tyrs chasing nymphs" versus the more recent and enlightened
position of "feminist scholarship" which has "challenged the innocence of that picture" and taken "the nymph's point of view."
This is preposterous. The hedonistic fantasy was the creation of
second-rate poets, decorative painters, and Isadora Duncan—
not academic scholars, who have tended to see the opposite, i.e.,
high-minded philosophy and moral meanings. That classical
scholarship sympathetic to and accurate about women only began
with contemporary feminism is a gross libel. Winkler's ignorance
of the corpus of long-established scholarship in this area is evident
when he calls the work of Sarah Pomeroy "groundbreaking." He
has been misled by others to think that Pomeroy's competent but
tepid *Goddesses, Whores, Wives and Slaves: Women in Classical Antiquity*
(1975) is somehow pioneering. That short book is simply an
unexciting and rather conventional compilation of basic material
well-known to classicists and yawningly familiar to anyone already working in the field of historical sex studies and systematically absorbing the 200-year scholarly record.

Next we are told: "For ancient Greece the questions about
sex itself were very excitingly posed by Michel Foucault, one of
the great thinkers of our age, who died of AIDS in 1984." Note
the Madison Avenue elements in this sentence: the questionable
claim "one of the great thinkers of our age" has come to Winkler
externally; it's a trendy tag line learned by rote, like "Winston
Tastes Good Like a Cigarette Should." Nothing in *Constraints*
demonstrates that Winkler has a shred of philosophical knowledge later than antiquity. Again: why is the medical information
here? Hovering in it is an implied false logic between having

AIDS and being an innovative thinker about sex. There is no such connection in reality.

Now we get a two-page section called "Anthropology and the Classics" that shockingly demonstrates Winkler's defects of knowledge. The account of anthropological history given here is so shaky and superficial that it would rate a C − in any rigorous college course. Winkler devotes only a few sentences to the Cambrige school, whose work, he states, "was received with great distaste by many of their contemporaries." Jane Harrison, in particular, was greeted with "frank revulsion," revealing "the white-washed, romantic, and racist image of Greece, which was so useful for pedagogical purposes in the North Atlantic states." Winkler, as the rest of the book lamentably demonstrates, is not deeply read in the work of Jane Harrison, and in this particular passage he shows he doesn't know a hill of beans about her enormous academic fame in her lifetime. He has bought into feminist agitprop that all great women have been spurned and stifled by the patriarchal establishment. And as for "racist," this is an inflammatory vulgarity beneath Winkler's dignity. The survey in the next paragraph of unspecified "important innovations" in twentieth-century anthropology—where structuralism, semiotics, and feminism have now wonderfully ensured that anthropologists "no longer condescend to their informants as backward" (when was that ever the rule—in the age of Diderot?)—is so vague and uninformed that one must regretfully conclude the presence of the word "anthropology" in the subtitle of this book is fraudulent, a sham.

Next comes a series of self-exculpations where Winkler tries to slap a fancy mask over the fact that "my studies have not been systematic." He is really practicing "equestrian academics"; he is offering us "an artist's pencilled outline"; the "variety of perspectives" in his mismatched essays show the "insight" of pluralism. But, a few lines later, here's the first thesis sentence we get: "Greeks insistently focused on dominance and submission, as constituted by phallic penetration." Welcome to the rigid, ugly, uninformed world of Foucault. At the end of the introduction, Winkler declares:

> I hope that these methods of anthropologically in-
> formed reading will help to discredit the ethnocentric
> interpretations which have dominated the English and
> German traditions of Classics for the past two hundred
> years. The rather cool culture of NATO Classicists
> has been a poor premise for interpreting the emotional
> and political protocols of Mediterranean people.

Are we to understand by this that Foucault is showing us a way
out of the alleged thermostat problem? But Foucault is one of
the dullest, most frigid and constipated theorists of sex ever; it's
trial by prune-faced ice-lock. And his generation of French philosophers was powerfully under the influence of the German
school of Heidegger. Winkler fails to see the luminous element
of ritualized Apollonianism in ancient Athenian culture, for which
the English and German classics traditions are in fact ideally
suited. As for NATO's "emotional" deficit: Joyce's *Ulysses* makes
great use of the legendary link and parallels between Greek and
Irish culture. Wales too, like Ireland, has a passionate history of
music, poetry, and heroic strife. The introduction ends: "I hope
these essays will show how much more interesting the Greeks
really were." I'm afraid Winkler's slightly gaga attitude toward
the sunny Mediterranean is painfully reminiscent of James and
Forster heroines on their first trip abroad. Too much of this book
reads like a corny rehash of *Never on Sunday* and *Zorba the Greek*.

The first essay, "Unnatural Acts," is about Artemidoros'
Dream Analysis. I like Winkler's use of the nonpolitical and nonjudgmental term "protocols" for social and erotic conventions.
However, the problem with this essay is that the conclusions are
already assumed in advance ("For 'Nature,' Read 'Culture,' "
says the opening section headline.) Winkler's lack of real anthropological knowledge is shown on the first page, with its bizarre footnote about the Manchu mother who would "routinely
suck her small son's penis in public." This gratuitous item is
cited from an article by another classicist, not an anthropologist,
and it is used in a flat, exploitative way, without any sense of the
larger questions governing display or manipulation of the body

in world culture. Winkler's lack of philosophical ability even to negotiate between the terms "nature" and "culture" is next indicated in his approving citation of this astonishing bit of tautology by a feminist classicist: " 'Nature' and 'culture,' as culturally defined rather than natural concepts, are unstable, historically relative assumptions." Should we laugh or cry? Neither Winkler nor the lady seems aware of the triple circularity, which would flunk opening-day logic class. This is an excellent example of the tenth-rate thinking currently epidemic in sex studies.

This essay demonstrates that Winkler has a conspicuous talent for translating pornography, which he treats honestly and well. But as an analyst of ancient materials, he was ill-served by his advisors, who pointed him in the wrong direction. Winkler is sensitive, tentative; he is best at fluid sensory effects. He wants to let go, to follow his own sensuality and aesthetic instincts. But again and again, compulsively, this openness is shut down by a hammering political terminology imposed by others. Fascist jackboots stomp all over these pages. Winkler wants sex, but the Foucault vending machine only dispenses sexuality. Apparently, there was no one to tell Winkler to read Freud (to whom he makes some gingerly and uncomprehending references, mediated through a negative essay by someone else) or, even more, Jung, who is desperately needed in this essay chock-full of vivid archetypal imagery that Winkler doesn't have a clue about how to interpret. The glancing treatment of incest and bestiality is quite unsatisfactory, again showing Winkler's lack of familiarity with the modern anthropological and psychoanalytic record, massive on the subject of incest. Dreams of a man having sex with his mother are said to refer to "the mother's central symbolic role in the household": note the prim Foucault social constructionism, far inferior to Freudian psychology, which would see questions of identity and eroticism turbulently flowing from our primal origins in the mother's body. Winkler's ill preparation for dream analysis.is clear in genial, mushy remarks like, "Many of us may like to think that sexual activities involving two people will be mutually pleasurable." He has no sense whatever of Freud's well-established and indispensable theories of anxiety, conflict, and ambivalence, the absence of which is disastrous for the third essay

in this volume. Finally, Winkler, aping Foucault, overstates Artemidoros' cultural significance. He evidently knows nothing
about the genre of popular dream books that, for example, flooded
the market in the Sixties or even with the still-flourishing trade
in advice-giving astrology handbooks; hence he sometimes ear-
nestly overinterprets in a poker-faced way details that are merely
tangential or whimsical.

The second essay is called "Laying Down the Law: The
Oversight of Men's Sexual Behavior in Classical Athens." The
trouble here is that Winkler's evidence is principally drawn from
the years 430–330 B.C.—in other words, from the moment (the
great plague) that classical Athens began its decline. The main
theme, announced by facetious headline, is "Anus-Surveillance."
We are asked to indignantly and automatically reject the virtually
universal identification of passive male anal intercourse with female or feminizing experience, which in my view has always been
based on a common-sense analogy with sexual anatomy: only
women are born with vaginas. It is understandable why gay
studies would like to detach the old popular imputation of effem-
inacy from gay men, who are sometimes very masculine, but
contemporary political wish lists must not be projected backward
to distort the historical record. The issue will remain in dispute,
but there may indeed be a subliminal and kick-producing gender-
crossing element in playful passive sodomy. Studying Freud helps
one to identify such contradictions and ambiguities in eroticism,
which is often intensified by theatrical reversals. My own examination of the bower theme in art has shown the actual dominance and control operating in female sexual receptivity. That
Winkler knows he's not on firm ground is shown by his sudden
emphatic citation of Stephen Greenblatt, who has no credentials
that I am aware of for theorizing about classical antiquity.
There's so much in this essay about "the protocols that polarized
penetrators and penetrateds" that after a while it feels like a shop
class in drill bits and how to know them. The simplistic Foucaldian active-passive dualism reflects a lead-footed and remarkably unsophisticated view of sex.

What is unattractive in this essay as it goes on is the im-
plication that politics is just an empty game. There is a curious

affectlessness about questions of honor, self-sacrifice, civic order, political virtue, or service to the nation. In the school of Foucault, institutions, first artificially reinforced, begin to dissolve. With Winkler, you start to get a slumming feeling: go to the capitol, go to the whorehouse—what's the difference? Winkler is at his best in the areas he was actually trained in: for example, his interesting examples of different usages of the Greek word *phusis* are well-chosen and succinctly presented. This is the kind of outreach work classics has been desperately in need of: lucid definitions and etymologies of ancient languages accessible to the general reader, not just the specialist. Unfortunately, the essay ends in a burst of Halperinisms—straw men and Halperin himself, presiding as an authority on Greek sexuality. These two books, perpetually citing each other, have a Tweedledum-Tweedledee redundancy.

The third and title essay is on "erotic magical spells." Here we see the tragic waste of American talents enslaved to French masters. This essay could and should have been a classic. But it is full of colossal blunders, caused by Winkler's lack of attention to some of the most distinguished scholarship in his own field. Two books by Jane Harrison are listed in the bibliography, but it is obvious Winkler has not given her the attention she deserves. This essay cries out for her insights into and formulations about magic belief. Incredibly, Winkler, wearing the blinders of Foucault, does not see magic spells in a religious or ritual context. They're nothing but representations of "social forces," showing "the deep tremors of hatred of women," evidence of "the institutions of terror that have circumscribed the experience of women over the centuries." Bonehead feminist theory is plopped on top of a wealth of uncanny archaic material, which burns and twists with all the dark daemonic energy of sex. Winkler, lacking Freud or even the shrewd Denis de Rougemont, can't believe love could innately produce this language of violence and warfare; he keeps bumblingly telling us what "we" mild, sane, tender creatures think of love. Does he know nothing about medieval romance, courtly love, Petrarchan sonnets, Goethe, Byron, Baudelaire? Has he never listened to the radio? The blues, torch, and pop tradi-

tions are boiling with anguish and aggress~~i~~
line between love and hate," says a Sixties h~~.~~

Winkler is busy, busy with ten-dollar te~~.~~
neutically sophisticated" (applied to himself),
have time to think about literary connections to
poetic refrain, formulaic utterance of all kinds, as i~~.~~ ~~..~~reet
curses. At moments here he starts to move away fro~~m~~ Foucault—
a love-sick man prepares "to enter the powerful underworld of
his own psyche"—but he catches himself and abruptly stops, not
daring to stray from social-constructionist orthodoxy. Any references in the spells to nature—night, the moon, the planets—
are ignored. As usual, there are misconceived generalizations
about the Mediterranean because of Winkler's lack of familiarity
with equivalent spells in old rural Northern Europe and Africa
and the modern Caribbean, with its voodoo or santería. Winkler
has feminist conniptions about a terra-cotta statuette showing a
woman with a sword in her neck and thirteen copper needles in
her body. To interpret that imagery, all you need is a little knowledge of the Tarot. The best things in this essay are when Winkler
cuts the crap and just follows his lascivious bent to tell us about
"penis ointments" and anti-wet-dream herbs.

The fourth essay is on Longus' *Daphnis and Chloe,* which
Winkler, obviously unfamiliar with gynecological surgery, keeps
bizarrely calling *D&C.* Here it is clear that Winkler's real talent
is for Cleanth Brooks–style New Criticism, the patient, scrupu-
lous attentiveness to the internal literary qualities of a text. An
example: "In the long, hot summer of Chloe's fifteenth year,
suitors come buzzing about her, bringing gifts to her father
Dryas." So simple, so vivid, so honest. This is the real Winkler,
old-fashioned and dreamy. But in the era of junk bonds, you can
be sure the shrapnel of "androcentrism, phallocentrism" will soon
fall. Again and again, Winkler, under the Foucault vow to hear
no biology, see no biology, speak no biology, misinterprets the
simplest things in Longus' tale of sexual awakening. He makes
ridiculous statements about the modern view of love; the hip set,
reading each other, evidently has no time for Stendhal, Balzac,
Swinburne, Wilde, Gide, Proust, Brecht, Lorca, Genet, or Ten-

..see Williams, all of whom contradict Winkler's claims. What is particularly inept in this essay is the crashing, jargon-jammed pseudo-anthropology, which is simply doing, very awkwardly, what the truly politically astute European and New York critics of realism in the nineteenth-century novel did so well in the Forties and Fifties. This is reinventing the wheel as a bone-jarring square.

That Winkler is way off base is hilariously proved by the story's closing wedding paragraph, where, he admits, there is a "mysterious and unexpected," an "exceedingly odd," an "amazing" note of "harsh unpleasantness" he cannot explain. It's a powerful infernal metaphor of "breaking up the earth with tridents," which of course reveals Longus' archetypal analogy between woman and nature, that brutal biological absolutism of sexual anatomy and sexual intercourse that the school of Foucault keeps trying to repress. Winkler has therefore misread everything. He strains to get out of this jam with a Vaseline-valedictory Halperinism: we must *not*, heaven forbid, put our critical faculties "solely in the service of recovering and reanimating an author's meaning." I burst out laughing at this. ("Oh, ship of fools!" I said to myself.) Winkler shovels so much manure at the end of this essay that we're knee-deep in it. He has no idea there have been a hundred years of complex commentary on sex, a body of work whose language, strategies, and patterns of argument, whose failures and successes can educate and refine the sensibility and skills of the student of sex. The born-yesterday French-besotted faddists, addicted sniffers of wet printer's ink, think they're starting on the ground floor; so they're condemned to another hundred years of trial and error. The rest of us can safely ignore them.

The fifth essay is on Homer's Penelope. The 32 verbose pages, heavily padded by dull plot summary worthy of Cliff's Notes, could be honed to eight of substance. The heart of the argument is a pedestrian New Critical analysis, uninformed in basic narratological principles one learned in college twenty-five years ago. For all his feminist posturing, Winkler cannot keep the women of the *Odyssey* fully in focus. He sees nothing of the archetypal house and home theme that runs through virtually every episode of the poem, nor can he evoke Homer's brilliant contrasts of Penelope with Circe, Calypso, and Nausikaa. His Penelope, whom he tries to hype as some sort of aggressive career mom, ends up rather boring and characterless. Putting her into action like a wind-up toy, he misses the real dramatic dignity of her majestic, melancholy stasis.

There's more grade-school anthropology in this essay, "It's a Funny World" anecdotes that belong in an airline magazine. Some of it is unbelievably offensive. For instance, we are told that "descriptions of life in rural Greece today" can tell us so much about "this wretched world of ours": "they open our urban eyes, accustomed to television and rear-view mirrors, to the clean dirt streets of pre-industrial societies, where the gossip of neighbors and the smell of goats are equally rank." An image flashed into my mind as I read this: WASPy, oh-so-fine Ashley Wilkes, chin in hand, mournfully recalling "the lazy days" and "the high soft Negro laughter from the quarters." Oozing benevolent liberalism, Winkler manages to insult most of the Third World, which lives with goats and camels and does not find them "rank." I am personally offended, since my grandfather loved to shop for goats and kept, behind his town house in upstate New York, a talkative goat named Giuseppina who remains the subject of much family mythology. Winkler should have taken his, not our, "urban eyes" on a little American journey to learn about his native land. As someone who spent many years amid the dirt roads and gossip of rural New York and Vermont, I think there's a lot about modern life he didn't know.

The first words of Winkler's sixth essay, on Sappho, are "Monique Wittig." It is contemptibly servile for a male classicist to court popularity in this way. Sappho and Emily Dickinson are the only woman geniuses in poetic history. Neither deserves to be introduced by one of our maudlin, run-of-the-mill feminist polemicists. In the next paragraph there is an outrageous slur against Denys Page, whose work, while "indispensable," is also "time-bound": he and all those other outdated scholars would not have "understood our matrices (feminist, anthropological, pro-lesbian)." Lobel and Page "assumed the validity of Victorian no-no's" and so were "deaf to much of what Sappho was saying, tone-deaf to her deeper melodies." The school of Foucault will apparently stoop to any lie. Winkler's repeated claim that Sappho needed contemporary feminism to liberate her prudish Victorian image is ludicrous. In 1966, while doing the reserve reading for our study of Sappho in Greek class, I was deeply impressed by the superb writing on her by male scholars before and after World War Two: Bruno Snell, Albin Lesky, Denys Page, and many others. I have continued to teach and research Sappho since then; last year, for another project, I did a full-scale review of the history of Sappho criticism, and again I was impressed. Feminism, in all fields, has yet to produce a single scholar of the intellectual rank of scores of these learned men in the German and British academic tradition. And as for them not being "anthropological"—absurd: they were true historicists. Furthermore, Page, in the deft readings of *Sappho and Alcaeus* (1955), boldly argued for the homosexuality of Sappho's lyrics, at a time when, unlike Dover's 1970s, it was risky to do so. Page is owed a public apology.

Winkler does lots of feminist calisthenics in this essay, but his view of Sappho is totally reactionary. Like all his women, she ends up bland and syrupy, an effect he tries to counter by grotesque overstatements: "Sappho's consciousness is a larger circle enclosing the smaller one of Homer." I am a passionate admirer of Sappho, but that has to be one of the stupidest sentences I have ever seen in a scholarly book. Winkler's account of Sappho's place in Ionian culture or in Archaic poetry generally is completely inadequate. He attempts to do a New Critical analysis of her major lyrics, but he takes forever to make simple points, such as that the Aphrodite ode has a multiple time frame and that Sappho is both in the poem and speaks it—the first and most elementary observations made in class by any sensible teacher.

Winkler's reading of "He seems to me a god," one of the great psychological documents of Western culture, is unpersuasive. The searing self-examination and language of agonized emotion, which, as Lesky points out, influenced male poets for a thousand years, are sponged away for a silly comparison to Odysseus' beach encounter with Nausikaa. The whole force of Sappho's poem depends on her mentally addressing a young woman who is not in fact hearing her (but who may be present in the audience when the poem is recited—a wonderful stratagem). The girl seems to be talking and laughing with a man across the room and paying no attention whatever to Sappho. Winkler, preening his feminist feathers, tries to get rid of the man, which won't wash. Odysseus, in contrast, is wittily addressing Nausikaa full-face. He stands naked, a branch over his balls; he holds her eyes so she will not glance down; he re-creates, through the power of aristocratic speech, his real rank. Nubile Nausikaa, sizing up the grizzled stranger, is impressed and thinks about snagging him. The flirtatious scene, ablaze with light, is full of the freshness of new beginnings. Sappho, however, is in torment. She sinks into spiritual isolation in a public place. Chills and fever overcome her. Love in Sappho, as never in Homer, is an affliction, a near-death experience. It is she, reaffirmed by her admirer Catullus, who created our romantic tradition of emotional ambivalence. Winkler's final contribution is to ransack Sappho's lyrics for references to clitorises. Her delicate archetypal fruit and flower imagery is wrung for lewd double-entendres. All this clumsy clitoris-brandishing is like dropping bricks into a goldfish bowl. But what can you expect from a book that begins, after all, with Michael's groin?

The concluding essay, "The Laughter of the Oppressed," has a promising theme but gets bogged down in rebutting Marcel Detienne's *The Gardens of Adonis* (1977). If only Winkler had used this same method of skeptical critique with the work of another inaccurate Frenchman, Foucault. The treatment of images of male and female genitals at Greek festivals fails to set the theme in an anthropological context of world religions. Winkler's identification of serpents as phallic symbols is a common but serious mistake, as Philip Slater pointed out more than twenty years ago. The dismissive reference to Frazer's theory of Adonis is cheap. The gushing promotion of new mini-articles by a feminist classicist, to the complete exclusion of substantive work done on the same topic forty years ago by Erich Neumann, is typical. The portrait of Greek women as jailed and oppressed fails to acknowledge the historical fact that male law and order also provided protection, security, and physical sustenance to women and children. At the end, the essay begins to slip out of Foucaldism toward an acknowledgment of biologic woman's cosmic power over the

cycle of birth and death, but Winkler is such a novice at con-
ceptualization that, a page later, he can end the book with a
manifesto of social constructionism without noticing the glaring
contradictions. The most telling phrase in this essay is Winkler's
lauding of "the corporate enterprise" of current scholarship. Yes,
academe has become a multinational corporation, and scholars
have become businessmen, mobile merchants on the make.

Some months ago, I received a terrible shock when I read
Martha Nussbaum's review of the Halperin and Winkler books
in *TLS*.[2] In high school in the early Sixties, I dreamed of intellectual work by women that would match the highest male standards and set men on their ear. A lot of women have written a
lot of academic books since then, but most of them fall far short
of that standard. In *The Fragility of Goodness* (1986), Nussbaum
achieves what I dreamed of. She and I were born the same year;
in a sense, her book and mine are opposite and complementary.
But in her *TLS* review, she seems to abandon for others the rigor
she imposes on herself. She calls Halperin and Winkler "judicious
and discriminating"; their two books are "meticulous and reliable
in scholarship, clear in argument." Winkler shows "exemplary
subtlety" and "grace and ingenuity," while Halperin's essays are
"clear and incisive," with "careful scholarly arguments and a
judicious, wide-ranging use of the evidence." Winkler's book has
"extraordinary originality and insight" and is "amazingly beautiful"; it is "a work that will over the years stand comparison,
one imagines, with the best writings of Nietzsche." The last sentence of the review announces Winkler's death from AIDS six
weeks earlier.

I would prefer not to think that Martha Nussbaum is so
unfamiliar with the many fields of knowledge dishonestly claimed
by Halperin and Winkler. It would be better to think that the
death of Winkler, who I assume was a professional associate,
inspired her with elegiac emotions. But when the *TLS* asked
Nussbaum to review these books, it asked not Nussbaum the
private person, who grieves for the sufferings of others, but Nussbaum the scholar, who has ethical obligations to a wider group,
the scholarly community, present and future, whom she does not
know. The review presented an ethical dilemma; I regret the choice

that was made. When Martha Nussbaum compares Winkler to Nietzsche, what standards are left, and who will defend them?

III

The current crisis in the humanities has been misinterpreted by both sides in the debate. We are feeling the impact of two developments of the late nineteenth century: first, the birth of American graduate education in a departmental structure artificially broken down and separated into national literatures and, secondly, the secularization of faculties who had earlier emerged from divinity schools. German historicism, inspired by an ideal of scientific objectivity, made the latter development possible. It also drove an opening wedge between American higher education and Protestantism, the dominant code, conveniently at the moment of the first waves of Catholic and Jewish immigrants, who would transform American life. Secularization was never fully achieved: it lingered, I submit, even in the New Criticism, which as a college student in the Sixties I felt as suffocatingly Protestant in its style and assumptions. Secularization is a welcome process if it allows us to analyze literature and art without moral preconception and sermonizing; but secularization is pernicious when it strips the spiritual dimension from experience. Today's crisis is really a chaos: both the rigorous learning of German philology and the practical discipline of New Criticism have been cast aside for an ill-understood French style of grand, self-referential, pseudo-philosophical speculation, which no American critic does well.

The number one problem today is not ignorant students but ignorant professors, who have substituted narrow "expertise" and "theoretical sophistication" (a preposterous term) for breadth and depth of learning in the world history of art and thought. The idea of expertise in any one area of the humanities, with its subsequent phenomenon of faculty recruitment by time-framed "slots," was always mistaken. It was inspired, in this masculine pioneer country that has never taken the arts seriously, by nervous emulation of the sciences, where one can indeed deeply and profitably specialize in moths, ferns, or igneous rocks.

But there is no true expertise in the humanities without knowing *all* of the humanities. Art is a vast, ancient interconnected web-work, a fabricated tradition. Overconcentration on any one point is a distortion. This is one of the primary reasons for the dullness and ineptitude of so much twentieth-century criticism, as compared to nineteenth-century belles-lettres. American professors have been institutionally impelled, by graduate education and then by the universities that employ them, to become narrower and narrower. The goal of comprehensive cultural vision predicated by German philology, which esteemed universal scholarship, has been dismissed as unrealistic in a modern alienated world of fragmentation and subjectivity. But the old German style, sober, practical, precise, lucid, and learned, is exactly what is needed to remedy today's confusions and excesses. Only small minds fail to see patterns and wholes. Both undergraduate education and commentary on the arts require teachers and scholars who understand the history of civilization in broad, general terms. Hollywood Bible movies of the Fifties, like *The Ten Commandments* and *Ben-Hur*, with their epic clash of pagan and Judeo-Christian cultures, tell more truth about art and society than the French-infatuated ideologues who have made a travesty of the "best" American higher education.

New Criticism was not the total rebellion against German research it at first seemed to be. In its analysis of the structure and aesthetic principles of a text, it was simply applying the empirical method of systematic investigation to the inner life of a work, imagined as a self-sufficient mechanism. One of the recent leftist libels about the New Critics is that they were obsessed hunters of irony and paradox—a charge far more accurate about the febrile word-chopping school of Derrida. Alas, most New Criticism was deadly earnest, in the Protestant way. The strength of New Criticism was that it was formulated by poets, men of cultivation and sensibility and—something conveniently forgotten today—broad mastery of the classics and literary history, including the Bible. The weakness of New Criticism was its agrarian Rousseauism, which suffused its artistic psychology with a sunny benevolence and made it stubbornly resistant to the darker, more turbulent, and conflict-based system of Freud. On the other hand, the closeness of the Southern New Critics to the land kept them attuned to universal archetypal imagery of nature, which has been banished from the French social-constructionist world-view. The New Criticism was a superb instrument for the up-close study of literature. In its word-by-word revelation of the power and complexity of language, it remains unsurpassed for intro-ductory classroom instruction and for teaching people how to think and write. Its absence in France explains much of the current French clumsiness with historical and literary documents, which are manhandled and misread with solipsistic drunken abandon.

The major problem with New Criticism is that it cannot stand alone as an approach to art. It needs to be supplemented by historical learning and by training in larger schemes of con-ceptual reasoning. The present crisis in the humanities originated in the postwar English Department, which was and is a parochial construction. The folly was in thinking that you could make critics by training them just in criticism. Criticism without learning is futile. It produces lightweights, poseurs, triflers. Only poets can practice ad lib criticism, out of their own originality and defin-itiveness of imagination. The rapid expansion of universities in the baby-boom era and the invention of the four-year Ph.D.—a disastrous move that devalued the doctorate and substituted hasty, pretentious, assembly-line makework for true research and learning—institutionalized the worst features of second-generation New Criticism. The Fifties English Department as a genteel, hermetic echo chamber can still be felt in the work of Helen Vendler, for whom the world began with Chaucer and ended with Wallace Stevens. The puritanical moralism of middlebrow New Criticism is illustrated by the way Vendler's 1975 book on George Herbert exiled all references to sex to the footnotes, to the periphery of the permissible. The sex problem of New Crit-icism would come crashing back upon it: one reason for the incoherence and mediocrity of women's studies is that so many of its leaders—Ellen Moers, Carolyn Heilbrun, Sandra Gilbert, Susan Gubar, Elaine Showalter—were produced by the Fifties English Department and so never had an ounce of preparation for social and historical inquiry, much less the most rudimentary knowledge of psychology and sexology. Moreoever, these aca-

demic feminists, unlike Vendler, aren't even good critics in
Mamie Eisenhower–era terms and seem to have drifted into wom-
en's studies by default, after failing in aesthetic analysis. One of
the biggest scams of contemporary education is the way these
conventional married women who never rocked a boat in their
life ripped off and sanitized the ideas of my fractious generation
of the Sixties and turned them into profitable public careers.

The New Criticism had to go. Or rather, it had to be absorbed and transformed. It was an American style, and there
was an American solution to its problems. I will argue that the
French invasion of academe in the Seventies was not at all a
continuation of the Sixties revolution but rather an evasion of it.
In *Tenured Radicals*, which treats trendy showboating professors
with the irreverence they deserve, Roger Kimball makes one
statement I would correct: he suggests the radicals of the Sixties
are now in positions of control in the major universities. He is
too generous. Most of America's academic leftists are no more
radical than my Aunt Hattie. Sixties radicals rarely went on to
graduate school; if they did, they often dropped out. If they made
it through, they had trouble getting a job and keeping it. They
remain mavericks, isolated, off-center. Today's academic leftists
are strutting wannabes, timorous nerds who missed the Sixties
while they were grade-grubbing in the library and brown-nosing
the senior faculty. Their politics came to them late, secondhand,
and special delivery via the Parisian import craze of the Seventies.
These people have risen to the top not by challenging the system
but by smoothly adapting themselves to it. They're company
men, Rosencrantz and Guildensterns, privileged opportunists
who rode the wave of fashion. Most true Sixties people could not
and largely did not survive in the stifling graduate schools of the
late Sixties and early Seventies.

The followers of Lacan, Derrida, and Foucault, far from
being political and intellectual sophisticates, are the real fossilized
reactionaries of our time. They seized on and dogged to death
ideas that were totally passé in America well before 1970. Foucault spoke of Beckett's *Waiting for Godot* as the pivotal liberating
experience of his generation of Parisians, emerging from existen-
tialism. When I saw that play in 1966 in college, I recognized it

as a repressive anxiety-formation of defunct modernism, which the Sixties revolution, energized by rock, had swept completely away. At that moment in America, popular culture, rude, vital, brassy, had triumphed. Warhol and Oldenburg, reanimating the commercial motifs of our daily life, had killed the European avant-garde forever. The spiritual history of the Sixties has yet to be written. Psychedelia, a profound reordering of Western perception, lost its documenters, who blew their brains out on acid. Elvis Presley, one of the most influential men of the century, broke down racial barriers in the music industry, so that my generation was flooded by the power, passion, and emotional truth of African-American experience. Aretha Franklin, Levi Stubbs, James Brown, Gladys Knight: these voices and a hundred others are seared into our consciousness. Black artists are the American paradigm of vivid, vibrant personality, dramatic self-assertion, and spiritual magnitude of the individual voice. By what retrograde lace-curtain shrinking from reality did our academics look to spinsterish French notions of the "decentered subject"? Of *course* the French felt decentered: they'd just been crushed by Germany. American G.I.'s (including my uncles) got shot up rescuing France when she was lying flat on her face under the Nazi boot. Hence it is revolting to see pampered American academics down on their knees kissing French bums.

Lacan, Derrida, and Foucault are the perfect prophets for the weak, anxious academic personality, trapped in verbal formulas and perennially defeated by circumstance. They offer a self-exculpating cosmic explanation for the normal professorial state of resentment, alienation, dithery passivity, and inaction. Their popularity illustrates the psychological gap between professors and students that has damaged so much undergraduate education. The disciples of Lacan, Derrida, and Foucault are ignorant: ignorant of nineteenth-century intellectual history, which originated and developed their arguments, and ignorant of America, which leapt far beyond European thought from the moment we invented Hollywood. Specifically, the French school of the Seventies was crashingly irrelevant to America's internal political dynamic. We already had a major theorist greater than all the postwar French after Sartre: Norman O. Brown. In *Life*

Against Death (1959) and *Love's Body* (1966), the deeply learned and classically trained Brown made an unsurpassed fusion of literature, philosophy, psychoanalysis, history, and politics. His two books had a spectacular impact on the American Sixties. At the same time were released in paperback the four volumes of *The Social History of Art* by the Marxist Arnold Hauser, a scholar of staggering erudition and brilliant precision in the German style. It was because of Brown and Hauser that Foucault seemed to me, from the moment I first saw his work in 1971, an absolute ninny.

But my generation was condemned to live out what was only imagined by the older Norman O. Brown. We put the myth of Dionysus into action, and we hit the wall of reality. The Sixties revolutionized consciousness, but on the road of excess by which we sought the palace of wisdom, many of us lost our minds, lives, or careers through drugs, sexual orgy, or (my vice) constant challenges to authority. The Sixties, rebelling against Fifties bourgeois conformity and respectability, took life to its extreme and explored the far edges of the possible. Altamont (December 1969) was our Waterloo: there the Dionysian forces released by the Sixties showed their ugly face. The film *Gimme Shelter* documents that turbulent day, when the Hell's Angels beat people with pool cues, when the Rolling Stones presided over a murder before the stage, when Grace Slick could not calm a surging crowd moaning and sighing with Dantean inner torment. Moon in Scorpio: Altamont was the end of Sixties illusions about the benevolence of human nature and mother nature.

In America we made a rapid transit from the ideal to the real, that motif of disillusionment of the nineteenth-century novel. Everyone who honestly explored Sixties ideals eventually had to confront the limitations of those ideals. Risk and loss, often permanent, were the price of discovery. What is outrageous in the French fad is that a grotesque head trip was imposed on us, who had learned our own lessons in our own way. France is a prisoner of its history and high culture. It had no mammoth popular culture like ours: its brief student revolt flickered and failed. Lacan, Derrida, and Foucault are virtuoso wordsmiths without historical or political expertise, even in their own country. Their American popularity has been an asinine episode in the musty academic chronicles. In the Sixties, amid the cloistered sterility of late New Criticism, we vowed: never again. Never again abstractions that kill art; never again the mind divorced from the body or the mind divorced from emotion. The Seventies French fad was a flight from Sixties truths, a reactionary escape into false abstraction and rationalism, masquerading as distrust of reason.

Last year, I attended a lecture at the University of Pennsylvania given by a prominent visiting Ivy League feminist. It was a dreadful experience, and I'm afraid I behaved rather badly. A small, frail, drably dressed but obviously very nice woman with a pale voice showed slide after slide of gorgeous ads and pictorials from fashion magazines and proceeded to demolish them with an ugly, ponderous, aggressive, labyrinthine Lacan machinery that surely not three people in the audience fully understood. Brutal language of "mutilation," "decapitation," "strangulation," "bondage," and "enslavement" filled the air. I began to writhe in my seat with pain; I could not stifle, to the annoyance of my neighbors, muttered cries of "oh!," "awful!," and "give me a break!" At the end, I waved my arms around and made an agitated speech, most graciously tolerated by the lecturer, denouncing the feminist inability to deal with beauty and pleasure, to which gay men have made such outstanding cultural contributions. Every young woman in the audience, intimidated by incomprehension into thinking she was hearing something brilliant, was intellectually oppressed by that lecture and that approach to life and thought. Lacan is a tyrant who must be driven from our shores. Narrowly trained English professors who know nothing of art history or popular culture think they can just wade in with Lacan and trash everything in sight. As I later wrote to the series sponsor, if the lecturer had done the same thing to, say, African art—cutting into a tradition without any regard for its history, methods, or iconography—a lynch mob would have formed. I now realize how lucky I was, in the total absence of role models, to have only men to rebel against. Today's women students are meeting their oppressors in dangerously seductive new form, as successful, congenial female professors who are themselves victims of a rigid foreign ideology. Let's dump the French in Boston Harbor and let them swim home.

Robert Caserio recently said to me, "The whole profession has become a vast mimicry. The idea that there is open debate is an absolute fiction. There is only the Foucault monologue, the Lacan monologue, the Derrida monologue. There is no room for creative disagreement. No deviation from what is approved is tolerated." These monologues are really one, the monotonous drone of the school of Saussure, which has cast its delusional inky cloud over modern academic thought. Never have so many been so wrong about so much. It is positively idiotic to imagine that there is no experience outside of language. I am in love with language, but never for a moment did I dream that language encompasses and determines all knowledge. It has been a truism of basic science courses for decades in America that the brain has multiple areas of function and that language belongs only to specific areas, injured by trauma and restored by surgery or speech therapy. For thousands of years, sages and mystics of both East and West have taught us about the limitations of language in seeking truth. When Dante must part from Virgil at the gates of Paradise, he is expressing the ancient insight that faith and vision occur in a realm beyond reason and language. My generation, inheriting the Beatniks' interest in Zen, made a spiritual passage to India, with its flaming avatars. We knew words, names, concepts had to be dissolved and transcended. Lacan, Derrida, and Foucault are termites compared to the art, culture, and archaic topography of India. One remedy for today's educational impasse: more India and less France. The followers of Derrida are pathetic, snuffling in French pockets for bits and pieces of a deconstructive method already massively and coherently presented—and with a mature sense of the sacred—in Buddhism and Hinduism.

The American academics who went bananas over Gallic theory were callow 90-pound weaklings, trying to pump themselves up with powdered tiger's milk. Their political and cultural naïveté is astounding. France suffers from an overstructured educational system that produces a vigorous but one-dimensional form of reasoning descending from the seventeenth century. Despite the French reputation for love, cultivated French personality is highly repressed. French high culture, like that of the Japanese, is insular and superbly artificial. Since Racine, the French language *is* French culture. It is cold, elegant, ironic, linear, constricting. Gautier, Baudelaire, and Huysmans were complaining about the excessive sanitation of educated French well over a century ago. The balanced phrase-forms and repetitious internal rhythms of French thought can be heard in virtually any French movie of the past fifty years, particularly when the characters begin to discourse on love. Their affectations, pomposity, and self-deceptions are a major source of comedy, exploited by Renoir, Buñuel, Truffaut, Godard, Chabrol. The French, locked in by overintellection, require radical deconstruction of their speech, persona, and world-view. Lacan, Derrida, and Foucault have no relevance to anything outside of postwar France. They are performing necessary acts of verbal and conceptual violence upon a culture as walled and arrogantly self-centered as the Chinese imperial palace. Most American academics are totally lost when trying to read French polemic. They have no idea that in French you can form sentences that are virtually content-free, that are merely rhetorical flourishes echoing, reversing, or sabotaging prior French sentences. Translations of Lacan and Derrida are pored over by earnest Americans, fatuously taking as literal truth statements that were merely the malicious boutades of the flâneur. Lacan and Derrida are meaningless unless you already have in your head the austere, sonorous, classical French sentences that they are twisting and wringing like a washcloth.

Our French acolytes, making themselves the lackeys of a foreign fascism, have advertised their intellectual emptiness to the world. In America, deconstruction is absurd, since we have never had a high culture of any kind. Far from being overliterate, we are still preliterate, accentuated by an image-dominated popular culture that was the all-embracing *paideia* of my generation. American personality, far from being trapped in decorum, is booming, pushy, manic, facilely optimistic. At its essence, it is infantile in its beaming, bouncing egotism, a character type seen in film in the bumptious newlywed husband of *Niagara*, the suburban Connecticut host mixing honey daiquiris in *Auntie Mame*, the griping yahoo spurning Venetian food in *Summertime*, or that

French favorite Jerry Lewis, whose giddy, tumbling spontaneity represents everything that is impossible in mannerly France. America is still a frontier country of wide open spaces. Our closeness to nature is one reason why our problem is not repression but regression: our notorious violence is the constant eruption of primitivism, of anarchic individualism. The Sixties attempted a return to nature that ended in disaster. The gentle nude bathing and playful sliding in the mud at Woodstock were a short-lived Rousseauist dream. My generation, inspired by the Dionysian titanism of rock, attempted something more radical than anything since the French Revolution. We asked: why should I obey this law? and why shouldn't I act on every sexual impulse? The result was a descent into barbarism. We painfully discovered that a just society cannot, in fact, function if everyone does his own thing. And out of the pagan promiscuity of the Sixties came AIDS. Everyone of my generation who preached free love is responsible for AIDS. The Sixties revolution in America collapsed because of its own excesses. It followed and fulfilled its own inner historical pattern, a fall from Romanticism into Decadence. In France, in contrast, the brief student and worker revolt was put down by government action, an external force. Armchair French leftists like Foucault went into a permanent sulk. They never saw the errors of their ideas because those ideas, through lack of French moxie, were never tested against reality by being put through their full organic cycle. Hence the utter madness of French leftist pretensions being flaunted by milquetoast academics in America, which as a nation had made an epic journey to the heart of darkness and returned with tragic truths.

The American Sixties already contained every revolutionary insight. We didn't need Derrida: we had Jimi Hendrix. In the blazing psychedelic guitar work of this black genius, time, space, form, voice, person were deconstructed. Floating Oriental suspensions released the categorizations of European mind. Hendrix's radical artistic statement, with its raw elemental sound-effects of earth, air, water, and fire, addressed both nature and culture and therefore dwarfed society-obsessed French thought. Psychedelia's deconstructions, unlike Derrida's, destroyed the safe and known for one purpose: expanded vision. The Sixties saw the cosmos and were awed by it. The French, frolicking in their miniature stone garden, haven't had a cosmic thought since Pascal. America, furthermore, by virtue of its overlapping and competing ethnicities—Jewish, Italian, Greek, Puerto Rican, Chicano, Irish, Swedish, German, Polish, Russian, Chinese, Japanese—had intrinsic to its character as an immigrant nation a multiplicity of perspective on life, language, and behavior that snobbish, homogeneous France, suppressing its resident Algerians, lacks. Derrida, an Algerian Jew, had his own private agenda in France that is not applicable to America.

The Sixties were also a great age of cinema. My generation, transferring to college campuses the cult atmosphere of urban art-film houses, sat in rapt, reverent silence (now totally lost) before hundreds of Hollywood classics and subtitled foreign films in a dozen languages. Through film we gained an international and transhistorical understanding, a mobility of mind that freed us from the parochial domestic Fifties. France was present, but as only one item in our cultural overview. Resnais and Robbe-Grillet's operatic *Last Year at Marienbad* dramatized the burden of history and, like Kurosawa's *Rashomon*, the relativity of time, memory, and narrative. Ingmar Bergman's bleak northern trilogy dealt with the death of God and meaning and, in *The Silence*, the death of language—significantly transcended by music. *Persona*, a masterpiece, showed the tyranny of medical authority, the breakdown of the social mask, the cruelty and amorality of the unconscious, the intermingling of fantasy and reality. Antonioni's *L'Avventura* followed, at trancelike length, the questing individual lost in the rocky landscape of modern desolation. *Blow-Up*, through its dissolving crime photographs, addressed the subjectivity of perception and, in its closing mimed tennis game, the fictiveness of community and social behavior. Fellini's films showed consciousress riddled and vexed by sexual fantasy and guilt, a daily war with spectral internalized censors. *Lawrence of Arabia* was a real-life parable of imperialism, racism, and power politics, of idealism collapsing into cynicism. Finally, the Marx Brothers, their popularity restored, performed elaborate surreal deconstructions of language, manners, public decorum—verbal, social, and sexual formulas of every kind.

What I am demonstrating is that anyone culturally awake in the American Sixties was already deeply immersed in all the issues that entered the academy, in grotesquely distorted programmatic form, through the French keyhole in the Seventies. Far from being *au courant* sophisticates, the French acolytes were toadying careerists, untouched by the Sixties. I will never forget the first time I heard the name "Lacan," pronounced by a fellow woman graduate student at a Yale cocktail party with a haughty, clarion-like, head-tossing, triumphant smugness of discovery that would have embarrassed Marie Curie. I saw the first clustering of yuppies around Paul de Man, who, because I was reading Freud, Frazer, Nietzsche, and Sade, thinkers of distinction, seemed to me bland and phony, an ideal model for Ivy League WASPs trying to resist the ethnic, sexual, and pop culture revolution of the Sixties. Hence de Man's delightful recent exposure as a Nazi sympathizer did not surprise me in the least. The Seventies theory explosion was a panic reaction by headlocked pedants unable to cope with the emotional and sensory flux of the iconoclastic psychedelic Sixties. It was a desperate search for new authority, new dogma. It misused and abused modernist concepts for personal cachet and professional advancement. Alienation, anxiety, and relativity, as embodied in film, still retained major principles stripped away by the theorists, with their fanatical, sterile mind-games: the beauty of the human face; the power of emotion; the allure of the visual; the presence of nature, in sea, moon, cloud, night; the virtuosity of the artist, as actor, cinematographer, or *auteur* director; and above all, the magnetism and complexity of sex. The French theorists are eros-killers. The smouldering eroticism of great European actresses like Jeanne Moreau demonstrated to my generation woman's archetypal mystery and glamour, completely missing from the totalitarian world-view of the misogynist Foucault. For me, the big French D is not Derrida but Deneuve.

The psychedelic Sixties were about opening oneself to sensations and messages from above, below, and beyond the social realm. We sought the oracular, the mystic, "vibrations" between persons and planets. A poem or film had a magic authority. The French Seventies, on the other hand, were about rigid mental control, power plays by the critic over the artist and text. Academics with the souls of accountants now approached art like a business deal, haggling over negotiable, movable clauses. The older Beat poets, by their disdain for material possessions, were a spiritual example to us in the Sixties. In *Howl* and *Kaddish*, Allen Ginsberg fused the American bardic tradition of Whitman with Jewish moral passion to deconstruct institutions, history, social class, and concepts of sexual and mental normality. Through his impact on Bob Dylan, Ginsberg changed rock and the world. What did the academic Seventies offer? Not a fiery holy man but plastic Ken dolls, beady-eyed, greedy, cutthroat. Ginsberg, like the pioneering Lenny Bruce, who turned comedy toward social critique, was influenced by the rich, melodious voices and syncopated jazz rhythms of black music. African-American culture is still rooted in the rural South, with its evangelical fervor and firebreathing preachers. The blues shouters and black gospel choirs are alive and ecstatic with "the spirit," which the French theorists wouldn't recognize unless it came up and hit them in the head. Walk in Philadelphia on a Sunday morning, and you will hear majestic Niagaras of sound pouring from the black churches. And who's doing the preaching in Ivy League humanities departments? Lily-livered, dead-ass, trash-talking foreign junk-bond dealers. The school of Saussure, nose in the dictionary, can't see the ancient art form of dance, the sacred poetry of the body, which has made America the envy of the world. Black teenagers, with brilliant virtuosity, push forward the frontiers of dance. Month by month on the street, they invent new movements that are recorded on music videos and beamed around the world, to the helpless amazement of European and Japanese admirers, who cannot imitate them. I have a dream: in my dream, based on the diner episode in *The Blues Brothers*, Aretha Franklin, in her fabulous black-lipstick "Jumpin' Jack Flash" outfit, leaps from her seat at Maxim's and, shouting "Think!," blasts Lacan, Derrida, and Foucault like dishrags against the wall, then leads thousands of freed academic white slaves in a victory parade down the Champs Élysées.

The French invasion of the Seventies had nothing to do with leftism or genuine politics but everything to do with good old-

fashioned American capitalism, which liberal academics pretend
to scorn. The collapse of the job market, due to recession and
university retrenchment after the baby-boom era, caused economic hysteria. As faculties were cut, commercial self-packaging
became a priority. Academics, never renowned for courage, fled
beneath the safe umbrella of male authority and one-man rule:
the French bigwigs offered to their disciples a soothing esoteric
code and a sense of belonging to an elite, an intellectually superior
unit, at a time when the market told academics they were useless
and dispensable. It is comical that these vain, foolish, irrelevant
people, so contemptuous of American society, imagine themselves
to be leftists. They understand nothing of America. And because
of their ignorance, Mercury, god of commerce, forced them into
a historical pattern they are blind to: far from being the lone,
brave dissenters against conservatism, as David Halperin ineptly
claims, the academic theorists were the first wave of yuppie spec-
ulators, the first corporate raiders of the Wall Street gilded age.

The facile industry of high-tech criticism is as busily all-
American as the Detroit auto trade. New! Improved! See next
year's model today! A false progressivism has goaded the profession into a frantic tarantella. Hurry up; get on the ball; you must
"keep up with," must stay in front. But the humanities, unlike
medicine, marine biology, and astrophysics, are about great enduring human truths that in fact never change but are rediscovered again and again. The humanities are about insight,
illumination, wisdom. French theory, with its empty word-play,
produces sophists, experts in getting ahead, getting worldly re-
wards. It allows a continuation not of Sixties leftism but of Fifties
prep schools, with their snide, slick style, a cool, insufferably
pretentious, nasal voice you can hear everywhere on Ivy League
campuses. French theory is brand-name consumerism: Lacan,
Derrida, and Foucault are the academic equivalents of BMW,
Rolex, and Cuisinart, the yuppie trophies. French theory is com-
puterized thinking, superclean and risk-free. It's the Macintosh
that drags the Icons to the Trash, and it's the Big Mac of fast-
food, on-the-run dining. The McDonaldization of the profession
means standardized, interchangeable outlets, briskly efficient academics who think alike and sound alike. Scholars have made

themselves into lock-step computer technicians, up on and hawking the latest gadget-of-the-month. French theory is like those
how-to tapes guaranteed to make you a real-estate millionaire
overnight. Gain power by attacking power! Make a killing! Be a
master of the universe! Call this number in Paris *now*!

The self-made Inferno of the academic junk-bond era is the
conferences, where the din of ambition is as deafening as on the
floor of the stock exchange. The huge post-Sixties proliferation
of conferences, used as an administrative marketing tool by colleges and universities, produced a diversion of professional energy
away from study and toward performance, networking, advertisement, cruising, hustling, glad-handing, back-scratching, chit-
chat, groupthink. Interdisciplinary innovation? Hardly. Real
interdisciplinary work is done reading and writing at home and
in the library. The conferences teach corporate raiding: academics become lone wolves without loyalty to their own disciplines
or institutions; they're always on the trail and on the lookout,
ears up for the better job and bigger salary, the next golden fleece
or golden parachute. The conferences are all about insider trading
and racketeering, jockeying for power by fast-track travelling
salesmen pushing their shrink-wrapped product and tooting
fancy new commercial slogans. The conferences induce a delusional removal from reality. They mislead fad-followers like Halperin and Winkler into beginning ridiculous statements with
"We"—we think, we say, we do this or that. No, we don't; that's
you, the teeming conference-hoppers, the plague of locusts and
froglets croaking in their tiny pond. In the conferences, a host of
Bartleby the Scriveners tippy-toe through showy verbal pirouettes and imagine they're running with the bulls at Pamplona.
But the menu, as the chorus chants in *Monty Python*, is nothing
but "Spam, Spam, Spam!" The conferences are lightweight shut-
tlecock scholarship, where the divorced can trawl for new spouses
and where people meet in an airless bubble to confirm each
other's false assumptions and certitudes. A new *Dunciad* is needed
to chart the reefs and shoals of this polluted boat-choked race
course, where no one ever gets anywhere.

Whole careers have gone down the tubes at the conferences.
Dozens of prominent academics are approaching the moment of

reckoning, when they and everyone else will realize they have wasted the best years of their professional lives on cutesy mini-papers and globe-trotting. By their books ye shall know them. A scholar's real audience is not yet born. A scholar must build for the future, not the present. The profession is addicted to the present, to contemporary figures,. contemporary terminology, contemporary concerns. Authentic theory would mean mastery of the complete history of philosophy and aesthetics. What is absurdly called theory today is just a mask for fashion and greed. The conferences are the Alphabet City of addiction to junk, the self-numbing anodyne of rootless, soulless people who have lost contact with their own ethnic traditions. Their work will die with them, for it is based on neither learning nor inspired interpretation. The conferences are oppressive bourgeois forms that enforce a style of affected patter and smarmy whimsy in the speaker and polite chuckles and iron-butt torpor in the audience. Success at the conferences requires a certain kind of physically inert personality, superficially cordial but emotionally dissociated. It's the genteel high Protestant style of the country clubs and corporate boardrooms, with their financial reports and marketing presentations. The transient intimacies of the conferences are themselves junk bonds. Dante would classify the conference-hoppers as perverters of intellect, bad guides, sowers of schism.

The conferences have left a paper trail of folly and trivial pursuit. True scholars are time-travellers, not space-travellers. Rattling away on their gerbil wheels, the conference-caged theorists replicate the rabid turf-wars of Paris, where an intellectual's every sentence is a calculated self-positioning against another intellectual, an incestuous Peyton Place solipsism impenetrable to gullible Americans. One of recent theory's most provincial conference-groupies: Eve Kosofsky Sedgwick, whose writing on sex is, in my opinion, completely factitious and without scholarly merit. But by the dogged determination that Richard Nixon showed on the rubber-chicken circuit, Sedgwick has managed to convert pedestrian critical skills and little discernible knowledge in history, philosophy, psychology, art, or even premodern literature into a lucrative academic career. Sedgwick is a notorious bloated-blurbist, turning out inflated dust-jacket encomia for

Halperin and, in perhaps the dopiest blurb of the decade (it mentioned ozone), D. A. Miller. She should be giving lectures in marketing and consumer science to business schools.

The junk-bond era has also spawned something that calls itself New Historicism. This seems to be a refuge for English majors without critical talent or broad learning in history or political science. Its style is Joan Didion crossed with the *National Geographic*, glossy, formulaic, unrigorous. New Historicism is of the yuppies, by the yuppies, for the yuppies. To practice it, you apparently must lack all historical sense. My idea of political analysis began with Thucydides and Tacitus. My interest in bridging the gap between disciplines was nourished by reading Vico, Tocqueville, Veblen, Durkheim, Weber, Spengler, Curtius, Panofsky, and Eliade, as well as Nietzsche, Hauser, and Brown. What do New Historicists read? Their contemporary, Clifford Geertz, who can't hold a candle to the magisterial, monumental Arnold Hauser. The anecdotal, microchip manner of New Historicism is yuppie grazing, *cuisine minceur* in a quiche-and-fern bistro. At its best, in Stephen Greenblatt, it is still too bright, crisp, clean, too dressed-for-success. As a student at Yale, Greenblatt had available as models two brilliant exemplars of his own spiritual tradition, the ascetic, poetic Geoffrey Hartman and the turbulent, brooding Harold Bloom. But Greenblatt's books, waving vaguely from a distance at Sixties ideas, go the old bland WASP route, where nothing is actually personally risked or exposed. There is no passion or suffering, no deep learning. Everything is carefully measured against its immediate reception. The New Historicists, carrying contemporary baggage into other eras, are simply repeating the cultural imperialism of British colonels laying out high tea in the jungle. New Historicism is the no-sweat, pain-free, careerist gentrification of authentic Sixties leftism.

Foucault is the ideal thinker for the yuppie age. He is the master of the quick fix, of make-it-to-the-top by any means. Twist the facts, doctor the balance sheet, toss out veteran employees, bring in the smart-mouthed brats, turn the world into one big power lunch. Foucault perfects the WASP alienation of mind and culture from emotion. There are no untidy ambiguities in his system. Everything is rigidly schematic, overdetermined, reducible to chart form. Contradictory evidence is never admitted. Foucault represents the final decadence of Western Apollonianism, a cold, desiccated fetishism of pure I.Q. divorced from humor, compassion, ethics, eroticism, wisdom. It is this same combination of maniacal abstraction with lust for personal power that led to the deranged orderliness of the concentration camps. There is a constant rush to judgment in Foucault. He is filled with specious generalizations, false categorizations, distortions, fudging, pretenses to knowledge in areas where he was ignorant. He had no ability whatever to discriminate among historical sources, where he makes terrible blunders. Foucault had the kind of clever but limited mind that is good at inventing acrostics, crossword puzzles, and computer programs. He had little major talent beyond this, except for a genius for self-promotion. The word "modest" recurs in descriptions of Foucault as a person and writer. To which I reply: there's a sucker born every minute. As a writer, Foucault was an arrogant bastard. He did not believe in truth and so never sought it. His books, clumsily researched but overconfidently argued, show language-obsessed Parisian parochialism become paranoia, delusional and obsessive-compulsive.

Foucault is the Cagliostro of our time. Nowhere is this more evident than in his treatment of Émile Durkheim, his true source. Those who, like Halperin, claim Foucault's descent from Nietzsche are simply Foucault's dupes. An entire book could be written applying Harold Bloom's theory of anxiety of influence to Foucault's desperate concealment of his massive indebtedness to Durkheim, to whom he barely, dismissively, and inaccurately refers. Innumerable discussions of Foucault, including J. G. Merquior's excellent *Foucault* (1985), which hilariously exposes the elementary errors made by Foucault in every area he wrote about, do not even mention Durkheim. This illustrates the kind of interdisciplinary incomprehension that has allowed Foucault to appear erudite, when he was not. The undeserved adulation of Foucault's *Discipline and Punish* reminds me of that priceless moment at the 1980 Oscars when Jon Voight, sitting in the front row as he listened to Laurence Olivier give fey, meandering, and parodistic thanks, was addled and overcome, mouthed a silent, mackerel-like "Wow!" and smacked himself in the middle of his forehead. American humanists, untutored in sociology, are knocked out by Foucault's daring: analyze crime and punishment, prisons and penal codes! Gee, I wish I'd thought of that! Well, Foucault didn't think of it either. It's in Durkheim's *The Division of Labour in Society* (1893). Foucault extends Durkheim's argument one step further but covers up the influence. Look at Durkheim's *Primitive Classification* (1903), and you will see the shadow of Foucault's phrases about taxonomy. Durkheim is everywhere in Foucault. The intricate complexities of analysis of organizations and power groups in Max Weber make Foucault look like a tyro. It is only ignorance of the social sciences that has allowed Foucault to rise to cult status among pitifully unprepared American humanists. I am not aware of any woman in the world doing work on a higher intellectual level than the British sociologist Gillian Rose: in *Dialectic of Nihilism: Post-Structuralism and Law* (1984), she administers a well-earned drubbing to both Foucault and Derrida that demonstrates their circular reasoning and misreading of basic sources.

Foucault is falsely used by naïve American academics as a scholarly source of information, as if he were Fernand Braudel. But you cannot trust a single fact in Foucault. His books should be called *Foucault's Diaries*. They have no relationship to historical reality. They are simply devious improvisations in the style of Gide's *The Counterfeiters*. They attract gameplaying minds with unresolved malice toward society, people who give lip service to rebellion but who lack the guts to actually rebel and pay the price. Derrida is smack for the spirit, but Foucault is the academic cocaine, the yuppie drug of choice of the Seventies and Eighties. In the Sixties, LSD gave vision, while marijuana gave community. But coke, pricey and jealously hoarded, is the power drug, giving a rush of omnipotent self-assurance. Work done under its influence is manic, febrile, choppy, disconnected. Coke was responsible for the plot incoherence of fifteen years of TV sit-coms and glitzy "high-concept" Hollywood films. Foucault is the high-concept pusher and deal-maker of the cocaine decades. His big squishy pink-marshmallow word is "power," which neither he nor his followers fully understand. It caroms around picking up lint and dog hair but is no substitute for political analysis. Foucault's ignorance of prehistory and ancient history, based in the development and articulation of cultures and legal codes, makes his discussions of power otiose. He never asks how power is gained or lost, justly administered or abused. He does not show how efficient procedures get overformalized, entrenched, calcified, then shattered and reformed. He has no familiarity with theories of social or biological hierarchies, such as the "pecking order" universally observed in farmyards and schoolyards. Because, in the faddish French way, he ridiculously denies personality exists, he cannot assess the impact of strong personalities on events nor can he, like Weber, catalog types of authority or prestige. He is inept in comparing different governmental structures. Because he cannot deal with flux or dynamic change, he is hopeless with protracted power struggles. An astute political analyst would have begun his reflections with the long conflict between Pharaoh and priesthood in Egypt or between Emperor and army in late Rome, patterns still observable in our century's ongoing power struggles between college administrations and faculties or between Hollywood corporations, banks, and studios on the one hand and directors, actors, and screenwriters on the other.

Foucault, like Lacan and Derrida, is forty years out of date. He does not see and cannot deal with the radical transformation of culture by new technology and mass media following World War Two. He overlooks the economic role of entrepreneurship, and he is blind to the dominance of personality in our pagan Age of Hollywood. Liberal academics are stuck in a time warp. Invoking the Foucault buzz words "surveillance" and "the police," they try to re-create the Fifties world of J. Edgar Hoover and *Dragnet*, the last, lost moment of liberalism's political authenticity, before it was destroyed by my generation's excesses. It is mildly nauseating to see this snide use of "the police" as a literary cliché coming from spoiled, wifty, middle-class academics who would be the first to shriek for the police if a burglar or rapist came through the window. And as for surveillance, Foucault-style language analysis seems lame and monotonous compared to the treatment of the same theme by Sade, Blake, Poe, Dickens, Dostoyevsky, Kafka, Brecht, or even Rod Serling in *The Twilight Zone*. The cultural mode of the post-Sixties era is not surveillance but voyeurism, *ours*. Eye-energy, thanks to omnipresent television, is going in the opposite direction. Institutions are the modern reality principle. Current academic liberalism cannot understand the fragility of institutions, or the ease with which order, due process, and civil liberties can be destroyed by assertions of anarchic selfhood. As a battle-scarred Sixties veteran, I learned this the hard way. Humanists like to childishly sneer and snort about the system, but they are quick to hide behind it, to pose from its forum at conferences, and to use it as a lifelong gravy train.

The academic popularity of Foucault, Lacan, and Derrida was produced by the poor educational preparation of American humanists, who appear to have slept through college. In the basic biology class of my first college semester in 1964, we studied the Pre-Socratics, with their competing and contradictory theories of the origins and constituency of matter. Heracleitus, in particular, to whom I had already been introduced by Walter Pater, contains everything that is in Derrida and more. We later studied the Western development of scientific classification schemes and the checkered history of evolutionary and genetic theories from Lamarck through Mendel and Darwin. In basic geology the next year, we learned how to think in huge time-frames and how to analyze multiple layering and inversions in mixed physical evidence. At no time in my education or reading was science ever presented as an absolutist, dogmatic methodology, the way it is constantly maligned these days by French-befuddled humanists. We saw, following Aristotle and his seventeenth-century admirers, that science is a system of provisional hypotheses, open to constant revision and disproof. In classical art and history, we were impressed with modern archaeology's tender solicitude for the tiniest chips and fragments of vanished cultures, with the excruciatingly slow and heroically self-abnegating excavation, measurement, numbering, photography, extraction, cleaning, cataloging, restoration, and preservation of artifacts. (It was exasperation and impatience with dull potsherds that ended my childhood dream of becoming an archaeologist.) In introductory social science, we learned that the nineteenth-century rise of anthropology as a discipline hastened a new cultural relativism that shifted Europe from centrality; we were shown how anthropology is a limited interpretation by aliens who inevitably alter the small societies they enter and observe. As for Saussure, from the moment we began Latin class in junior high school, we were told, in simple, common-sense terms, that language is an arbitrary, self-enclosed system that varies from culture to culture, a point obvious to everyone studying languages for the last 200 years. Even the hot-dog vendor on the street would never mistake the word *elephant* for a real elephant. The French school, tickling its own buttocks, is in a state of dementia about the actual facts of modern thought. It has nothing whatever new or important to say.

The English professors who ran off after the French, like the stampede of silly knights whom Spenser's bemused Britomart watches disappearing after the (to me) False Florimell, were demonstrating an inadequate grasp of their own literary tradition. Blake's conceptual "mind-forg'd manacles"; his exploited chimney sweeps coerced and brainwashed by adult maxims; the barely verbal ego and primitive sensory state of "Infant Joy"; the oppressive institutional walls of "London"; the Orc-Urizen cycle of rebellion and repression; the spiritual combat of delusional mental emanations and projections in the long poems: here, at the birth of Romanticism, is every major theme that ends up as stale French pretzels at the last gasp of modernism. Lytton Strachey, notably in his treatment of Florence Nightingale as a secret imperialist, has Foucault's debunking method already. Sensational Fifties prison and sanitarium movies, like *The Snake Pit* and *Suddenly Last Summer*, make Foucault's points more entertainingly. In 1952, in his study of schizophrenics in *Psychoanalytic Explorations in Art*, Ernst Kris demonstrated that artistic creativity is a distortion of received categories, supporting the connection between art and madness that had been a truism for centuries. Bob Dylan's "Subterranean Homesick Blues," "Desolation Row," and "Ballad of a Thin Man"; the Rolling Stones' "Sympathy for the Devil," "Jumpin' Jack Flash," and "Street Fighting Man"; Jim Morrison's line for the Doors, "Send my credentials to the House of Detention": these angry Romantic statements, haunted by nature *and* culture, are the true voice of our time. My idol is Keith Richards, the Rolling Stones rhythm guitarist who made menacing music out of the Dionysian darkness never seen by society-obsessed Foucault. The thunderous power chords of hard rock smash the dreary little world of French theory. The French have no sense of elemental realities. They could never have produced a D. H. Lawrence, a Neruda, an Allen Ginsberg.

If the history of ideas, including science, were properly taught, the French influence would shrivel to nothing. Foucault, crippled by his ignorance of antiquity, never saw until it was too late that Enlightenment scientism was a revival of Greek Apollonian taxonomies. Rather than admit he had been dreadfully wrong, he devised campaign after campaign of further deception and self-concealment. His style is to pretend to find symmetrical little categories, actually as random as the rolling plums on a slot machine. American humanists, who can't think their way out of a paper bag, gape in wonder at these lofty displays of false logic. Foucault's orderliness is that of a scowling, squinting, round-shouldered person ramming knitting needles into a great pile of badly mixed, sticky bread dough. The humanists are blinded by the flashing skewers (what "matchless penetration," breathes the dazzled Halperin), but informed scholars recognize a blob when they see one. And skewer-ramming is no way to bake bread. Foucault's taxonomies are always arbitrarily imposed and never generated by the evidence. He treats his material and readers in exactly the fascist way he claims society treats the body—as a mannequin without its own animal energy or internal processes. As a flunky of Saussure, Foucault has to keep nature invisible at all times. This makes it impossible for him to honestly explore the necessary role of repression in such features of education and child-rearing as toilet training, simple basic issues never far from our minds in America, with its strong tradition of practical and social psychology.

There are two main areas where Foucault is severely deficient. First is his picture of consciousness, which is trapped in the contours of French language and culture in ways he never remotely saw. But beyond this, Foucault does not understand global or associative clusters of meaning. Most disastrously for someone claiming to discover the "epistemes" intrinsic to a period, he has no feeling for metaphorical or symbolic thinking.

Without metaphor, literature and art are incomprehensible. Without symbolism, love, religion, and patriotism are incomprehensible. Reading or teaching Joyce's *Ulysses* requires more nimbleness with multiple linguistic and cultural codes than was ever displayed by Foucault. The most serious flaw of Foucault's system is in the area of sex. I view his hurried, compulsive writing as a massive rationalist defense-formation to avoid thinking about (a) woman, (b) nature, (c) emotion, and (d) the sexual body. His attempt to make the body the passive property of male society is an evasion of the universal fact so intolerable to him: that we are all born of human mothers. By turning women into ciphers of men, he miniaturizes and contains them. Most of Foucault is just recycled, denatured Rousseauism. His police state is a third-rate *film noir*, but significantly missing the beautiful, mysterious woman. Foucault sees power everywhere except where it is greatest: the female principle. It is no surprise he attracts mostly men, who are always ready to believe that the verbal and rational explain everything. Foucault's antiseptic world has neat hospital corners. He has scrubbed away woman's messy emotional centrality. The fruits of Foucault are wormwood. He was a Herod without a Salome. This was a man of mutilated psyche: if what I have reliably heard about his public behavior after he knew he had AIDS is true, then Foucault would deserve the condemnation of every ethical person.

Six months ago, perusing the new releases at the library, I came upon Robert Drews's *The Coming of the Greeks*. In the next two days, I read this slim book with electrified attention and with tears in my eyes. Here is the great Western analytic tradition that my generation of trendy yuppies has thrown out the window. There are 2,500 years of continuous philosophical, scholarly, and monastic practice behind this logical, luminous, transparent style. Drews, speculating about an early period of European population migration for which the evidence is scanty, presents and argues his controversial case with absolute honesty. There is no propaganda, no distortion, no sleight of hand, no intention to deceive—none of the academic immorality that swept the profession in the Seventies and Eighties. Every syllable of this book is precise and painstakingly qualified. This is the real sophistication, the real theoretical expertise. Drews has the scholarly power so advanced that it makes him invisible. Fine fabrics, which last forever, can be recognized by an experienced eye from across the room. Drews's writing has the weave, the texturing, the stitching of high intellectual quality. Academe has been flooded by French knockoffs, shoddy *pret à porter* merchandise. Robert Drews has the Anglo-American goods for all seasons.

What is needed now is a return to genuine historicism, based on knowledge of and respect for the past. The fashionable French posturing—"there are no facts"—has got to stop. There are no certainties, but there are well-supported facts which we can learn and build on, always with the flexible scholarly skepticism that allows us to discard prior assumptions in the face of new evidence. If there were no facts, surgeons couldn't operate, buildings would collapse, and airplanes wouldn't get off the ground. Critics got themselves into a muddle by trying to study literature alone, without mastery of the other arts. The word-created subjectivities of literature, particularly in modern non-mimetic fiction, have lured feeble minds into believing nothing exists in the universe outside academe. Familiarity with the visual arts, which must prepare physical materials like paints and metals in scientific ways, would have prevented many of the idiocies that have poured from literature departments in the past twenty years.

The skepticism claimed by deconstruction is a bookworm affectation by tunnel-vision careerists. That art is its own self-contained, transhistorical system I also believe, following my study of Gautier, Baudelaire, Pater, and Wilde. But that every work of art is by definition stylistically or conceptually self-referential is simply ridiculous. This principle does apply to certain kinds of ironic, late-phase works, like *Tristram Shandy, Finnegans Wake*, or Duchamp's doctored *Mona Lisa*, but it makes no sense at all with classicism, most of High Romanticism, or the major nineteenth-century social-realist novels. It was in reading *Tristram Shandy* for class in graduate school that I noticed how it is primarily men who gravitate toward the gameplaying self-reflexive style. There is an alienation from emotion in it, a Nervous Nelly fear of letting go and being "exposed." As an attitude toward life, it betrays a perpetual adolescence. Those who hurled themselves after Derrida were not the most sophisticated but the most pedestrian, most pretentious, and least creative members of my generation of academics. Bergman's *Persona* is a masterpiece not because the film jumps its sprockets at the end ("I am a movie") but because it confronts and explores the emotional, psychological, and moral tensions of Western personality. The epic saga of life and art cannot even be seen, much less understood, by the toy techno-trinkets of the French school.

We have available to us two great Western traditions of skepticism and disputation, the Hellenic and the Judaic. Our educational and legal systems have been heavily influenced by Greco-Roman philosophy, rhetoric, and oratory, partly transmitted through the Catholic church, whose theology was born in the Hellenized eastern Mediterranean. Jewish thinkers, because of their ancient heritage in religious law, have been pioneers in legal philosophy since the Middle Ages. Modern America has a strong Jewish presence in the literary, legal, medical, and scientific worlds. There is nothing more thrilling than listening to two New York rabbis aggressively debate each other on a radio talk show. The intellectual vigor of Talmudic disputation puts the theory wing of American academe to shame. It is no coincidence that my mentors have always been Jews. We have right here on native soil a superb high-energy model of subtle inquiry, humanistic compassion, and profound learning. It was from Jews (beginning at T. Aaron Levy Junior High School) that I learned how to analyze politics, law, business, and medicine, how to decipher the power dynamics of family relationships, and how to plan pragmatic strategies of social activism. The Jews know there *is* a story in history, for they have suffered it. Those who deny there is meaning or order in events have their heads in the sand. One of the most unpalatable aspects of the French fad is the way it has shown ambitious academics drifting from and selling out their own cultural identity. Foucault is white bread and mayo for the assimilated Jews.

America had another vivid analytic style of informed commentary and dissent: that of male homosexuals in the pre-Stonewall period. Gay liberation, allowing greater freedom of assembly, sexual expression, and personal style, also unfortu-

nately diverted toward recreation energies which had earlier been
absorbed in aggressive, witty discourse. In college, I was stunned
and exhilarated by the bold free thinking and cruel irreverence
of gay men, who respected no conservative or liberal piety, even
of the humanitarian polio crisis. My admiring memory of their
revolutionary, philosophe-like iconoclasm makes me most re-
gretful about recent infringements of free speech by a few over-
zealous AIDS activists, who have made themselves the arbiters
of a new dogma and enforced it with terroristic tactics. Injustice
cannot be remedied by injustice. The examples of Gandhi and
Martin Luther King show that civil rights movements best succeed when they are guided by ethical principles. Gay men, even
more than Jews, have the most to lose from unilateral suspensions
of civil liberties. As the gay community became a crowded, glit-
tery, fast-paced world unto itself, gay men began to lose the
brilliant mental edge that they had had in the old haunted world
of masks, where comedy was born of suffering. Ironically, as
public acceptance has increased, gay commentary on the straight
world has gotten more strident and less insightful, partly through
a bad influence from sloppy feminist rhetoric. The Halperin and
Winkler books show the sad decline in quality of thought from
corrosive independence into self-righteous groupthink. Once gay
men were the enemies of jargon, cliché, and cant. Once gay men,
through their avant-garde study of the minute history of art,
antiques, interior design, fashion, music, opera, Broadway shows,
and Hollywood movies, were masters of an archaeology of culture,
hypersensitively acute to chronology, style, tradition. Only the
drag queens, my heroes, have preserved the old gay aesthetic,
which elevates eternal beauty and imagination over politics. It
is not too late to restore it to centrality. And it is not too soon
to start talking about ethics. Gay studies, if it expects academic
legitimacy, must follow the scholarly lead of the rigorous James
Saslow, not the slipshod David Halperin.

IV

My proposals for academic reform are meant to put learning
back at the center of the profession. Mastery of historical facts

and dates, with interpretation a necessary but secondary process, should be strictly required of both faculty and students. The present highly subjective, essay-centered humanities curriculum preserves bourgeois Protestant models of discourse that discriminate against those of other cultural backgrounds or temperaments and that encourage a calculating, careerist style of student response. Literary essay-writing, perfected by the prep schools, has turned into a con game. In my experience with freshmen from minority urban or Southern rural families, the fairest educational method reduces the course to orderly bodies of material that can be approached and mastered by anyone, given sufficient application. This is true equality of opportunity. Success in a humanities course, as much as one in medicine or law, should be contingent upon present effort, not upon skill in facile word-games learned elsewhere. At the same time, I would like to liberalize classroom teaching, to free it from the iron yoke of the prefab daily syllabus and allow more room for improvisation, especially in lectures. The teacher is present as a living, breathing embodiment of the humanities. Interpretation begins with the teacher's ability to think out loud and to follow the beguiling stream of associations, often inspired by the students themselves, in their many moods from euphoria to narcolepsy. This liberalization is not inconsistent with an overall tightening of standards. There should be an imposing roster of primary and secondary texts for independent study, assessed by long and gruelling exams. The classroom should be heaven, the exam room hell.

Teacher training, recruitment, and review require extensive reform. Specialists are the last thing undergraduates need. We have a generation of latchkey children, the product of divorce and absentee working parents. Many were raised by permissive Sixties parents loath to impose repressive religion on their children. Consequently, our students are anxious, adrift, often self-destructive. They are desperately searching for meaning. We need reconstruction, not deconstruction. All undergraduate teachers should be generalists. The curriculum should be radically restructured. There would be three large areas: science, social science, and humanities. All present humanities departments would be dissolved into each other. The graduate schools would begin preparing for this shift by forbidding specialization in any one art form, much less one period within an art form. Graduate students need cultural broadening and expansion, not narrowing and concentration. They would be required to become conversant with a minimum of two art forms, in all world cultures and periods. If necessary, they would be forced to take undergraduate courses to remedy their deficiencies. There is no need for specialized graduate course work in literature or art history. The materials for such study are fully available in the library. Exams alone could test mastery for degree certification. The undergraduate curriculum would be severely stripped down. Pork-barrel specialist courses, a form of gross exploitation by which professors have made students do their research for them, would be abolished. All courses, except those dealing with major thinkers and artists of the rank of Plato, Dante, Shakespeare, Michelangelo, and Picasso, would have to be interdisciplinary and cover a minimum fifty-year span. The freshman and sophomore years would consist of basic courses required of all students. All professors, no matter how famous, would be compelled to teach in the basic program. A rigorous history of ideas framework would be devised, on the Columbia model, taught by both humanities and social science faculty, who would have to interact in preparatory meetings and thus begin to find the common ground between disciplines. All upper-level courses would be rotated. Courses would be assigned on the basis of what a professor does *not* know, rather than on what he does. This would put learning at the heart of the enterprise and keep the institution in a constant dynamic ferment of discovery and exploration.

Academe needs deprofessionalization and deyuppification. It has to recover its clerical or spiritual roots. Scholarship is an ideal and a calling, not merely a trade or living. Every year at commencement, we put on medieval robes that connect us to a great monastic past. We should be in the world but not of it. Our vocation is a ministry. There is no truth, but as thinkers we are obliged to seek it. The present system is geared to producing careerist academics rather than scholars or intellectuals. Specialization belongs only to personal professional research; it has no place whatever in undergraduate education. I call for a total abolition of the annual Modern Language Association Convention sessions (699 over four days in December 1990) for three reasons: they splinter the profession into political special-interest groups like Washington PAC lobbyists; they encourage the midget format of the "talk," which is simply a vehicle for cozy relationships and networking; they occur too close to the formal marketing apparatus of the profession and are therefore corrupted by it. The MLA Convention crams the moneychangers into the Temple instead of driving them out. Job recruitment should seek these qualities in a candidate: (a) overall mastery of the Western artistic and intellectual tradition; (b) ability to relate our tradition to other great world traditions; (c) a passion for learning; (d) an interest in communicating that passion to undergraduates.

Attendance at conferences must cease to be defined as professional activity. It should be seen for what it is: prestige-hunting and long-range job-seeking junkets, meat-rack mini-vacations. The phrase "He or she is just a conference-hopper" (cf. "just a gigolo") must enter the academic vocabulary. I look for the day when conference-hopping leads to denial of employment or promotion on the grounds that it is a neglect of professional duties to scholarship and one's institution. Energies have to be reinvested at home. The reform of education will be achieved when we all stay put and cultivate our own garden, instead of gallivanting around the globe like migrating grackles. Furthermore, excessive contact with other academics is toxic to scholarship. Reading and writing academic books and seeing academics every day at work are more than enough exposure to academe. The best thing for scholars is contact with nonacademics, with other ways of thinking and seeing the world. Most of the absurdities of women's studies and French theory would have been prevented by close observation of ordinary life outside the university. There should be more flow between the university and society. Politicians, businessmen, soldiers, artists, engineers, scientists should be brought in for regular visits and an exchange of views. Instead of schmoozing with other academics at conferences, faculty should be required to do outreach work via general-interest community lectures at public schools, libraries, and churches. A sense of the general audience must be recovered. All literary criticism should be accessible to the literate general reader. That there is such a general audience, which has been arrogantly blocked out by obscurantist theorists (laughably claiming leftist and populist aims), I know from letters I have received about my own book. Literature and art are never created for scholars but for a universal audience. If academics cannot see that audience, they cannot see art. Students are the nascent general readers among us.

The postwar "publish or perish" tyranny must end. The profession has become obsessed with quantity rather than quality. At top universities, two published books are becoming the minimum even for an associate professorship. Burger King now rules the waves. One brilliant article should outweigh one mediocre book. Real contributions to knowledge take time. Scholarly time is very slow. Right now, young academics are caught in a bind which pits scholarly integrity against their economic self-interest, particularly if they are responsible for children. Scholarship is a life of study leading to a mature production of the mind. Completed chapters of a substantial ongoing project, submitted to outside review, should be acceptable for employment or promotion. Rushing people into print right after grad school just leads to portentous fakery, which no one reads anyhow. Maynard Mack was already saying in 1969 to our graduate seminar that "95% of what is published in any given year should be ritually burned at the end of that year." The pressure on shaky novices to sound important and authoritative makes for guano mountains of dull rubbish. Good writing and teaching require a creative sense of play. In American academe, as opposed to Great Britain, playfulness and humor, as well I know, are suspect, suggesting you aren't "serious" enough. But comedy is a sign of balanced perspective on life and thought. Humorlessness should be grounds for dismissal. Eccentric individualism, in the style of the old German scholars, must be tolerated. Teachers should not be conformist clones. Graduate students must be encouraged to let their personalities flower in the classroom. Teaching is a performance art.

A feeling or respect for the past is the great gift we can

bequeath to our students, trapped in the busy, bright, brazen present. Even leftist professors these days lack a sense of history. Arguments against the canon have come suspiciously often from banal, uncultivated careerists who, whatever their current prominence, lack scholarly distinction. Individual authors or works may go in and out of favor (both Shakespeare and Bach had to be revived by Romanticism), but the overall line of Western culture will never change. Every woman, black, or Oriental raised and writing in English is a product of that main line. The piddling ignoramuses who deny there is a distinct, discernible, objective Western tradition are just woozy literati. That line is absolutely, concretely manifest in the visual arts: at the temple complex of King Zoser at Saqqara are the papyrus-capped pillar forms invented by Imhotep which would be transmitted to us by Greece and Rome. Freshmen from the poorest neighborhoods are amazed to discover that, cresting the columns of Philadelphia banks, churches, museums, libraries, and civic buildings, are the fronds and curls of Egyptian plant life, in 4,500 years of historical memory. The whole racial argument about the canon falls to nothing when it is seen that the origins of Greek Apollonianism were in Egypt, in Africa. Go down, Moses: even Judeo-Christianity sojourned in Egypt.

The freshman year should be entirely devoted to basic science (biology and geology) and to ancient world history and art, up to the early Middle Ages and the birth of Islam. Sophomore-year coverage would extend from the High Middle Ages and Renaissance to the present. In the first year, comparative religion would allow the social science and humanities faculties to fuse their instruction. The sacred texts of all major world religions would be studied, beginning with the Bible, knowledge of which has disastrously eroded. Students adore paleontology and archaeology, which, particularly in its underwater branch, brings together science, history, and art. Artifacts, monuments, and sacred sites and rituals from European, African, Far and Near Eastern, Pre-Columbian, Native American, and Oceanic cultures would be closely studied. The method would be rigorously old historicist. There would be no melodramatic victimage scenarios, that drippy amateur soap opera which fuzzy academic liberals, suppressing recognition of their own innate aggression, aggressively project backwards. The human record is virtually universally one of cruelty barely overcome and restrained by civilization. Imperialism and slavery are no white male monopoly but are everywhere, from Egypt, Assyria, and Persia to India, China, and Japan. Current events should be systematically but sparingly worked into the ancient picture by teachers. For example, I like to show freshmen the elegant Arch of Titus in the Roman Forum. There, in the bas-relief of the great menorah being carried from the Temple by Roman soldiers at the sack of Jerusalem and Diaspora, we see the beginnings of the political problems that still seethe in the Mideast.

Modernization means Westernization. The modern technological world is the product of the Greco-Roman line of mathematics, science, and analytic thought. The academic pop-politicos, pandering to students, rob them of their future. Education must simultaneously explore and explain the world's multiculturalism while preparing the young to enter the Apollonian command-system. But ethnic descendants should, as much as possible, retain their creative duality. I feel Italian but love America. Oprah Winfrey shifts wonderfully back and forth, with jazzlike improvisation, between her two voices. African-Americans must study the language and structure of Western public power while still preserving their cultural identity, which has had world impact on the arts. We must expose the absurdity of our literary ostriches who think we need the death-by-sludge French theorists to tell us about multiple "discourses." The established scholarship of comparative religion, anthropology, and art history had already prepared us with a flexible, accurate methodology for negotiating among belief-systems and identifying the iconography and symbol-schemes of different cultures and periods. I call for an immediate end to undergraduate "Theory of Criticism" courses, which force pastel hangers on people who have no clothes yet. Such courses should be reconstituted, by less trendy faculty, as "History of Aesthetics," to take in all world art forms, including dance, which has to be rescued from the Phys. Ed. department and given its true eminence. The Greek organic triad, Archaic/High Classic/Hellenistic, is the paradigm for the study of style, just as the rise, flowering, and decline of Rome, so lavishly well-documented, is the paradigm for the study of politics. Classicism trains the eye. Knowledge of it is essential for artists and for everyone who claims to be interested in art. The simplicity, clarity, and proportion of classicism remain major principles of architecture and theater and opera sets, and they profoundly inspired important fashion designers like Chanel, Adrian, and Halston. The mythic pattern of Western culture is Greek revival: again and again, objects are lost and refound, overvalued, devalued, then revalued. But the classics always return. Naturally, tastes may vary from person to person: I myself think *Auntie Mame* the best novel since World War Two, and I infinitely prefer *Antony and Cleopatra* to *King Lear*, which puts me to sleep, except in its campy opening scene. But I also recognize that no one in the world can claim to be educated without knowing *King Lear*. The real marginalizers are the panderers, who would condemn our students to perpetual second-class status.

Great works of art have their own life and will outlast us. We hold these things in trust. Academe should be a savings and not a spendthrift institution. Like public museums, universities are essentially conservative, curatorial. Yes, art works seem to shift from generation to generation, but it is the mercurial gleaming of Proteus, the metamorphosis of imagination. It is up to us to choose the works best suited to enter the dream life of our students, works that will retain their value and give the best return over time, lasting sources of consolation and enlightenment. In the predatory go-go era of quick-turnover junk bonds and windfall profits, there has been no interest in long-term investment of time and energy by either faculty or students. Tired of literature and piqued by *au courant* linguistics? Why, just binge and purge with Saussure: swallow him whole, then vomit him out. Don't bother doing the real work that linguistics requires— painstaking mastery of ancient and modern world languages. The theory years were pure sloth, a pig-rut of pretension and megalomania. In this disgraceful academic scandal, we have people dismissing science and psychology who know nothing of science or psychology; people spouting politics who know nothing of political science or history; people claiming to do anthropology who know nothing of anthropology; people throwing around philosophical terms who know nothing of philosophy. For the first time ever, we have pedantry without learning.

The spiritual vacuum of recent academe is responsible for the popularity of false teachers like the mushy Joseph Campbell, who gives people the long view of traditional mythology, and for the spread of New Age mysticism, whose hoaxer channelers satisfy the craving for ancestral voices. We need back-to-basics reform on every level of education. Old German philology was culture criticism at its learned, comprehensive best. Let us put an end to the yuppie buffet, the designer drugs and watered-down, piss-poor Molotov cocktails served with crudités and French canapés, hot now, stale later. Perhaps the French flunkies should leave academe and form their own associations, like the Shriners, where they can moon over their idols and exchange photos like bubble-gum cards. There are precedents for this in the cults of Swedenborg and Madame Blavatsky. Enough already of Lacan, Derrida, and Foucault poured like ketchup over everything. Lacan: the French fog machine; a gray-flannel worry-bone for toothless academic pups; a twerpy, cape-twirling Dracula dragging his flocking stooges to the crypt. Lacan is a Freud T-shirt shrunk down to the teeny-weeny Saussure torso. The entire school of Saussure, including Lévi-Strauss, write the muffled prose of people with cotton wool wrapped around their heads; they're like walking Q-Tips. Derrida: a Gloomy Gus one-trick pony, stuck on a rhetorical trope already available in the varied armory of New Criticism. Derrida's method: masturbation without pleasure. It's a birdbrain game for birdseed stakes. Neo-Foucaldian New Historicism: a high-wax bowling alley where you score points just by knocking the pins down. Hey, fellas: there's something out there that electrocutes people on beaches, collapses buildings like cardboard, and drowns ships and villages. It's called nature. The next time the western horizon flames with crimson, remember that this is what Foucault never saw. Foucault was struck down by the elemental force he repressed and edited out of his system. Science, disdained by Foucaldians, is our only hope for controlling the retrovirus and marauding infections of AIDS. Science and society are our frail barriers against the turbulence of cruel, indifferent nature.

How does the mind work? This is the psychedelic question. Sensation, perception, emotion, memory, dream, imagination: French theory is hopelessly inadequate for explaining art and life. An American psychedelic criticism would see through and disrupt while also intensifying and enhancing. Teachers who assign Lacan, Derrida, and Foucault to unprepared students are fools. There is so much else to learn and know. The French fad is now a skeleton wreck. Seventy years of the school of Saussure are crowded onto a solitary ice floe: as we steam by or fly overhead, we should simply say to our students, "Look, my child, there on that wandering island heaped with bones is where the Saussurean Sirens sang and where so many lost their lives and careers." A word-drunk profession driven by conferences and cronyism turns itself into a seething herd of lemmings, weasels, and coy duo-dog acts, at MLA or on the road.

Women's studies is institutionalized sexism. It too must go. Gender studies is no alternative: "gender" is now a biased, prudish code word for social constructionism. Sexology is an old and distinguished field. As sex studies, frankly admitting it is sex we are tirelessly interested in, it would take in the hundred-year history of international commentary on sex; it would make science its keystone; and it would allow both men and women as well as heterosexuals and homosexuals to work together in the fruitful dialogue of dislike, disagreement, and debate, the tension, confrontation, and dialectic that lead to truth. Women's studies is a comfy, chummy morass of unchallenged groupthink. It is, with rare exception, totally unscholarly. Academic feminists have silenced men and dissenting women. Sunk in a cocoon of smug complacency, they are blind to their own clichéd Rousseauist ideology. Feminists are always boasting of their "diversity" and pluralism. This is like white Protestants, in the nineteenth and pre-Sixties twentieth centuries when they controlled American politics, finance, and academe, claiming diversity on the basis of their dozens of denominations. But blacks, Jews, and Italian Catholics, standing on the outside, could clearly see the monolithic homogeneity that the WASP insiders were blissfully, arrogantly unaware of. If any field ever deserved a punishing Foucaldian analysis, it's women's studies, which is a prisoner of its own futile, grinding, self-created discourse. Women's studies needed a syllabus and so invented a canon overnight. It puffed up clunky, mundane contemporary women authors into Oz-like, skywriting dirigibles. Our best women students are being force-fed an appalling diet of cant, drivel, and malarkey. Pioneering work in sex studies will come only from men and women conservatively trained in high-level intellectual history.

American feminism's nose dive began when Kate Millett, that imploding beanbag of poisonous self-pity, declared Freud a sexist. Trying to build a sex theory without studying Freud, women have made nothing but mud pies. In Great Britain and France, feminists did not make this silly mistake, but unfortunately their understanding of Freud has been tainted by the swindling Lacan. Now the missing but indispensable Freud is being smuggled back into America by the Lacan feminists, with their paralyzing puritanism. It's all ass-backwards. Just read Freud, for pity's sake, and forget Lacan. It's outrageous that women undergraduates are being made to read Lacan who haven't read Freud and therefore have no idea what Lacan is doing. Freud is one of the major thinkers in world history. One reads him not for his conclusions, which were always tentative and in process, but for the bold play of his speculative intelligence. He shows you how to conceptualize, how to frame long, overarching arguments, how to verbalize ambiguous, nonverbal psychic phenomena. Reading him, you feel new tracks being cut in your brain. Cheap gibes about Freud, epidemic in women's studies, are a symptom of emotional juvenility. American feminists, snivelling about Freud without reading him, have sentenced themselves and their work to mediocrity and irrelevance.

Simone de Beauvoir's brilliant, imperious *The Second Sex*, now forty years old, is the only thing undergraduate sex studies needs. Add Freud to de Beauvoir, and you have intellectual training at its best. The later French women choking the current syllabus don't come up to Simone de Beauvoir's anklebones: that damp sob sister, Hélène Cixous, with her diarrhea prose, or Luce

Irigaray, the pompous lap dog of Parisian café despots doing her grim, sledgehammer elephant walk through small points. American feminism is awash with soupy Campbellism: schlockmeisters like Marija Gimbutas, the Pollyanna of poppycock, with her Mommy goddess tales conveniently exalting her Lithuanian ancestors into world-class saintly pacifists. The chirpy warblers Gilbert-Gubar, those unlearned, unreadable bores, with their garbled, rumbling, hollow, rolling-trashcan style. Carolyn Heilbrun, Mrs. Fifties Tea Table, who spent her academic time, while my generation was breaking its head against social and sexual convention, spinning daydreams about a WASP persona, Amanda Cross, and who spoke out only when it was safe to do so. Heilbrun's late self-packaging as a feminist is a triumph of American commerce. The gauzy, ethnicity-evading style of her dazzlingly research-free books is the height of wishful, reactionary gentility. Women's studies is a jumble of vulgarians, bunglers, whiners, French faddicts, apparatchiks, doughface party-liners, pie-in-the-sky utopianists, and bullying, sanctimonious sermonizers. Reasonable, moderate feminists hang back and, like good Germans, keep silent in the face of fascism. For fifteen years, the established women academics irresponsibly let women's studies spread uncritiqued and unchecked (I call this period "While Vendler Slept"). Great women scholars like Jane Harrison and Gisela Richter were produced by the intellectual discipline of the masculine classical tradition, not by the wishy-washy sentimentalism of clingy, all-forgiving sisterhood, from which no first-rate book has yet emerged. Every year, feminists provide more and more evidence for the old charge that women can neither think nor write.

Most current academic leftism is specious, because post-Sixties liberalism is moribund. My anti-liberal position should not be mistaken for conservatism: I am radically pro-pornography, pro-prostitution, pro-abortion, and pro–legalization of drugs. The leftist attack on the traditional Western canon has primarily come from politically weak thinkers who are the product of English departments. Genuine Marxism, which I respect, requires accurate observation and rigorous economic analysis of present social conditions. The academic leftists merely parrot outworn formulas and slogans from the prewar era. It's a literary game, without the deep conviction of personal sacrifice. Gerald Graff's *Professing Literature* is most interesting and well-written when it is on the firm ground of the birth, development, and decline of New Criticism. But Graff's account of nineteenth-century classical education is appallingly deficient, full of coarse bias, selective use of evidence, and elementary errors in historical reasoning. Its major problem is its failure to consider, in due detail, the cultural transition from eighteenth-century Neoclassicism to Romanticism, in its several nineteenth-century phases. Graff's presentation of classics as dry, dead, and pointless is pure propaganda.

Richard Ohmann and Terry Eagleton are clear, vigorous, combative writers whom I take seriously and enjoy reading, even when I strongly disagree with their facts and conclusions. Both are good examples of the Marxism-that-isn't. Their picture of the contemporary world simply shows they do not live in it. Ohmann notes that he entered college in 1948 (a year after I was born). He has no understanding of the way mass media formed the imagination of my postwar generation. Protesting "the tyrannies of this culture," he urges us to overturn "bourgeois culture" and "the rule of our dominant classes." Condescension and paternalism mar his hoary, stereotypical portrait of the poor, passive, "powerless proletariat" helplessly manipulated by "the ruling class," the managerial oppressors coldly wielding their awful brainwashing tool, the media.[3] Ohmann is snobbishly scornful of the actual tastes of the very people he claims to speak for. Pop culture *is* mass culture. The people live in it and through it. By the electric nerve-reflex of commerce, television vividly speaks their thoughts and dreams, and with their own confident, aggressive energy, which so overwhelms and confuses bookish academics. Through mass media, African-Americans have revolutionized the arts and taken over the world stage. Ohmann's passing remark about Italians made my blood boil. His insulting, maudlin picture of the embarrassed Italian immigrant cowering in a World War One–era Shakespeare class and, because of "invincible ignorance," condemned to the humiliation of being "a laundress or parking attendant" shows just how delusional ivory-tower leftism gets.[4] The Italians I know came here, from

1895 to 1935, gung-ho for education; from Cincinnatus through Renaissance artisans to the present, Italians have believed in the nobility of physical labor; working-class people, unlike academics, love cars and like to be around them; laundry has a huge positive symbolism in Mediterranean culture, visible as early as Homer's Nausikaa episode and strikingly evident in stories from my family heritage. I could go on and on. Academic Marxism is a fantasy world, an unctuous compassion-sweepstakes, into which real workers or peasants never penetrate.

Terry Eagleton is a deft, witty summarizer of other people's ideas. Applied Marxism is, oddly, his weakest point. He also goes limply soft on academic feminism, whose bourgeois prudery, moralism, and Protestant word-fetishism he does not see. Eagleton's thought-provoking arguments against the canon are unfortunately vitiated by the fact the he seems to have little feeling for art. Is education to be gutted merely because Terry Eagleton wandered into a profession for which he discovered, too late, that he had minimal talent? Like Foucault, Eagleton continues to push into one new field after another, restlessly searching for success in something. He has certainly been successful in convincing literary critics that he is a Marxist. Sociologists and political scientists might think otherwise.

The signal failure of the academic Marxists is in their obliviousness to the transformations of modern labor. In the age of mass media, power has shifted its meaning and loci. Capitalism, whatever its problems, remains the most efficient economic mechanism yet devised to bring the highest quality of life to the greatest number. Because I have studied the past, I know that, in America and under capitalism, I am the freest woman in history. Unionized blue-collar jobs now routinely pay higher salaries than are earned by most teachers. Physical labor, as a concrete skill occupation, is free of the soul-destroying office politics suffered by the Marxists' demonized managerial class, who take their jobs home with them and are in a continual funk of anxiety and neurosis. Performance assessment at the top, as in academe, is a murky mire of words, gossip, connections, stroking, conspiracy, backstabbing. Unharried weekend leisure time is the center of working-class American life in ways the academic Marxists, resentfully marking papers and endlessly pressed for time, simply don't see. I have no idea what Eagleton's jobs were before Oxford, but while Ohmann was attending conferences and enjoying his tenure (received, he admits, before he became a Marxist), I was making ends meet by teaching Sophocles and Shakespeare to warmly receptive black and white factory workers in on-site night classes at the Sikorsky Aircraft plant a half hour away. So much for the irrelevance of the canon. The Marxists fail to see the simple archaic conservatism of the working class, as well as the endurance, worldwide, of its warrior code, an individual ethic, related to athletics, of courage, honor, and stoicism. Academic Marxism, based on neither observation nor experience, has turned into cocktail chat for the carriage trade.

I now address the graduate students. This is a time of enormous opportunity for you. There is an ossified political establishment of invested self-interest. Conformism and empty pieties dominate academe. Rebel. Do not read Lacan, Derrida, and Foucault, and treat as insignificant nothings those that still prate of them. You need no contemporaries to interpret the present for you. Born here, alive now, *you* are modernity. You are the living link between the past and future. Charge yourself with the high ideal of scholarship, connecting you to Alexandria and to the devoted, distinguished scholars who came before you. When you build on learning, you build on rock. You become greater by a humility toward great things. Let your work follow its own organic rhythm. Seek no material return from it, and it will reward you with spiritual gold. Hate dogma. Shun careerists. If you keep the faith, the gods may give you, at midlife, the sweet pleasure of seeing the hotshots who were so fast out of the gate begin to flag and sink, just as your studies are reaching their point of maturation. Among the many important messages coming from African-American culture is this, from a hit song by Midnight Star: "No parking, baby, no parking on the dance floor." All of civilized life is a dance, a fiction. You must learn the steps without becoming enslaved by them. Sitting out the dance is not an option.

The children of the Sixties have returned. Twenty years have passed, and many of us, through folly, hubris, or mischance, have died or been left sleeping in the land of the Lotus-eaters. The palace has been taken over by shallow upstarts, raiding and wasting the treasury laid up by so many noble generations. It's time to clean house.

NOTES

1. *Christianity, Social Tolerance, and Homosexuality: Gay People in Western Europe from the Beginning of the Christian Era to the Fourteenth Century* (Chicago, 1980), pp. 330–32.

2. "The Bondage and Freedom of Eros," June 1–7, 1990, pp. 571–73.

3. *English in America: A Radical View of the Profession* (New York, 1976), pp. 335, 65. *Politics of Letters* (Middletown, Conn., 1987), pp. 2, 12.

4. *Politics of Letters,* p. 14.

THE M.I.T. LECTURE:

CRISIS IN THE

AMERICAN UNIVERSITIES

Transcript of lecture given September 19, 1991, at the Massachusetts Institute of Technology in Cambridge. Introduction given by Kenneth Manning, Professor of the History of Science, on behalf of the Writing Program.

———

Thank you, Professor Manning, for that most gracious introduction. And may I say what a pleasure it is to be here, a mere *stone's throw* from Harvard.

I address you tonight after several sex changes and a great deal of ambiguity over sexual orientation over twenty-five years. I am the Sixties come back to haunt the present.

Now, speaking here at M.I.T. confronted me with a dilemma. I asked myself, should I try to act like a lady? I can do it. It's hard, it takes a lot out of me, I can do it for a few hours. But then I thought, *Naw*. These people, both my friends and my *enemies* who are here, aren't coming to see me act like a lady. So I thought I'd just be myself—which is, you know, abrasive, strident, and obnoxious. So then you all can go outside and say, "What a bitch!"

Now, the reason I'm getting so much attention: I think it's pretty obvious that we're in a time where there's a kind of impasse in contemporary thinking. And what I represent is independent thought. What I represent is the essence of the Sixties, which is free thought and free speech. And a lot of people don't like it. A lot of people who are well-meaning on both sides of the political spectrum want to shut down free speech. And my mission is to be absolutely as painful as possible in every situation.

So I've been attacking what I regard as the ideology of date rape. At the same time as I consider rape an outrage, I consider the propaganda and hysteria about date rape *equally* outrageous from the Sixties point of view, utterly reactionary from a Sixties point of view. And I will continue to attack it. And I will continue to attack the well-meaning people who think they're protecting women and in fact are infantilizing them. Right now in the current *SPIN*, I'm going after a few other things, like battered women and snuff films. And I'm going to be as painful as possible, until Gloria Steinem screams!

The problem of the last twenty years is that people think that "liberal" and "conservative" mean something. The liberal and conservative dichotomy is dead. The last time it was authentic was in the Fifties, when there really was an adversarial voice coming out of people I really respected, the New York Jewish intellectuals like Lionel Trilling and the people of *Partisan Review*. There was an authentic liberal versus conservative dichotomy at that time. But my generation of the Sixties, with all of our great ideals, destroyed liberalism, because of our excesses.

We have to face that. And we have to look for something new right now.

The situation right now is that we have on one side people who consider themselves leftists but to me, as far as academe is concerned, are phonies, people who have absolutely no credentials for political thinking, have no training in history, whose basic claim to politics is simply that nothing has happened to them in their lives. A lot of these people have money. I'm sick and tired of these New Historicists with trust funds. I'm so sick and tired of it. And because they're pampered, their whole lives have been comfortable, because they've kissed asses all the way to the top, they have to show they're authentic by pretending sympathy for the poor lower classes, the poor victims.

The whole thing is nothing but a literary game. I'm exposing it. And I'm exposing it from the inside. I attended a public university, Harpur College of the State University of New York at Binghamton, which was sort of like Berkeley East at that time, seething with real radicals. I know what *real* radicals look like—and they did not go on to graduate school. When I got to Yale for graduate school—I spent four years there and barely survived that experience—it was the last point that scholarship in literary studies was authentic, when it was solid. And it began to wander away from that base in the last twenty years. It's something I'm trying to reform at the present time.

What we have right now is this ridiculous situation where if you criticize liberals, people say, "She's a conservative!" Now, what kind of a lack of information is this about intellectual history? Liberalism is only 200 years old. There are other points of view on the world besides that of liberalism in its present decayed condition. We of the Sixties were often in revolt against liberals. Lenny Bruce, when he recited all those dirty words, was trying to offend liberals, not conservatives. So in the present situation I don't know what to call myself. I would maybe say "libertarian" or something like that. I'm trying to create a new system—I call it "Italian pagan Catholicism." But that may be too esoteric! I'm thinking that I want to bring about an enlightened center. I would like to call it, maybe, "pragmatic liberalism," that is, a liberalism that has learned the political lessons of the past twenty-five years.

What I don't like right now is that there's a kind of knee-jerk, intimidating way of calling someone "neoconservative" if they happen to criticize the liberal academic establishment—"Right, you're a neocon." Now, when people call *me* a neocon, what kind of idiots are they? I'm someone who is on the record as being pro-pornography—all the way through kiddie porn and snuff films. I'm pro-prostitution—I mean *really* pro, not just pro-prostitute and against prostitution. I'm pro-abortion, pro-homosexuality, pro–drag queens, pro–legalization of drugs. *This* is neoconservative? What kind of amateurishness is out there that people in the press—including *The Village Voice* and *Mother Jones* and things like that, which should be the voices of liberalism—what kind of stupid amateurish thinking is this to label me a neoconservative?

Now, this just shows you what's going on and why the situation is as bad as it is, because if people are trying to critique from within the academic establishment and they're getting tarred with the word "neoconservative," you keep on doing that long enough, people will get used to hearing it about themselves, and they will *become* conservative. We don't want that situation. My feeling is that a lot of people have been driven toward the neoconservative side by the failure of the liberal academic establishment to critique itself. So rather than blaming *The New Criterion* or Roger Kimball for all the problems of the world, it's time for the liberals of academe to critique themselves, to reform it from within. Over ten years ago it was obvious there was a problem, a terrible problem, but the academic establishment just sat on its duff, until the neoconservatives got hold of this issue. The reform of education is *not* a neoconservative issue! It is an issue facing the entire nation. So what I'm trying to do is to mobilize and radicalize the liberals who have been silent and who have let academe be taken over by these opportunists, these sickening, disgusting, ass-kissing opportunists.

Now, the enlightened center that I envision would mean that I want to pull back toward the middle the people who have drifted toward the neoconservative side. Because I think some of them are really not conservative. I think some of them can be pulled back, if there is an authentic debate within liberalism, an authentic self-critique of the academic establishment. At the same time, I want to awaken and bring out of their silence all kinds of vestiges of the Sixties that I know are out there. They're writing to me now. It's very moving to me to get the kinds of letters that I'm getting. Like when this huge, nasty exposé I wrote for *Arion* at Boston University came out, and the *San Francisco Examiner* magazine made it its cover story this summer. They asked me, by the way, "Would you pose as Madonna for our pages?" And I said, "No, but I'll do something just as good." So I posed in a purple miniskirt with a whip and chains in front of a porn store. I thought for San Francisco I should do that—make an extra effort!

So at any rate I got these wonderful moving letters from San Francisco and from the Bay Area—people who said that they were weeping, crying as they read my piece. They said that "for twenty years I've seen our Sixties ideals seem to be betrayed—I felt lost and uncentered—and when I read your piece I remember again the fire that we felt in the Sixties, I remember again what we were working for in the Sixties." Okay, so this is what I'm doing. I'm trying to bring back out of the woodwork all these Sixties people. Come out, come out, wherever you are! Come back. Take over the cultural center again! And as for the Lacan, Derrida, Foucault people, who needs them? Put them on an island and let them float out to sea. This is what *I* say!

I like very much Blake's idea of Innocence, Experience, and then Redeemed Innocence. And I think that's what happened here. We of the Sixties had wonderful ideals, but then we were very arrogant, and God knows—if you think I'm arrogant now— *ha*! I'm a shadow of my former self! My attitude was that of the Doors: "We want the world, we want it now!" Very impatient; very rude—I'm still rude. I mean, I really had to learn a lot of lessons. I had to learn political lessons. My generation failed in many ways. We have to *face* that, that we failed. That we had wonderful ideas but that we were naïve about the length of time it takes to effect institutional change. It was almost like a great wave came and knocked us down. It's like a great wave that just smashes you down. That's what I feel. I'm an astrologer—people don't mention this! I mean, everyone's attacked me for everything else. I mean, I'm an astrologer—it's right in my book. I *endorse* astrology. I believe in astrology. Will someone attack me for that? No!

So I believe in cycles, okay? And I think that the last twenty years have been *hell* for those of us of the Sixties. I mean, I feel that I've come back from the dead. Honestly, I feel that I in some sense died. I, like, hit the wall. All of us did, I think, in some way, from the Sixties, either from the drugs or from the sex, which led to the sexually transmitted diseases of today. People don't want to talk about this. They want to say, "No, there's no connection between behavior and the sexual diseases of today." But please, let's not be stupid. Let's not rewrite history. There is a terrible reality which we must face. I've said it again and again: "Everyone who preached free love in the Sixties is responsible for AIDS." And we must accept moral responsibility for it. This idea that it was somehow an accident, a historical accident, a microbe that sort of fell from heaven—absurd. We must *face* what we did.

With me it wasn't sex, it wasn't drugs, with me it was challenging authority and just being absolutely *impossible* in every situation. And I just had to learn my lessons. My career has been a disaster, an absolute disaster. I could not get hired *anywhere*. There was no university that would hire me. And I've been teaching at art schools for twenty years. Now, as the Rolling Stones say, "You can't always get what you want, but you sometimes get what you need." So that's how I feel. Having worked at art schools for twenty years, I feel how fortunate I am because I have been spared all these poisons that have swept over the Ivy League and so on, and I've been dealing directly with artists, rather than people from prep schools. You know, when I have to cross the river in Philadelphia and use the library at Penn, and I hear those voices, those prep-school voices—well, let me tell you! You know, the kind of students I have are poor, they have a talent, often they are Hispanic or African-American dancers who come out of poor neighborhoods, who've been given scholarships and so on. I have them in my classes. I have enormous rapport with them and love of them, and I feel how lucky I am to have this kind of direct experience.

Whereas people like, um, Stanley Fish—whom I call "a totalitarian Tinkerbell"—that's what I call him. Uh-huh. Okay? How *dare* he? What a hypocrite! People at Duke telling us about multiculturalism—those people who have never had anyone outside of a prep school in their classes. It's unbelievable—the preaching! That whole bunch of people at Duke—all of them in flight from their ethnicity—every one of them—trying to tell us about the problem of the old establishment. The problem with the old establishment was that it was WASP. So what's the answer to that? Be *ethnic!* Okay? Every one of them—every one of them—look at the style that they write—this kind of gameplaying, slick, cerebral style. Those people have an identity problem!

So, at any rate, my career has been a disaster. And before my book was finally published at Yale Press, it was rejected by seven New York publishers, I could not get published throughout the Seventies and Eighties, I was completely poor. For the first time in my adult life I'm out of debt as of three months ago. I've been on the unemployment line. I have taught in factories. I'm probably the only major voice right now in academe who's actually taught factory workers. As opposed to these people who are the Marxists [*makes prancing, dancing, hair-preening gestures*], oh yes, these Marxists, like Terry Eagleton at Oxford. Do you know what he makes? Do you know the *salary* that man makes? Oh, it just disgusts me. This is why he has to wear blue jeans, to show, "Oh, no, I don't have the money." These people are hypocrites! They really are. It's all a literary game. There's no authentic self-sacrifice, no direct actual experience of workers or working-class people. It's appalling, the situation. It's everywhere, it's everywhere in the Ivy League.

Now, one of the reasons I'm so angry. I really went on the warpath last year, especially about feminism. I consider myself a feminist. I began my revolt when I was just a little child. I was born in the late Forties. And I absolutely could not *stand* the way the culture demanded that women be feminine. I did not relate to my sex role *at all.* I have been a totally alienated sexual being since I was a tiny child. And it began with dolls—this was the thing—*dolls*! My parents learned soon enough not to give me dolls—they knew I didn't want them. But I think my first experiences of social alienation would have been when we would go visiting or something, and people would say, "Oh, a cute little girl is coming. We'll get a cute little doll for the cute little girl." And so my parents wanted me to be polite, you know, they trained me to be polite, and so these horrible surreal scenes would happen, where I would be surrounded by all these, like, glowing, smiling, ten adult faces smiling at me and handing me this lump of humanoid rubber and expecting me to be glad about it, and I would just think, "*What* am I going to do with *this?—UGH!*" And meanwhile I have to smile—and this is when I knew I didn't fit in, okay?

You know, I'm really happy there wasn't all this talk about sex changes back then, since I probably would have gotten this fantasy that I was a man born wrongly in a woman's body, and I think I might very well have become obsessed with the idea of a sex change, which would have been a terrible mistake. Because I think I absolutely am a woman, but I was just a woman born ahead of my time. I was a kind of pioneer, and decade by decade I've acclimated myself to my sex role—thanks to my friendships with gay men and drag queens! Drag queens have influenced me enormously. Their analysis of the mythology of male and female, and the theater of gender and so on, I've absolutely taken into myself. I used to be—"tomboy" would be underestimating the word. I was an Amazon, an *Amazon* when I was very young. I mean, I was just so—People *remember* this. I mean, before feminism was, Paglia was! Out there punching and kicking and fighting with people. No one understood what I was doing, but from my earliest years I had this burning desire to *do* something for women, to do something *so massive* for women, to demonstrate that women should be taken seriously.

So by the time I got to college, I had been thinking about sex for *years*. I always had a scholarly turn of mind. I wanted to be an archaeologist early on. I think that that is one of the things that separates me from others in literary studies today. My sense of time-frame is so vast compared to that of people in English departments. When I think about sex, when I think about *anything* in culture, I'm thinking about a 10,000-year time span, you see, and this is what causes a communication problem with feminists, because most of them, as far as I can see, tend to have their specialties in the late eighteenth century or following. There are a few who have training earlier, but they tend to be very narrowly focused even in that one area. I think my broad expanse of learning and my already world-consciousness—coming from my early passion, when I was, like, *four* practically, to be an Egyptologist— I was just fascinated with Egypt and began studying it very early on—I think that huge time-frame that I have has been enormously advantageous. And it's one of the reasons, again, why I'm not understood by feminists, though I *am* understood by historians. The fan letters—I mean, it's absurd—the fan letters that I get from historians, from political scientists, from philosophers, from art historians, and so on and so forth. The bunkers are just the literature departments and the feminists—they're all in league with each other: "Oh, no, she's *horrible*! She's horrible!" Why? Because I'm challenging the scholarship of everything. I'm challenging *their* scholarship, which I think is absolutely amateurish. It will not serve women to base a sex theory on shoddy scholarship. We cannot *have* this. We cannot have this second-rateness. It's epidemic everywhere.

Let me just continue with my little overview here. There was a point where feminism and I agreed. I was thirteen though. It was 1960, okay? That was a time when I said, "Men are terrible. The sexes are the same. Men must change. Society must change. And all the problems between the sexes are coming from the fact that men are so awful." I was thirteen! That's an unevolved position. It's thirty years later, girls! Let us move *on*! Oh, *God*! So I continued studying and, at this point, I became notorious in Syracuse, New York, where I was going to high school, for my Amelia Earhart obsession. The newspaper actually reported this. For three years—this looks forward to *Sexual Personae*—for three years, I did this Amelia Earhart research. The biographer of Amelia Earhart told me I had done more research in the primary sources than *he* had! I spent every Saturday in the bowels of the public library going through all these materials, old magazines and newspapers, before microfilm. Everything was falling to pieces. I probably destroyed the whole collection! I was covered with grime. Amelia Earhart to me was an image of everything a woman should be. It remains that for me. Amelia Earhart, my obsession. She is woman alone. Not woman hand-holding in a group and whining about men. Woman *alone*! Okay, all right? Woman goes up in the plane. If she crashes, she doesn't go, "You *men* did this to me!" She knows that *she* is responsible. It's *her* skill, *her* preparation. And then nature. Something that's not in her control can be her opponent: *nature*!

No one wants to talk about *nature* now. Meanwhile, the entire student population of the world is thinking about nature, the environment, they're thinking globally, but our faculty are off in their little corners talking about social constructionism. They haven't thought about nature in twenty years, okay, they are *so* behind. You mention the mere word "nature"—"*Essentialism!*" That's *it*. What—? I *mean*—! The thing about the Sixties is that we had a comprehensive world-view. We saw the injustices of society, and we wanted to remedy them. We focused our negative energy against society to change it. At the same time we saw the enormity of nature. And we *honored* the enormity of nature. It is appalling, the situation now, that you could *think* about talking about sex without thinking about nature. That you could claim that you are an expert in gender without knowing about hormones! The contempt for science that's going on among humanists is contemptible.

My idea of an integration between science and the arts goes way back to my earliest years. There was a doctor, a Jewish refugee in my hometown of Endicott, New York, Dr. Julius Gattner. He had fled from Hitler. One of my earliest memories is his office. It was a kind of replication of the great culture of the late nineteenth century, the comprehensive culture of German philology that I still esteem. You went to his office, and while you were waiting there were pedestals, Greek columns, with Chinese vases on them. Then inside the office—he would be in his white coat—there'd be the medical instruments, and there were also glass-paneled furniture and books with beautiful bindings. Behind his desk was a bust in black of the *Hermes* of Praxiteles. This is like Freud, you see. It's this combination of the sciences plus the arts. "Impossible," you say, today? "Impossible—we're too specialized for that, we're too expert." No, this is *exactly* what we need. We have to bring this back, this idea of all of culture integrated. This is what we must do for the next generation of students. We *must* do this. We must make radical reforms of undergraduate and graduate education, to give students this kind of comprehensive vision of culture.

Back to Amelia Earhart and so on. Okay, so meanwhile, I get to college. I'm, like, the only feminist. People never saw a feminist before. I was already out there. By the time Betty Friedan's book came out, I was already out there doing all this obnoxious stuff. By the time I got Simone de Beauvoir's book, I was sixteen. I read that, and I thought, "*Yes!* Yes! Instead of writing a book on Amelia Earhart, I will write a mega-book that will take *everything* in." So there's the birth, you see, of *Sexual Personae.*

So by the time the feminist movement broke out in 1969, as an outgrowth of the Sixties, I had so evolved in my thinking because I was in a scholarly way studying the evidence of world history and world culture. To talk about sex, you must do that. You must take personal responsibility for your research. This idea that somehow sex-theory was born from the head of Athena in 1969—"Boom!"—like that—and no one's worth reading before 1969—this is *ridiculous!* Because there was nothing for me to read—thank *God* there wasn't all this women's studies crap for me to read. I instead went about systematically absorbing a hundred years of the history of psychology. The idea that all of that is irrelevant is so stupid! Beginning with Krafft-Ebing and Freud and Karen Horney, Melanie Klein, Ferenczi—I mean, there are so many of them—all of the papers of psychoanalysis in the journals and so on. I absorbed all of that. It's fantastic. It is not completely vestigial stuff that we have to keep in the archives of the library. This was work by people who were learned, who had a sense of history. The disaster of women's studies today is that women are being prevented from understanding that there's a hundred-year history of sex-theory, sex-commentary. Instead they're being forced to read these very narrowly trained contemporary women. And most of it is *junk*! It's *junk*! It's appalling!

One of the main reasons that I am so angry is that last year at the University of Pennsylvania I went to a lecture—and I'm going to start identifying her. I haven't for a year, but I just spilled the beans to a Cornell magazine, so I might as well keep doing it. It was Diana Fuss of Princeton, a very prominent feminist theorist. She seems to be a very nice woman. This is the *pity* of it! She was such a nice woman. I had never heard of her, I didn't know her. I went to this lecture and I thought, "This is *awful*, what is happening here!" A lecture hall filled with young women from the University of Pennsylvania, okay, and this Diana Fuss, this really nice, very American kind of a woman—we're not talking, like, cosmopolitan here, and I mean cosmopolitan with a small *c*!—what she did was show a series of slides that she had made of contemporary ads and pictorials from *Harper's Bazaar* and so on.

Let me tell the full story of what happened that night. Now, normally if you're in a boring lecture, you can, like, tune out. You know, you can plan your meals, do your laundry in your head, and things like that, okay? In this case, it was *torture* to me, because she was showing these *gorgeous* pictures up on the screen, beautiful pictures that were stimulating the mind, stimulating the imagination, you understand? And at the same time she was *trashing* these pictures with this horrible Lacan, labyrinthine thing. So I was just out of my—I was out of control. People turned around and said "*Shh!*" to me. I was *writhing* in my seat [*imitates electrocution-like spasms*]. It was *awful*. Let me give you an example. There was a Revlon ad of a woman in a blue pool of water, and she was beautifully made up, and there was obviously a reflector being used to shine the sunlight especially intensely on her face. This was a beautiful ad. And Diana Fuss was going, "Decapitation—mutilation."

Then there was a beautiful picture from *Harper's Bazaar*, I think, of a black woman wearing a crimson turtleneck. But instead of the collar turned over, you know, it was up like this, around the chin. It was very beautiful. It was like a flower. And she was wearing aviator glasses that I recognized, from the 1930s!

Now Diana Fuss said, "She's blinded." *I* would have said, "She has mystic vision." Anyway, with the turtleneck, what do you think? "Strangulation, bondage!" It went on like this, picture after picture after picture. I thought, "This is *psychotic*." Such radical misinterpretation of reality is psychotic. But it's a whole system. Psychosis is a system. People within that system feel it's very rational.

Now, what I hated about this was you had two hundred young women, who didn't understand a *word* of what she was saying—it was all that Lacan gibberish—and they're all going, "Ohhh, *wow*! The woman from Princeton—a big woman from Princeton. She's so brilliant!" And I thought, "This is *evil*." Diana Fuss is not evil. She's a nice woman. But if what you're *doing* is evil, I'm sorry, it has to *stop*. This is perverted. It really is perverted. When you destroy young people's ability to take pleasure in beauty, you are a pervert! So I stood up, I was very agitated— and she was such a good sport. I mean, here was this maniac she never heard of, my book had just come out, and I was waving my arms around. I said I didn't mean to condemn her, because I understood that what she was doing was the result of ten years of feminists doing this. But nevertheless, I asked, why is it, why is it that feminists have so much trouble dealing with beauty and pleasure, I said, to which gay men have made such *outstanding* cultural contributions? *Why*—if gay men can respond? This is why I get along so well with gay men, and I don't get along with lesbian feminists. This is why my sexuality is a complete neuter! I don't fit in anywhere! I'm like this wandering being, the Ancient Mariner—it's just awful.

So anyway, afterwards I went down to speak to Diana Fuss because I wanted to find out how much she knows about art, because she's a product of English departments. And I spoke to her a little bit, and I could see she knew nothing about art. And I also could tell she knew nothing about popular culture. Now you see the problem here. You cannot just suddenly open a magazine and look at a picture of a nude woman and then free associate, using Lacan. You cannot do that! Because fashion magazines are part of the history of art. These are great photographers, great stylists—and gay men have made enormous contributions to fashion photography. Anyway, I made a huge statement that night—the whole audience gasped. I went, "The history of fashion photography from 1950 to 1990 is one of the great moments in the history of art!" And everyone went, "*How* can you *say* that?" Because obviously fashion is an oppression of women.

And beauty, according to, um, Miss, um, Naomi Wolf, is a heterosexist conspiracy by men in a room to keep feminism back—and all that *crap* that's going on. I call her, by the way, "Little Miss Pravda." She and I are head to head on MTV this week, in case you want to know! But I won't appear with her. *Oprah*'s tried to get me on with her: I won't go on with her. A talk show in Italy wanted to fly me over to appear with her. *No.* I always say, "Would Caruso appear with Tiny Tim?" If you want to see what's wrong with Ivy League education, look at *The Beauty Myth*, that book by Naomi Wolf. This is a woman who graduated from Yale magna cum laude, is a Rhodes scholar, and cannot write a coherent paragraph. This is a woman who cannot do historical analysis, and she is a Rhodes scholar? If you want to see the damage done to intelligent women today in the Ivy League, look at that book. It's a *scandal*. Naomi Wolf is an intelligent woman. She has been ill-served by her education. But if you read Lacan, this is the result. Your brain turns to pudding! She has a case to make. She cannot make it. She's full of paranoid fantasies about the world. Her education was completely removed from reality.

Now, I want to totally reform education, so that we get really first-rate, top-level intellectual work by women. We're not going to get it. There's a lost generation of women coming out of these women's studies programs—a lost generation. If you spend your whole time reading Gilbert-Gubar, Hélène Cixous, and all the rest of that French *rot*—thank God, I didn't have that. Thank God, I had only men and Simone de Beauvoir— and Jane Harrison and Gisela Richter. There were great women writers as well, great women scholars. I held myself to *the highest standards*. I didn't say, we're going to make new standards, women's standards, and give us women's awards, the women's sweepstakes, and all that stuff. No one takes women's work seriously

right now. Do you think that men take it seriously? Do you think
anyone reads Gilbert-Gubar? I mean, who reads Gilbert-Gubar?
or Carolyn Heilbrun, that mediocre, genteel crap, coming from
a woman who's Jewish and who is still writing in a genteel style.
This is feminism? *This* is feminism? This is third-rate, tenth-rate
stuff. It's appalling that our young women are being assigned to
read things like Lacan when they're sophomores and haven't read
Freud. What good does it do to read Lacan if you haven't read
Freud? All of Lacan is just a commentary on Freud. This is
ridiculous. It's a *horrible* situation. We need massive reform,
at every level.

Now back to my little survey here. So by the time the wom-
en's movement broke forth in 1969, it was practically impossible
for me to be reconciled with my "sisters." And there were, like,
screaming fights. The big one was about the Rolling Stones. This
was where I realized—this was 1969—boy, I was bounced *fast*,
right out of the movement. And I had this huge argument. Because I said you cannot apply a political agenda to art. When it
comes to art, we have to make other distinctions. We had this
huge fight about the song "Under My Thumb." I said it was a
great song, not only a great song but I said it was a work of art.
And these feminists of the New Haven Women's Liberation Rock
Band went into a rage, surrounded me, practically spat in my
face, literally my back was to the wall. They're screaming in my
face:"Art? Art? Nothing that demeans women can be art!" There
it is. *There it is!* Right from the start. The fascism of the contemporary women's movement.

Feminism is 200 years old. Ever since Mary Wollstonecraft
wrote that manifesto in 1790. It's 200 years old. It's had many
phases. We can criticize the present phase without necessarily
criticizing feminism, I want to save feminism from the feminists.
What I identify with is the prewar feminism of Amelia Earhart,
of Katharine Hepburn—who had an enormous impact on me—
that period of women where you had independence, self-reliance,
personal responsibility, and not blaming other people for your
problems. I want to bring that back. And my life has been a good
example of it. Because my career was a disaster, but I did not
blame it on anyone. I took personal responsibility for my own

work. If I could not be published in my own lifetime, I would leave it beyond the grave, as Emily Dickinson did, and torture people in the next life!

So in 1969 I saw immediately—and still we have this problem, twenty years down the line from the birth of contemporary feminism—that there are two huge areas that feminism has excluded that need to be integrated within it. That's what I'm doing. That's my contribution. One of them that was excluded was aesthetics. Right from the start there was a problem with aesthetics, a difficulty with dealing with beauty and with art. If you think that's an old problem, it isn't. The present prominence of Naomi Wolf and her book indicates that what I'm criticizing is still a contemporary problem. The accolades on the back of that book from leading feminists, including Germaine Greer— who said, "This is the most important book—since my *own* book!"—show that that's still an issue.

So: aesthetics. Because one of my earliest faculties was my responsiveness to beauty. I think it may be something innate in Italians, I honestly think it may be. There's an art thing, an art gene that we've got. Early on, I was in love with beauty. I don't feel *less* because I'm in the presence of a beautiful person. I don't go [*imitates crying and dabbing tears*], "Oh, I'll *never* be that beautiful!" What a ridiculous attitude to take!—the Naomi Wolf attitude. When men look at sports, when they look at football, they don't go [*crying*], "Oh, I'll *never* be that fast, I'll *never* be that strong!" When people look at Michelangelo's *David*, do they commit suicide? No. See what I mean? When you see a strong person, a fast person, you go, "Wow! That is fabulous." When you see a beautiful person: "How beautiful." That's what I'm bringing back to feminism. You go, "What a beautiful person, what a beautiful man, what a beautiful woman, what beautiful hair, what beautiful boobs!" Okay, now I'll be charged with sexual harassment, probably. I won't even be able to get out of the room!

We should not have to apologize for reveling in beauty. Beauty is an eternal human value. It was not a trick invented by nasty men in a room someplace on Madison Avenue. I say in *Sexual Personae* that it was invented in Egypt. For 3,000 years at the height of African civilization you had a culture based on beauty. We have two major cultures in the world today, France and Japan, organized around the idea of beauty. It is *so* provincial, feminism's problem with beauty. We have *got* to get over this. Obviously, any addiction—like if you're addicted to plastic surgery—that's a problem. Of course it's a problem. Addiction to anything is a problem. But this blaming anorexia on the media—this is Naomi's thing—oh *please!* Anorexia is coming out of these white families, these pushy, perfectionist white families, who all end up with their daughters at Yale. Naomi arrives in England, and "Gee, all the women Rhodes scholars have eating disorders. Gee, it must be . . . *the media!*" Maybe it's that *you* are a parent-pleasing, teacher-pleasing little kiss-ass! Maybe you're a *yuppie!* Maybe *you*, Miss Yuppie, have figured out *the system*. Isn't it interesting that Miss Naomi, the one who has succeeded in *the system*, the one who has been given the prizes by the system, she who is the princess of the system, *she's* the one who's bitchin' about it? *I'm* the one who's been poor and rejected—shouldn't *I* be the one bitching about it? *No*—because I'm a scholar, okay, and she's a twit!

The second area where feminism is deficient is in its psychology. Right from the start, Kate Millett banned Freud as a sexist. And so we have this horror that has arisen over the last twenty years of feminism trying to build a sex theory without Freud, one of the greatest masters, one of the great analysts of human personality in history. Now, you don't have to *assent* to Freud. I don't read Freud and go, "Oh, wow, he is the ultimate word in the human race"—that's not how I *read!* I follow him, and I go, "This is interesting. Now maybe he needs to be supplemented." So I'll supplement from wherever—a little bit from Jung, a little bit from Frazer, whom I very much admire, sometimes from astrology. I mean, I find all kinds of things everywhere. Soap opera—I love soap opera—Lana Turner—I'll take it from anywhere. I've very syncretic. I'm very eclectic. But I mean Freud has to be the *basis* of any psychology. We should be reading him first, not these minor women, and build up from there. All this obsession with "Well, did you read Jeffrey Masson's thing on the seduction theory?" Oh, please, who *cares?* All this "Let's unmask Big Daddy"—this obsession with the weaknesses

of big figures. This is infantile. It's infantile. You read major
figures not because everything they say is the gospel truth but
because they expand your imagination, they expand your I.Q.,
okay, they open up brain cells you didn't even know you have.

So we have these two large areas: we have aesthetics missing
from contemporary feminism and we have psychology. It's an
incoherent psychology right now. Another thing, I feel, and others
might not agree, is that its politics is also naïve, a politics which
blames all human problems on white male imperialists who have
victimized women and people of color. This view of history is
coming from people who know nothing about history. Because
when you think of the word "imperialist," if you automatically
just think "America," then you don't know anything. Because
someone who's studied the history of ancient Egypt knows that
imperialism was practically invented in Egypt and in the ancient
Near East. If you want to talk about imperialism, let's talk about
Japan or Persia or all kinds of things. It's not just a white
male monopoly.

What we need, you see, is really systematic training in political science and history. It's obvious there's a need for this now.
There was, following the Sixties, an appetite for history, but the
people in academe were not willing to do the work necessary to
master history and anthropology and so on. Instead, it was sort
of like, "Hey, we need history! Let's see. Oh—there's Foucault!"
It was sort of like that. It's sort of like ducks when they're born—
the first thing they see, you know? So if they see a vacuum cleaner,
they think it's their mother. They'll follow the vacuum cleaner.
That's what happened. Foucault is the vacuum cleaner that
everyone followed.

All I can say is thank God, by the time Lacan and Foucault
appeared on the cultural landscape, I had already done all my
preparations. I had been reading very deeply not only in college
but especially during graduate school in the Yale library, so by
the time they arrived I was intellectually prepared to see how
specious they are. And therefore it never affected me. And now,
of course, there are people who spent twenty years of their lives
on these characters, and now, of course, they're a little irritated
when someone says, "Oh, that was a waste." It's sort of like a

period where people were told, because they had no taste of their own, that they should furnish their house in zebra Naugahyde furniture. So they went heavily into this, okay, their whole house is furnished in it. Then suddenly, twenty years down the road, someone like me appears and says, "Guess what—that's *out* now. Not only that, but it was in terrible taste to begin with." So you can see why they're mad at me. They're mad because they're stuck with that furniture! They have twenty years of furniture!

But time for something *new*. I think, you know, that there's something happening. I can really feel it. Like for twenty years, no one would listen to me. I just hit a wall. No one heard what I was saying, no one understood anything about what my book was doing, people just looked at me with blank faces. And suddenly people are listening. It's not me that's changed. The culture is changing. Something is happening. It's a twenty-year astrological cycle that's happening. I was very moved, a few months ago—Arsenio had on the Fifth Dimension, reunited! The Fifth Dimension, which had quarreled, the catfights, all that, they had reunited, and they were singing "Aquarius" on *Arsenio*! I was very moved! I said, "Something is happening. The Sixties are coming back." Some of the lines of that song I really identify with: "The mind's true liberation." This is what I stand for: "The mind's true liberation."

And unfortunately what's happening today, with this kind of very sanctimonious and sermonizing talk about sex that's coming out of the rape counselors and so on, people do not realize, with all their good intentions, how oppressive this is to sex, what a disaster this is to the mind, what a disaster this is to the spirit, to allow the rape counselors to take over the cultural stage. Now the work that they do is good, and it's wonderful that they're there. But we cannot have this scenario being projected of male rapaciousness and brutality and female victimage. We have *got* to make women realize they are *responsible*, that sexuality is something that belongs to them. They have an enormous power in their sexuality. It's up to them to use it correctly and to be wise about where they go and what they do. And I'm accused of being "anti-woman" because of this attitude? Because I'm bringing common sense back to the rape discourse?

Now when people say to me, "Oh, you're always talking about feminists as if they're monolithic. We're not monolithic. We're very pluralistic. We have so many different views." No, excuse me: the date-rape issue shows that I am correct. Because there is *one voice* speaking about date rape from coast to coast, *one voice*, one stupid, shrewish, puritanical, sermonizing, hysterical voice. And where are all these sophisticated feminists supposedly out there? Where *are* they? Totally impotent, locked in their little burrows wherever they are, whether they're in the East Village or Harvard. Wherever they are, they're impotent. There's not one voice raised to bring some sense into this hysteria. Now, I am an experienced teacher. I sympathize with the problems of freshmen, and so I believe that date-rape awareness is an excellent thing to do when students arrive, not only for the men, to warn the men that breaches of civilized behavior will not be tolerated, but also to warn the women, because unfortunately to me what's happening is that we have a white middle-class problem. I don't notice so many Hispanic women and African-American women going around and carrying on like this.

Like just this weekend—I'm getting so sick and tired, so nauseated by what's been happening—down in Philadelphia, where I work at the University of the Arts, there were two incidents at Temple University, and I think they're just a disgrace to women, these incidents—*as reported*—we don't know what really happened. The girl has met the guy once before, this is the second time she met him, they were at a party, she invites him back to her room, its three A.M., she falls asleep, and then suddenly something happens, and she charges him with rape. Now, pardon me, wake up to reality! This is a ridiculous situation. If a real rape occurs, I will help to lynch the guy from the nearest tree. I will be absolutely ferocious. I will get my switchblade knife—given to me by a reporter, by the way!—I will help track down the rapist and punish him. But this sort of thing is disastrous. We cannot have this, these white middle-class girls coming out of pampered homes, expecting to do whatever they want. They don't understand what's going on, that there's a sexual content to their behavior, that maybe there's a subliminal sexuality, a provocativeness in their behavior. "Don't say 'provoc-

ative'! Because then you're *blaming the victim!*" Well, women will
never be taken seriously until they accept full responsibility for
their sexuality.

We have got to let the mind open *freely*, freely toward sex,
and understand that from the moment you're on a date with a
man, the idea of sex is *hovering* in the air—*hover, hover, hover*, okay?
I'll tell you what *I'm* bringing back. I'm bringing back *lust!* A
friend of mine, Robert Caserio, said in a recent lecture at Ann
Arbor, "There's a lot of talk about gender on campus these days,
but not much about sex." And he said there's a kind of "antisepsis
in the classroom." And I think this is really true. There's a real
Puritanism about the way sex is being discussed and "managed"
in the current ideology of women's studies. Now, you know that
recent song, "Sadeness," from the Euro-pop disco album by
Enigma. There's another great song on there, "The Principles of
Lust." And I thought, "*Yes*, that's what I'm doing in my work."
I am discovering and articulating the principles of lust.

And lust should be a positive force. It should not be something that *men* are directing toward *us*—"Yuk! Pooh!" It shouldn't
be like that. So I am *proud* to be in the current *Playboy*. Yes, I am.
I am proud to be there, okay, I am proud to be next to the section, "Women of the Big Ten." People say to me, "Oh, you must
be against *Playboy* taking pictures of women on campus," and I
say, "Not at all! If *Playboy* is kidnapping women to photograph them, then I will help you lynch the people from *Playboy*.
But as long as women want to pose, I applaud it." It's nice to
see a bosom that's not amplified with silicone, it's nice to see it.
[*Imitates leafing through magazine*] "Mmm—they look good to *me!*"
I'm proud to be there, very proud. And *Penthouse* will be next!

I'm pro-pornography. I feel *that* was the liberation of the
Sixties. And it's been *lost*. I feel that the sexual ideology of current
feminism is reactionary and repressive and puritanical and pho-
bic. And it's being produced by many of these women who have
succeeded, you see, in the women's studies programs and who
don't understand the degree to which their own careerism, their
own opportunism is enwrapped with these ideas. They don't
understand. They're not sophisticated women, many of them.
They're not. They're not cosmopolitan women. To talk about

sex, you have to know about literature and art. Literature and art are the best way into the psychology of mankind, because of the ambiguity and mystery. Because that is where you feel the flux, the *flux* of our sexual desire, the way our spirit is not in these rigid categories of oppressor and victim. Everything is flowing. Fantasy and imagination and all these things, they're always flowing. That's why Freud has been so useful for me, because of the way he is able to study the dream process and to find words to articulate these ambiguous nonverbal phenomena. It's a very, very good exercise for anyone trying to talk about sex. So the present situation is just appalling—just appalling. The language that is being used by these people, the way social-welfare issues have taken over the agenda. We cannot have this.

What's happening on campus is—I started feeling it twenty years ago, actually, the way the campus in America was drifting away from intellectual life, the way the campus was becoming a summer camp, the way the universities were beginning to focus their strategies on getting parents to pay money to send their children there, so we're going to give the kids "*a nice experience.*" So now, you see, the Student Services departments are taking over. This is leading to the speech codes and so on: "Oh, my God, we can't have a child coming here, with someone *paying* for them to come here, and then for them to hear a nasty thing about them! We must *squelch* that." The universities must be centered around the idea of intellectual discourse, intellectual inquiry. We cannot have any speech codes. This is absurd.

And you know what's so ridiculous about this is that these people want "multiculturalism," they want to talk about various ethnic groups. At the same time they want to deny there's any difference between those ethnic groups. This is insane! It's illogical. It's incoherent. If you're going to have the ethnic groups and if you're going to draw a firm line separating those groups, then surely those groups have characteristics that separate them and that should be the subject of comment. But *no*—the amnesiac liberal establishment wants to draw lines and erase all of our mental life within those lines. It's appalling. It's appalling. It has to stop.

So anyway I believe, you know, that we should be as nasty

as possible, at all times! It serves *nothing* to just try to squelch speech. It changes no one's opinion of anything. Now, I am Italian—*very* Italian. I'm so Italian that this has crippled me in my advance in academe. I noticed this early on, even while in college—although I had a wonderful experience in college. Wherever I'm surrounded by Jews I'm happy—it was a very Jewish college. It was, like, eighty percent poor New York Jews from downstate, and I just feel very happy around Jews because they respect my mind. My mentors have always been Jews, Harold Bloom and so on, and they're the only ones who can tolerate my personality! But at any rate, when I got to Yale . . . whoah! culture shock! Because I saw the way the WASP establishment had the Ivy League in a death grip. In order to rise in academe, you have to adopt this WASP style. It's very laid-back. Now, I really can't do it, but I call it "walking on eggs at the funeral home." You have to talk like this [*lowers voice to unctuous, monotonous whisper*], you have to talk as passionlessly as possible, you have to be totally blank and very decorous and never crack a joke. *Whimsy* is permitted. No belly laughs!

Now, I'm *loud*. Did you notice? I'm very loud. I've had a hell of a time in academe. This is why I usually get along with African-Americans. I mean, when we're together, "Whooo!" It's like I feel totally *myself*—we just let everything go! It's like *energy*. This was the Sixties: energy. *Energy* was the Sixties! Now I really hit the wall of academe, boy, because no one could take me seriously. First of all, a fast-talking woman? Joan Rivers made my life a lot easier, when she appeared on the scene. Now when I talk, people go, "Oh, Joan Rivers." Before, they went, "Whoah—*freak!*" And, you see, people would discriminate against me because they thought, "Well, a fast-talking, little woman. She can't be serious." Because, you know, to be a deep thinker you have to be *slow*. So you'd notice this—like the men at Yale were slow. You'd ask them a question and—[*long pause, staring*]. I could write a chapter in the time it takes them to answer a question!

So at any rate, my ambition as a Sixties person was to utterly transform academe and bring this kind of ethnic intensity and passion to academe. And I flunked miserably. I really was just *crushed.* I saw many of my peers at Yale graduate school sail onward and upward to big positions where they all are now, at Johns Hopkins and Harvard and Berkeley and Chicago, and they're just up there at the very top of the profession. And meanwhile I was totally invisible, as obliterated in my own time as I could have been. But I accepted this. I *accepted* this. Emily Dickinson's example really was very inspiring to me, you see, because she was not published in her own time. Her few poems that managed to get published, they doctored. They altered the rhyme or tried to smooth them out and so on, and she was appalled by that and never put her poems out to be published again. But she never swerved from her vision of her own voice. And so she died, and they found all these poems in the bureau drawer. And then, *because* she never swerved from her vision, a hundred years later we read her and now we, her true contemporaries, understand her. So I thought this was going to be my fate. And the point is, a scholar should prepare for the future. A scholar should write for the future, not for the present. See, the problem of the last twenty years is that we have these careerist academics who are simply trying to maneuver for position *now* and who are writing things for consumption *now.* That is not scholarship. That's, like, advertising. And it's *bad* advertising.

So—[*looks at watch*] oh, I'd better keep on moving here, or otherwise this is going to be like *The Exterminating Angel*—you know that movie where guests arrive at a dinner party and can't leave? Here's a major point I want to make. *The New Criterion* has come into being and has flourished due to the failure of academic leftism in this area of aesthetics. People keep thinking of it in political terms. Hilton Kramer was an *art critic*. See what I'm saying? The vacuum around aesthetics in academic liberalism has produced *The New Criterion.* Now I want the liberals to start thinking in these terms. Instead of saying, "Oh, those awful people in *Commentary* and *The New Criterion,*" start saying, "What have *we* done? What have we *failed* to do that has produced this reaction to the right?" And until the liberals begin to critique themselves and to take control of academe and to admit their sins and to atone for them, the neoconservatives will continue to flourish, which is not good. We cannot have a situation where the neoconservatives are writing literate, lucid, learned prose and you have the leftists writing garbled, labyrinthine *junk*. As long as that goes on, okay, the neoconservatives *deserve to win*!

[*voice calls out from audience*] What's my sign? Who asked that? Who asked that question? I'm an Aries. What do you *think*? Bette Davis, Joan Crawford—*please*!

Now for a series of minor points. The idea that feminism is the first group that ever denounced rape is a gross libel to men. Throughout history, rape has been condemned by honorable men. Honorable men do not murder; honorable men do not steal; honorable men do not rape. It goes all the way back through history. Tarquin's rape of Lucretia caused the fall of the tyrants and the beginning of the Roman Republic. This idea that somehow suddenly feminism miraculously found out that women were being exploited and raped through history is ridiculous. We have got to remove things like rape from the women's studies context and pull it back into ethics. It belongs in *ethics*. We have to ask how should *everyone*—not just men—how should everyone be trained as a child to behave in society. We must put it in a general philosophical context. This idea of focusing in, suddenly, at the freshman year of college—it's too late! Guess *what*—you're not going to convert anyone with a few films on date-rape education, a few demonstrations, and a few pamphlets being passed out, you're not going to change anyone's mind. Look—ethics has *always* condemned such abuses. You do not have this endless series of atrocities through history. Men have also protected women. Men have given women sustenance. Men have provided for women. Men have died to defend the country for women. We must look back and acknowledge what men have done *for women*.

Men's creation of the technological world of today has made *me* possible. I remember my paternal grandmother on the back porch in Endicott, scrubbing the clothes on a washboard. She had nine children. I remember that. I, her granddaughter, could have the leisure to write this book, thanks to the technological world and modern capitalism, which has such a bad rep. Look around the world, okay, and see what the reality is. Oh, I thank God I was born an American, I thank God. When I got to Europe—I feel the smog of convention hanging everywhere in

Europe, even in England, which is a very free-speaking and free-thinking country. In America, woman is at her freest. Never in history have women been freer than they are here. And this idea, this bitching, bitching, kvetching about capitalism and America and men, this whining—it's infantile, it's an adolescent condition, it's *bad* for women. It's very, very bad to convince young women that they have been victims and that their heritage is nothing but victimization. This is another perversion.

All right. Here's something: Germaine Greer. What a loss. What a *loss*! If that woman had stayed on her original track, all of feminism would have been different. She was sophisticated, sexy, literate. What *happened* to her? After three years, she turned into this drone, this whining, "Woe is me, all the problems of the world!" Something went wrong in feminism. This often happens in history. Revolutions begin laudably but sometimes almost immediately degenerate into ideology or into partisanship and so on. Every revolution eventually needs a new revolution. That's what I'm trying to do. I'm not trying to get rid of feminism. I'm trying to reform it, to save it, to bring it into the twenty-first century, in a way that allows the sexes to come together instead of being alienated from each other, that allows sex to be *hot* and not have, like, wet blankets of sermonizing thrown over it.

Sontag. Ohhh. Another woman. Both these women, Germaine Greer, Susan Sontag. What *happened*? When people say, "Oh, men keep women back," look, in our own time, two major women self-destructed. These women should have been leaders. These women should have been Madame de Staëls. Their work should have astonished multitudes. Both these women had the attention of the world, and they lost it. Through their own failings. Sometimes women have failings. Sometimes everything is *not* because of male conspiracy. Sometimes women do stupid things, okay, and become vain and conceited. In those two cases, those are *major* losses.

I feel that Susan Sontag should have been a leader in critiquing feminism but instead just played this role—whatever the role is that she plays—Miss Mandarin in her New York apartment. I don't know what the hell she's been doing for twenty years. She thinks she's a novelist. That's what she's doing right now, writing a novel. That's just what we're all waiting for, huh? Another novel by Susan Sontag! She has no talent whatever for fiction-writing. It's just a delusion. This is a woman who should have been a leading intellectual. This is a woman who should have provided that median link between academe and the world of popular culture. She started doing it. And then she pulled back when people attacked her. They said, "What are you doing? You're not serious!" And now she says silly things to *Time* magazine like, "Oh, well, I don't know why people talk like this. After all, I never wrote a whole essay on the Supremes. I merely mentioned them." Oh, come *on*! I would *love* to write an essay on the Supremes. In fact, I *have*—there's a whole section on them in Volume Two of *Sexual Personae*.

Sontag should have provided this link. This is what we need. We have a split between the world of the media and the world of academe that has been bad for both. And we need to bring the two audiences together. *She* should have done that, and I'm going to be trying to bring serious intellectual issues into the public domain and similarly bring public concerns back into academe. Because for all the talk of academic feminism about how they care for women—they think they speak for women— they don't speak for women! You go out in the street, most women on the street have contempt for feminists. Why? It's because of the excesses of feminism. They like to go through this ritual, "Oh, yes, we have such solidarity with Third World women." They don't know anything about Third World women! So much of academic feminism today is nothing but the complaining of white upper-middle-class women. They don't even realize the extent to which they're trapped in their own class. They don't realize it. And they just have to be broken out of it.

Let me go on. I have a whole list here of reforms. I'm going to sound like Martin Luther! A couple of things. The abuse of language has got to stop. Throwing around words like *racist* and *homophobic* and so on. Now, *homophobic* has a specific psychological meaning. It means someone who's *obsessed* with homosexuality, so that you go out and maybe kill or maim someone who is homosexual because of your own inner fear that you may be having homosexual impulses. It's a true phobia. We cannot allow

the word *homophobic* to be constantly used for anyone who says,
"I don't like gay people" or "I think homosexuality is immoral,
according to the Bible." We cannot be misusing this word. We
cannot condemn as *bigotry* everything that we don't agree with.
Words like *bigotry* have to go. Or you don't get enough money
for AIDS: "Genocide!" When you use words like this—this is
what they were shouting up in Kennebunkport when Bush was
on vacation on Labor Day—"Genocide!" Now what does this
do? I mean, you totally destroy the true meaning of genocide as
it was authentically embodied under Hitler. That's what you do.
You destroy meanings, you anesthetize people, and you turn
people off. You turn the mind off. You kill the brain. We cannot
have this. We cannot have this abuse of language going on.

Let me give you another example. There were anonymous
posters put up recently all over New York, with Jodie Foster's
picture: "Absolutely Queer." *Absolutely* queer? I thought we got
rid of absolutes! I thought that's what Nietzsche had done a
hundred years ago. Now we've got *gay* people talking about what
is *absolute*? This is fascism! This is fascism! It's going to drive
people back into the closet. We cannot have this. Jodie Foster—
I'm trying to challenge her to come out and to do what I have
done. In the *New York* cover story last March, I tried to make a
lead for her. I was trying to influence her. It hasn't succeeded
yet! Because obviously the problem for her is that she also now
and then dates men. I would like her to be able to say, "Look,
so? I'm not comfortable with the word 'gay.' " I want her to *say*
this. Because I think it's necessary to say. The word *gay* is becoming oppressive. It itself is becoming oppressive. I want her
to say this. I want her to say "I'm not comfortable with that
word"—and others like Sandra Bernhard must say it too: "We're
not comfortable with that. We don't feel that word describes what
we *are*. Yes, we've slept with women. Yes, we've slept with men.
But I do not want a word like a badge that tells me what I'm going to be or how I'm going to feel in the next 72 hours!"

Now, you know what I hate? This thing of, say you have a
man who's married, he has children, and maybe every month or
every few weeks he goes out and picks up a guy. Today in this
fascist atmosphere it's "You're *gay*! You're gay, and you're se-

cretly homophobic! You are self-loathing! You are hiding behind the mask of respectability!" What if he's just married and likes to sleep with men now and then? What's *wrong* with that? They're doing that in the Near East. They've done that in China and Japan. True liberation for homosexuals, for lesbians, will happen only when we can break through these stereotypes and allow for the free flow of desire, for spontaneity, for humor. I don't like the situation because right now it's bad for gay people! Right now, people are afraid. Often a woman is afraid to go to bed with another woman because she's afraid that if she does that, even though she's attracted to her, she'll be "*gay*"; she'll have to have an identity crisis, be gay, and all that other stuff. *Why? I'm* influenced by the great foreign films of the late Fifties and Sixties where you had Catherine Deneuve and Jeanne Moreau and Dominique Sanda floating around from bed to bed with a man, then with a woman, then with a man, then with a woman. I *like* that! I think *that's* sophisticated!

In terms of my history, you know, for a long while in my life I felt that, well, I have to be gay, because I'm so attracted to women, but then in a way it's living a lie, because then I have to repress my attractions to men. So after a while I thought, well, why do I have to give myself any label? Why can't I just respond from day to day and just go with the flow in the Sixties way? I think that is healthy. A healthy psychology goes with the flow and responds to situations and stimuli as they occur. It reminds me a little bit of Holly Woodlawn, the great Warhol drag queen, who was on an early Geraldo show. And Geraldo said to Holly Woodlawn: "Are you, like, a man who should be a woman, or are you a woman who was a man, or are you a man/woman?" And Holly Woodlawn said, "Oh—who cares? As long as you look *fabulous*!"

So part of what I want to do is liberate contemporary sexuality from the *new* rigidity of gay activism, which I think is getting a little too definite in the line it's drawing between gay and straight. Because I don't think that such a sharp line actually exists in real life. Many people deny that bisexuality exists. I happen to feel that women have a natural capacity for bisexuality. I don't like the situation today where young women are arriving at college, and the Student Services and the deans want to be very "compassionate" and "caring" right now. So when you arrive at college and a girl is sleeping with another girl: "Oh, you're gay. Isn't that nice? How *nice* that you're gay! This is wonderful. We're going to help you be gay. Really, there's no need to—" Maybe she's just sleeping with the other girl! What's wrong with *that*? Stop imposing the heavy burden of "identity" on people. Just let them live and breathe! I feel that life should be an art form. It should not be like a factory assembly line.

Now let me give my list of reforms. In my exposé, "Junk Bonds and Corporate Raiders" for *Arion*, I had these reforms, and then I will have others that are new. The ones I said there are first of all that the present concentration on essay-writing at the heart of the humanities curriculum is actually discriminatory against people of other cultures and classes. I think it's a game. It's very, very obvious to me, having been teaching for so many years as a part-timer, teaching factory workers and teaching auto mechanics and so on, the folly of this approach. You teach them how to write an essay. It's a *game*. It's a structure. Speak of social constructionism! It's a form of repression. I do not regard the essay as it's presently constituted as in any way something that came down from Mount Sinai brought by Moses.

I feel that *learning* has to be brought back to the center of the humanities curriculum. I can see what happened. What happened was that the old bibliographical style of literary scholarship had become totally enervated and dead, and then New Criticism rose up in the Twenties, Thirties, Forties—and then it really started dying in the Fifties—as a way to talk about the literary and artistic qualities of a text. And then unfortunately that detached itself entirely from any historical context, and you got a whole generation of critics who came through who have absolutely no historical sense whatever—they haven't been trained to think in historical terms. So we have a situation today where you're tested for a literature course on your ability to write an essay. I think again that something's wrong with this. Sure, perhaps an essay should be part of a larger exam. But I think we should go back to demanding mastery of fact and even rote memory. I think rote learning has a bad press. I think rote learning is one way that you train your mind. It's almost like weight training, in the physical sense.

Next, in terms of classroom teaching, there have *got* to be small classes. What kind of education is it, like at Harvard, where you have 800 people in a class? Is this education? People pay all that money to go there, for what? To sit in a huge class—why not get a videotape? Why not go read the lecture? This is not teaching. Teaching is when you have one person, a teacher in a room, doing improv with a class. *Looking* at the students, looking at them as people. And *all* faculty should be made to teach freshmen. This idea that "Oh, the freshmen—let's leave that to the graduate students, the slaves." That's absurd. The freshman year is the most important year, especially for people coming from deprived backgrounds. The teacher must confront the student face-to-face. Look at the student, watch the way the students are changing from year to year, care for them as individual beings. This has got to happen. The reform of education will be achieved when we *do* that, when we give personal attention to the students.

And one of the ways to do that is to cut off a couple of big things. The "publish or perish" thing has got to *stop*. We should say to young faculty: "We expect you, in twenty years, to produce a work, and we hope that you're constantly working toward it, and now and then we want to look at maybe chapters or pieces of the work that you're doing. But *your* number one responsibility is to *teach* and to develop yourself, and to expand your learning. You come here, you have an English Ph. D., you know nothing about art? That's your obligation. Learn about art. Learn about music, dance, history, politics, learn Chinese, go fishing. Do anything, but *don't* go to conferences!"

I demand that the profession go *cold turkey* on the conferences! There must be an accounting. Every college, every university, we must ask for an accounting. The funds that are being used to send people on plane trips to Monte Carlo and around the world should be going to the students and to development. You should give the money to a young faculty member for course development, not to go to a conference. Do you know the hundreds of thousands of dollars that are wasted on these plane tickets and these hotel reservations and all that? It's appalling.

It's a *scandal*. It's mini-vacations, boondoggling. *No more conferences*! And the MLA can begin by abolishing those stupid sessions, all 800 of them.

And also I've said in *Arion* I expect teachers to be generalists. Merely because you have as a professional scholar an area of specialty does not mean that you should be teaching that specialty to your students. No! Undergraduate education demands general education. It's no place to be having your students run little errands for you, doing your research for you. That has got to stop. Now, I have in *Arion* demanded really radical restructuring of the curriculum. And what I'm asking for is a *true* multiculturalism. Not this *phony* stuff, where you have these people who say [*imitates smug, airy woman professor*], "Oh, I'm multicultural because to my novel course I've added, yes, two novels by black women and one by a Chinese-American woman. See—I'm multicultural!" *That's* not multicultural! If you were really multicultural, you'd be studying, the way we did in the Sixties, Hinduism and Buddhism. You'd be studying other world cultures. These people are lazy, good-for-nothing pretentious people! Hypocrites! Hypocrites masquerading under this flag of multiculturalism.

What I'm calling for is true multiculturalism, that is, a restructuring of the curriculum, so that we have a two-year program. What I'm asking for is to begin in remotest antiquity, begin with archaeology in all the great world traditions. Year one would go from the beginning, from prehistory, all the way to the birth of Islam. And then the second year would go from the High Middle Ages all the way to the present, in all the great world traditions. We must study comparative religion. You cannot understand *any* other culture until you understand the religion of that culture. Sacred texts of all religions should be the basic readings of the first year, as I see it. *This* is the true multiculturalism, not that other stuff.

Next I'm asking for an arts-based, arts-centered humanities curriculum. I expect all humanities professors to be conversant with all the arts, a true cosmopolitanism. And what goes with that is that you cannot be graduating from an American liberal arts college without knowing about *black music*. This is a great art form we have given to the *world*. Jazz, blues, Billie Holiday,

Coltrane, Charlie Parker—there is no true liberal arts education in this country without that. We must do something to the curriculum to *build that in*. Right now dance, which is this enormous form, the most ancient of all art forms, is off there in the Phys. Ed. department—you go and take an aerobics class! You are not a liberal arts graduate until you know about dance—you *know* about it. You know about Martha Graham, you know about ballet, you know about the incredible contributions that African-Americans have made to dance. And every week it's going on and on and on, the sophisticated developments of dance that are going on in the streets of this country, but nowhere is it registering in our liberal arts curriculum. Instead, they're wasting all that time with Lacan! Who *needs* that guy? Get rid of him! Get *rid* of him! And *all* that stuff! There's plenty of room in the curriculum for what I'm saying, *plenty* of room, let me tell you.

Also in *Arion* I'm calling for an end to women's studies as presently constituted. That is, I'm asking for a development not into gender studies, because I think the word *gender* has become this code word for social constructionism, but rather I'm asking for something called "sex studies," admitting that it's *sex* we're interested in—*sex! lust! sex! Yes!* And I don't think gay studies is a good idea. I think we have got to have sex studies, a broad-based curriculum where you have men and women in the program and gay and straight in the program, talking to each other. We have got to have that. I think this ghettoization that is happening is bad for everyone. We cannot have a situation where you say [*imitates busy administrator*], "Okay, well, all right, we're going to get gay literature into the curriculum. Let's find a gay person. Put out an ad. Oh—are you gay? Okay, you can teach!" This is not good. We don't want this. We want the subject matter of homosexuality to be integrated with the curriculum. We want everyone to be responsible for these subjects.

I think that women's studies has made an error, because it's way off on one end. The way women's studies was thrown together, you see, was very pernicious. That is, suddenly, gender was in the air. *My* generation of the Sixties put it on the cultural agenda. And then the administrators were absolutely callow and weak in the way they put it together. They said, "Okay, um, let's see, um, you over there in the English Department, um, you're an expert in Jane Austen. You could do this, couldn't you? Women's studies?" [*imitates not-too-bright woman*] "Yeah, I could do that. Yeah, sex. *I've* had sex. I could do it." That's the way it was put together. It was put together in this ramshackle shanty way, and we're paying the price for it *now*. It's a disaster.

Now, here's the parts that are new, that weren't in *Arion*. I'm calling for an end to the corrupt practice of advance blurbs on books. Now, blurbs where you take something from a review, a published review that's in the open media and so on, and you put it in subsequent ads or the dust jacket of the book, that's perfectly legitimate, okay? But this advance blurb thing is absolutely appalling, because it means that they send your book around to your friends, they scratch your back, and you scratch theirs. This is part of the coziness of the profession that I think has just been pernicious. Where people say "*brilliant!*," "*mind-boggling!*," "shakes the foundations of the Western world!" That has got to stop.

Now, this one you're not going to like, probably. I do not like any kind of "minority" designation. I think the word *minority* is an insult. I'm speaking as an Italian-American. My mother came over here at six not knowing a word of English, and when she arrived they didn't say to her, "Oh, you poor person, you poor Italian-American, all you can understand is things about Italian-American culture, that's all we'll tell you, and oh, you can keep Italian. *Sure*—we wouldn't *dream* of imposing English on you." No. They said to her, "This is a disciplined American school. You will learn English." My mother, not speaking a word of English, and because of the support of her family, got straight A's all the way through, and look, within one generation, what you get: *Sexual Personae*. One generation! I write English better than the English! Now, for Hispanics to continue allowing this "minority" designation is extremely shortsighted. It's a disaster in the long run, because it cripples people to allow bilingual signs, to allow the use of Spanish in schools.

I think what we need is a kind of creative duality as ethnics. I am very proud to be an Italian, very proud. Ethnic people— African-Americans, Italian-Americans, Jews, Greeks, Hispanics, and so on—they should have this sense of duality. I feel that Oprah Winfrey does this very well, the way she has that double sense, the way she uses two voices. She vamps back and forth between her two voices. That's how I feel. I feel in between. *This* is the great richness of our country. But we cannot have a situation where people are being crippled because they're being allowed to retain their native language for years and years. This is a recipe for second-rateness. It is condescending, it's insulting to them. I think that the "minority" designations have served their useful purpose and should be dumped. And I know that's very controversial.

Next. Part-time teachers: we should upgrade their status and their benefits to allow for a couple of things. Number one for women to remain home with their children, if they wish, for the first three years. And number two, to allow people who are poets and artists or people who are informing themselves about the history of art, and so on, to give them the time to *do* that. I feel that the universities will be enriched by this raising of the status of part-timers.

An end of hostility to the media. Right now, the leaders of the MLA are off sitting on their duff and saying things like, "*There's* no problem. The media's making it up. There's no problem in the profession. And it's all a neoconservative plot anyway." The leaders of the MLA say things like [*imitates chirpy dowager*], "Gee, I mean, when we're in the media, look at it, we're like *this* [*makes one-inch pinching gesture*]. But *we* know we're not that small! We're *large*! We're *big*! We're not that small." Guess *what*? The media is seeing you *accurately*! There you have it, the eye of the media, looking at academics, sees them in their true size, okay, and sees the issues in their true absurdity! And people who are removed from the media think, "That can't *be*! I mean, why, that's not true! *I'm* not that. I'm not that little cartoon figure." [*sotto voce*] *Yes*, you are . . . .

And finally, in terms of the public schools, I feel that the education that was given to the immigrants for a hundred years, and now has collapsed, has to be brought back. There was discipline and order in those public schools. And don't tell me—those Italian-American boys of yesteryear were the biggest roughhousers. I mean, the principal would stand there with a truncheon, dealing with the boys—slap! slap!—into his palm. Order and discipline in the schools: we have lost the will to insist upon that. Because now [*imitates do-gooder bureaucrats*]: "We don't want to harm the socialization of the poor children. We wouldn't want to expel them—what a shame! We wouldn't want to expel them—what a scandal! We wouldn't want to keep them back in their grade, because that would harm their socialization." This coddling is a disaster! People were not coddled in the age of the immigrants. If you flunked, you flunked! The end result is we're graduating into college people who cannot read. This is not doing anyone any good. Expulsion used to be used. "Oh, we don't want to do that, because that just puts the problems out on the street." Well, why *not* put the problems on the street? Why not save the schools for those poor, deprived children who would like to, of their own will, make it?

I am very grateful for a public-school education. Look what happens when you have that kind of order, when you have that kind of rigorous, disciplined teaching that I had in the old public-school era. This is what allows you to develop your identity. This idea of "self-esteem"—*ugh*! The idea that "self-esteem" should be the purpose of education. This is social-welfare propaganda. Development of our intellect and of our abilities has to be the focus of education. Then we can have these extraneous agencies that can pick up the slack of the "self-esteem."

You build *identity*. Maybe identity comes through *conflict*. For example, my struggles with gender, my struggles with sexual orientation, my anguish over so many decades *produced* my work. We have to understand that, that sometimes conflict is *creative*. You will not get a book like *Sexual Personae* again for another thirty years, because now, whatever you want *goes*. If there's no pressure on you, there's no pressure to create. So we have got to stop this idea that we must make life "easy" for people in school, make it nice and easy [*imitates soothing, unctuous, paternalistic voice*], "We want you to have a pleasant time, we want to 'make nice' for you." *No*. Maybe the world is harsh and cruel, and maybe the world of intellect is challenging and confrontational and uncomfortable. Maybe we have to deal with people who *hate* us,

directly, face-to-face. That's important. You develop your sense
of identity by dealing with the things which would obliterate your
identity. It does not help you to develop your identity by putting
a cushion between yourself and the hateful reality that's out there.

On that note, I will close and let you go. Oh, no, no, I
understand there's going to be an S & M session now. As a fan
of Robert Mapplethorpe, I can't object to being abused in public!

Question (young man): Could you please expand on what you
mean by a feminist aesthetic?

Answer: Well, I was saying simply that I thought there was a
lack of an aesthetic. That is, the question of beauty has been a
very perplexing one to feminists. Since beauty has been expected
historically of women. It was for my generation a kind of—we
felt it as a burden. I certainly was part of this revolution against
the necessity for beauty. In the late Fifties and early Sixties, when
I was in high school, before the Sixties liberation, there was a
certain way you had to look. Blondes were big, for example.
Blondes ruled the world in the Fifties in ways you cannot possibly
understand today. Or maybe you sort of can. But I mean there
was Debbie Reynolds, there was Doris Day, there was Sandra
Dee, there was Carol Lynley, oh my God, you can go on and on
with this endless chain of blondes. And one felt that certainly the
pecking order—the high-school food chain, in dating and so on—
it certainly favored the blondes and a kind of frail, translucent
beauty. Okay now, here I am at midlife, and I'd like to report
that, over time, blonde beauty doesn't last. What you're left with
at midlife is bone structure, honey! The cheerleaders aren't
lookin' so good now, uh-huh.

So you see one reason why the first wave of feminism in the
late Sixties revolted against beauty. That's why. For example, in
the Seventies, I did not own a dress, and I boasted I would *never
again* wear a dress. It was a badge of *servitude*. Well, see what
happens? [*flashes her skirt*] I wore, like, Frye boots, and I *used*
them, boy! And then the culture changed, I think, as the result
of feminist success. Around 1980 you felt the culture changing.
And women of my generation began to recover the language and
the historical paraphernalia of female sexuality. And we're com-

fortable with it. I think there's been an *enormous* evolution. That's why Naomi Wolf is completely out of sync with what's happened.

There were certain role models on TV like, first of all, Joan Collins on *Dynasty*, who made it possible to be glamourous and also this businesswoman. But I think even more so, Donna Mills as Abby Ewing on *Knots Landing* did something for the persona of the American woman, rather than that kind of florid drag queen style of Joan Collins. I really admire what Donna Mills did. It's, like, she's very understated, very breathy, it's very feminine. And I think this had a real impact across the country not just on women in business but on housewives and so on. She redefined contemporary women. It's possible to be this *bitch*, this total businesswoman, shrewd, mentally alert and keen, and then also very sexy. Part of it is that she's a dancer. I always like actresses who have dance training. It's the graceful way she uses her body and so on.

So I think what's happened is that the culture has changed and moved backward toward beauty and recovered beauty, while feminist ideology has not. It's having trouble dealing with it, because it insists on interpreting it in ways that *were* true in the Fifties and early Sixties. That is, once it *was* something oppressive. You *had* to be this as a woman, or you were nothing. And now it's a matter of our option. Now and then there's a case like the one in Boston where the woman was fired for not putting on makeup, but these are rare cases. Now, I think, we women of my age, in our forties, feel *more* powerful in sexual clothing, in erotic clothing. That is, I enjoy wearing cosmetics now, I enjoy wearing high heels. I would *never* have *dreamed* this twenty years ago, when I was into my militant Amazon feminist phase, *never!*

So I'm trying to get other feminists to evolve and to understand that the culture has changed and for us to recover— here's the thing—to recover our full sexuality. Now here is a very controversial opinion that I have. Once I thought that militant lesbianism was an answer; as the years have gone on, I have begun to feel it is *not*. I have not seen the results that I would have liked. I now feel that part of a woman's power is her power over men, her sexual power. And I'm not saying stop sleeping with women, I'm not saying stop being a lesbian. I'm saying that a lot of gay women have closed down half of their brain and half of their sensorium, and that when you open that thing toward men, then the sex with your girlfriend will be hotter!

Q (middle-aged man): My question to you is, do you ever admit that you're wrong?

A: My grandmother, Vincenza Colapietro, was never wrong. Even when she changed her opinion 180 degrees, she was never wrong. So I have inherited that particular thing. I can't explain it, a kind of confidence that comes with the genetics of my Italian ancestry. I don't apologize for it, it's part of my accomplishments. Confidence is one of my great characteristics.

Q (young man): I'm Eliot Morgan—

A: *The Harvard Crimson*!

Q (con't.): What do you believe actually launched the reaction by people like Irving Howe and other people who usually kept silent for a long time about "p.c."? What do you think actually started the full reaction against the speech codes and so forth that were going on on campus?

A: What do I think has started the reaction against "p.c."? I'm not sure what began this. I'm very superstitious. I just feel that something went full circle. It's like a Zeitgeist. That moment that we went from the Eighties to the Nineties, you know, the period of greed and materialism, the Gilded Age of Wall Street. Was it Malcolm Forbes who died on New Year's Eve? There was the fall of Trump, there was the fall of Leona Helmsley, and suddenly— I honestly believe in big cultural weather patterns. I don't know what happened. It could have been Mars, or whatever, went into Aquarius! I don't know. But there's no doubt something has started. And people are very concerned. I think that up until now a lot of the liberals in academe have remained silent because they didn't want to be as crass as these other opportunists around them who are constantly jockeying for position and power. And so they've just gone off and done their own work, even though they're *very* unhappy about what's been happening.

Now, I think—I feel very hopeful about things because I think there's a concern for the students. We're starting to see the bad results on students, the impoverishment of their education. Like there's a very prominent woman writer and academic whom I'm trying to bring out of her hiding. She was talking to me about her campus, a well-known Northeastern college. She once told a student in impatience, "You want to do something really radical? Read Chaucer and Shakespeare." She could see that what they were reading—they were so up on the latest hip thing, and on these minor academics and so on. I think that once people see the result on the next generation, they will act. They will put themselves on the line not for themselves but for the future, for this generation and the next generation. So I am very hopeful that people are going to be heard from who have not been heard from up until now and who will be occupying, again, this great center. We must create an enlightened center. We must stop this fascism of the right and fascism of the left that's going on right now. Everything is much too polarized.

Q (young woman): You talked about beauty. You talked about it again and again. You condone the emphasis placed on beauty on women. You made the analogy of sports and seemed to condone that. One thing you didn't mention any time you talked about beauty was the passivity implied in the image of a beautiful woman. Sports again, in the dichotomy *you* brought up, sports is active, beauty is passive. The verbs in these magazines are often passive. The goal is to *be* admired, to *be* looked at, to *be* appreciated for how beautiful you are. Women are not doing anything besides that of their own accord—

A: Let me just answer that. I would like to adjust that interpretation, because I know that is the current one. I do not believe that a beautiful woman being looked at is "passive" beneath the "male gaze." I feel that that is a distortion. It's not correct. I'd rather think of it in terms of the Helen of Troy motif, that is, a woman in the glory of her sexuality. I'm trying to say that when we absorb the full history of art and then look at a fashion magazine, we won't *have* this feeling of passivity. Because if you look at the great statues of men—let's say the statues and paintings of men in Egyptian art—they are as beautiful. And the men wore cosmetics and jewellery and so on. The idea that a beautiful body that we're looking at is "passive" to our gaze seems to me so absurd. For example, to me the greatest images of beauty right now are in the back of gay newspapers, *male* newspapers. You look at those ads, and you see these *gorgeous* guys. Okay, now, *please*—do we honestly believe they are "passive" to our gaze? That is *absurd*! We are admiring their beauty, when we say, "Look at how beautiful the human body can be!" We're *admiring* it.

Q (con't.): But you brought up the example of Helen, and again that is a good example of passivity. The men went out and did the fighting over Helen. Helen just sat back and was beautiful. When you say men are beautiful, women are beautiful in the same sentence, you're ignoring historically that passivity has been associated with that and women have adopted that. And that again is dangerous to ignore because that is the basis of date rape! Women feel like they have to be passive. They've been taught this historically. You absorb any of the images throughout history, starting with Homer, starting with the story of the Trojan War, and Helen being the passive woman, being fought *for*, not fighting, *never* fighting, okay?

A [*sighing*]: I just think it's *so sad* if we're at that point where you have 10,000 ships destroyed for the beauty of a woman, when you have the old men on the gates of Troy in Homer looking at her and, like, they haven't felt any sexual desire in years, in decades, and they look at her and they say, "*Look* at that beautiful woman. It was *worth* it." If that's what we're reduced to, taking one of the greatest and most dominant images of mythology of the power of a woman's sexuality and reducing this to "passivity," what a sad and totalitarian life we're living now, with no literature and no art and nothing but these *sermonizing lessons* that we must learn!

And I'm calling for women actually to be *more* active in terms of their relationships with men, see, that's what I'm saying. I'm saying for women to stop floating into a fraternity party and saying [*dippily*], "Okay, what'll happen now?" I want women to take control and decide—

Q (con't.): That's historically what they've been taught—

A: I'm sorry, *no*! These are white middle-class pampered yuppies who are getting into this trouble right now. We of the Sixties said to the colleges, "Get out of our sex lives!" When I arrived in college in 1964, we women were locked in the dorms at eleven o'clock at night, and we said, "Get *out* of our sex lives, and let us take the risks!" Now these women of today are pampered. They don't understand that with freedom comes responsibility. I want them to decide: *What* do you want? Do you want sex or *not*? If you don't want it, stay home and *do your nails*!

Q (second young woman): You've got to spend an hour in the gym and another getting dressed. There's nothing passive about it!

A: There's *nothing* passive about female glamour—right! Take control!

Q (middle-aged woman): When it comes to making and implementing public policy, regardless of the institution or community, national, local level, and so on, whose aesthetic and whose values do we decide to use and on what basis?

A: Well, I think there are several issues. I mean, there's an issue within colleges, okay. I think that would be separate from a kind of agency that does outreach to the community. Each community would have its own needs. What I don't like about this negative attitude toward beauty is that, in my experience of teaching over twenty years, Hispanic and African-American women are very beauty-centered in a very positive way. In Philadelphia on Sunday morning, you'll see sixty-year-old African-American women coming out of church looking so fabulous. They're wearing violet suits and hats with veils, and they look fabulous. And African-American men have incredible style and a kind of dandyism that I relate to strongly, because there's a tradition of dandyism in Italian culture too. So what I don't like is I feel that feminism today doesn't realize the degree to which it's been co-opted by a certain kind of Puritan *whiteness*. It doesn't realize the extent to which it's very parochial in its viewpoint about beauty. Because

I think this beauty argument doesn't go anywhere with African-Americans at all.

Q (young woman): This refers more to your book than to your lecture. You characterize the woman artist as the Emily Dickinson or Emily Brontë who is basically the lesbian. Have times changed? Do women have to spring out of the head of Zeus, of a man, to be an artist?

A: Well, I didn't say that either one of them was a lesbian. I said that they're lesbian-*tending*. I said if we find any eroticism in them, it might be going toward love of women, but certainly I don't feel either of them was sexually active. And certainly that's not true of Jane Austen. It's not true of George Eliot. And Virginia Woolf was sort of sex-phobic, in general—we can't generalize about her! But no, I don't think it's necessary to be a lesbian. I'm just saying that in this particular case, these two great artists that I studied, I just thought that that was the direction of their eroticism, but they were really celibate. And I think that that's one of the options. Of course, I'm *Catholic*! And I have a cousin who's a nun, and I would have been a nun in Italy. I'm practically a nun *now*, believe me! I'm such a sexual *mutant*. I mean, I *can't* get a *date*, let me tell you! Gee, I wonder why? I get marriage proposals but no dates! [*Here a man leaps up in the audience and asks for a date. Audience cheers.*]

I didn't mean to truncate that question, but there's a lot to be said for celibacy, for the concentration of your mental and physical energy. I have a strong sense of vocation, like a nun. There's a monastic tradition not just in the West but also in Hinduism. It's not just that we're "prudish" about sex or whatever here. A lot of people and newsmagazines today say, "Oh, there's *no option*. We have to give condoms to all the high-school students, because we'd never dream of telling them about abstinence." But as a matter of fact, Balzac has written very feelingly in his *Cousin Bette* about the concentration of energy that you get through celibacy. And Balzac himself, in the great period when he was writing his major novels, was celibate. That more interests me.

Today there's this thing of "You can do it all. You can have

it all. You young women today, you can be a mother, you can
be a wife, *and* you can be a career woman." And I think that
women are getting more and more frazzled, more and more crazy,
because of these pressures. Whereas Katharine Hepburn, my
idol, has said, "You can't do it all." She and I are unmarried,
childless, and so on, and we're just like career egomaniacs. And
I think to get a book like mine, you have got to be an egomaniac.
Most women aren't willing to *do* that. Most women aren't willing
to rupture the fabric of social relationship to the degree that I
have and to the degree that Katharine Hepburn has. Then we
end up like crackpots, you know, in old age, but it's a life of
accomplishment. The women I admire were those prewar ladies,
the battle-ax maiden ladies, you know, at Bryn Mawr, at Vassar,
at Smith, those ladies with the monocle [*imitates fierce fist-on-hip
stance*]. That's the tradition I identify with. That to me was the
fount, the crucible of feminism. In this current phase of feminism,
there was a good, a very laudable attempt to bring in the concerns
of ordinary women, of housewives and so on, not just the all-
achieving superwoman of the Bryn Mawr era. But I think that
again it's gone astray, that feminism, for all its *claims* to be helping
or to be speaking to and speaking *for* those women, has ceased
to do that. In point of fact, it has become too mired within middle-
class assumptions. A book like Suzanne Gordon's recent book,
Prisoners of Men's Dreams, is terribly caught in the upper-middle-
class white experience in degrees to which it doesn't even realize.

Q (middle-aged man): You used the word "evolution." Isn't it
just early? What can we seize to bring us further in this evolution?

A: The context in which I used it, I think, is that I was saying
that I felt that feminism has not evolved. Let me give you an
example: Gloria Steinem. A friend of mine, the writer Heidi Jon
Schmidt, said about Gloria Steinem recently, "Once we needed
her, and now we're stuck with her." See, there's been no evolution
in Gloria Steinem's thinking. I mean, this was a very important
figure on the scene. It was she who made the image of a feminist
"normal." She, with her soothing voice, her wonderful television
manner, and her very mature style, really made it possible for

people to think of feminism as something legitimate and not just a bunch of bra-burning fanatics, you know?

But the thing is, feminism is stuck in that groove. It has not made any evolution. For all the great numbers of women writers that there are now, we are still in that posture of, like, whining and demanding that men must change. And what I'm saying in my work is that many of the problems between the sexes predate our social relationships. Many of them have to do with profound power struggles that are going on beneath the surface. Many of our problems with sex are half-conscious or unconscious. We get involved in the wrong kind of relationships, all kinds of things. The mystery of human motivation seems to me so profound. And in order to understand it, we have to read all the great writers from Dante to Aeschylus to Shakespeare and so on. So what's happening with feminism is that they're just reading each other. That's what I'm saying. That's what hasn't evolved.

Q (con't.): I meant with respect to "the mind's liberation." Where are we in the evolution?

A: Oh, you mean about the Sixties. I feel that the Sixties have not been fully understood. That is, the Sixties were looking for a fully expanded consciousness, and that's what the drugs were doing. The drugs were a means for the Sixties to expand the mind. But unfortunately the drugs turn on you. Drugs turn on you. And I think that that was one of the problems of my generation, the loss of the visions and the knowledge obtained by the most daring members of my generation through their drug experiences. They damaged their brains, and they never came back. In fact, Mick Fleetwood of Fleetwood Mac said a few months ago on *Entertainment Tonight* about the founders of that band that he feels very lucky to be in good condition, because when he goes to see them—he went like this [*knocks on forehead*]— "They're not the same people I knew once." And I think that's true of many people I know. Some of the most brilliant minds I know did not continue in academe, the ones I talk to still. The drugs gave vision, but they deprived the person of the ability to translate those visions into material form. I feel lucky I never was attracted to drugs. I am an addict of my own hormones, obviously, my own adrenalines! So, I thank God, that's why I'm alive today to be telling the story, or trying to tell the story.

So what I'm saying is that what happened in the Sixties, "the mind's liberation" in the Sixties, was something that has *never* been fully documented. The psychedelic element of the Sixties is a joke today, like Donovan or tie-dye shirts and so on. I'm saying it *was* no joke, okay? I'm saying that that was one of the most creative moments in Western history, the moment of that clash between Western religion and Eastern religion. I'm not a practicing Hindu, I'm not a practicing Buddhist, I'm not a practicing Catholic. But for me as a Catholic that coming together of all those world-religions at that moment was profoundly liberating. I feel that we *hear* it in Jimi Hendrix's guitar, we *hear* it in the music of the Sixties. That story has never been fully told. I want to do that. I can sense in my students for the last five years, I've been sensing, when I talk about the Sixties to my students, they all are listening, they're listening very intently. Something is happening. The whole Sixties thing is returning through the students of today. I feel very, very hopeful about the end of the century and the millennium, *very* hopeful.

Q (second middle-aged man): Robin Williams said, "Anyone who can remember the Sixties wasn't there." I remember in 1961 that I understood what the terms *right* and *left* meant when you were talking politics. How do you take *right* and *left* to mean in 1991? I don't understand them at all anymore.

A: Yes, I think that they no longer have any meaning. I think that the Sixties idealism of progressive politics is still or should be still alive, but we *must* take into account the lessons that we have learned, the political lessons of the Seventies and Eighties. Last month I saw the film, *Berkeley in the Sixties.* It moved me deeply, because that film absolutely shows what went wrong. It shows what went wrong, okay? When I saw those faces, I just felt I was *back* there again, the passionate faces of the first demonstrators at Berkeley, so committed, many of them Jewish. I felt I was back there. The way that Jewish intellectuals of that time had such a political astuteness and such a pragmatism. Then you see it *happen* in that movie, you see things starting to go wrong. You see it suddenly being taken over by a kind of [*jives back and forth, popping fingers*] white middle-class gameplaying. It turns into People's Park, it turns into, like, "Oh let's just provoke the university into a response. Let's play this *game*—let's, like, spit on the pigs—let's tip over these cars—let's ravage this lower-middle-class neighborhood." That's when it was *lost*. Even the people *in* this movie are commenting on it.

Idealism is fine. Then you must find the practical politics to embody and to sustain your idealism. And that's where we failed. I'm saying that we must bring back the idealism of the Sixties and find the practical politics for it today and stop tripping off in Cloud Cuckoo-Land, where you have all these ideas—"*Yes!* Racial equality! *Yes!* Feminism! *Yes!*" Ideals without any sense of the practical realities to put those things into action. So that's what I think we're looking for now. We want a return of idealism but with a profound sense of political realism.

Q (third middle-aged man): You started out your talk as sort of the last remaining, standing member of the liberatory Sixties generation, and you ended your talk with a call for order and discipline, which were the values that the Sixties rebelled against. And I'm trying to understand how you got from A to B.

A: Well, that's what I just said. That is, in the Seventies and Eighties, it was like this wave shoved us down, our faces were just shoved down. We *failed*. We failed because of our inability to understand that institutions change *slowly*. When I arrived at my first job at Bennington in 1972, my attitude was, "Hey, who *are* these people? And let's get some changes *now*! Who are these middle-aged types—*humph*!" And I had my agenda—[*snaps fingers like a martinet*] this and this and this—endless energy, all night long, blah, blah, blah. Oh, *boy*. Then over time I realized something. I realized that when institutions change fast, then there's the danger of abrogation of civil liberties. You must have *slow* change, not rapid change. Rapid revolutionary change can produce the counterreaction of conservatism or fascism. This is the lesson of history. We must move slowly, consistently, with a practical sense of realism. That's what I'm calling for. I've learned my lessons, boy.

Q (young woman): Do you see that the relationship between the natural and the psychical is something which is a really fundamental problem to be worked out in sexuality in terms of politics, in terms of philosophy, and theology, and so on?

A: You're asking about nature and culture? Yes! People think, because I'm talking about hormones and biology, that I am an "essentialist." In point of fact, I said right in the first pages of my book that sexuality is an "intersection" between nature and culture. It's fantastically intricate, *fantastically*. And it requires all of the learning that we can muster, in science as well as in anthropology, sexology, and everything like that. I'm saying that the kind of sophisticated discourse that's necessary to talk about sex and gender in history is missing from the current women's studies program and that we're far better off by training young women in high-level intellectual history—in Hegel and so on. I mean, it's unfortunate that these are *men*, okay? Isn't that *too bad*? Because these men were the sons of *women*, they were *produced* by women, for heaven's sake!

So I think that this kind of provincial attitude, that women should be best trained by reading women—again, there's a whole lost generation here. It's like sending a woman to train for the Olympics and saying, "Well, I'm sorry, but women have only produced these particular weights, you can only have them, they're not as heavy as those things over there." You train the brain in the same way as you train the body. And I feel that the most difficult and challenging texts should be put before women. That's the only way we're going to get real achievement. I don't think we should be dragging young women students today *down* in contemporary issues. I think we should train them in the past and allow *them* to make their leap *forward*. *Go* for it! *Speak* for your generation! *Don't* listen to us. Here are the great things that helped us to develop our minds. Now *you* go ahead and make your visions. I think that's the only way it's going to happen.

Q (middle-aged woman): I heard you make a lot of sweeping generalizations—

A: I'm known for that!

Q (con't.): —and I've also heard you severely criticize a number of individuals. I would just be curious to know if there's anyone else in the United States, any humanities faculty, that you admire? Are you actually the only one who's got things straight?

A: I would say that, in terms of political astuteness, I respect Edward Said very much. I think that he's a truly politically astute man, and I think that he is also an aesthete. This is a man who has broad training in both art and politics. I think that in terms of women, Martha Nussbaum, the moral philosopher at Brown— whom I've criticized recently for something else—is working at a very high intellectual level. I feel that Gillian Rose, the sociologist in England, is working at the highest intellectual level. That is not the level that is being achieved in feminism. There is not one single woman working in feminism who has achieved the level of either of those two women. We must set the highest standards for ourselves. In just the humanities—?

Q (con't.): I read your piece in *Arion*, and it was pretty generalized about the humanities.

A: Yes, well, I think the situation is appalling in the Ivy League. I think these people who have risen to positions at the top—I *know* some of these people, or I know *of* them through mutual friends, and so on. I know how they got to the top, okay? I mean, I remember seeing this when I was in graduate school. See, silly me, silly me—I thought to be a scholar was to master the whole history of everything. I had no idea that to succeed in academe you had to learn the *game*, the art of rising. Silly me—at the end of class, I would, like, *go*—go to the library, gotta do something, go to a movie, right? And I would see some of my fellow graduate students clustering around the teacher in this odd way, and I thought, "What are they doing?" And then at the end of lectures by famous people, I would see them, and there's a weird motion they would get. I've talked about that in my book. I call it "the court hermaphrodite"—like Rosencrantz and Guildenstern. And it's sort of like a zombie look they get on their faces, and their bodies begin to *undulate*, you know the way seaweed does [*imitates undulating seaweed*]. They're moving into *Toady Mode!*

I had no idea *that's* what you had to do to get a job in academe, to rise in academe, to curry favor with people in power. Oh, that *disgusts* me! It would disgust *any* member of the Sixties, this kind of thing, okay? This has got to *stop*, the sort of thing that you need to do in a Wall Street law firm. This is not the way you should get positions at Harvard. But some of those people at Harvard, that's the way they rose. I mean, there's a very prominent woman over there who's a Paul de Man toady, that's the way she rose, okay? And now it's her great contribution to take Paul de Man and Derrida and apply them to African-American culture. Wow! Hey! Let's applaud *that*! That's really gonna help us, isn't it? To apply deconstruction to African-American culture! Great! We should be just giving them the *raspberry* over there!

[A description of the circumstances surrounding the lecture can be found in the Appendix (pp. 306–307).]

APPENDICES

A MEDIA HISTORY

CARTOON PERSONAE

PROFILES, INTERVIEWS, DEBATES,
EXOTICA

A MEDIA HISTORY

It all began in March 1990, one month after the uneventful release of *Sexual Personae* by Yale University Press. I received a letter from a stranger, Herbert Golder, a professor of classics at Boston University who was editor of the newly revived scholarly journal *Arion*. He asked whether, in view of the admiring attention paid by my book to homosexuality in ancient Athens, I would be interested in reviewing two new classics books in gay studies. I had never heard of the authors, David Halperin and John Winkler, but I consented.

The order of events here must be stressed. The editor of *Arion* has since been accused of exploiting my media reputation. In fact, I had no reputation of any kind at that point. There had been a February review in the *Washington Post Book World* and a March review in *The Village Voice*, but even *The New York Times Book Review* did not publish its review of *Sexual Personae* until July 1990. And my personal, inflammatory presence in the media did not begin, as we shall see, until long afterward, in December of that year.

When I received the two books from *Arion* and began to read them, I was horrified. Their sloppiness and trendiness revolted me, and I began to feel that serious issues of scholarly ethics now faced the profession. I wrote to Herbert Golder, detailing my concerns and asking what length he would set for a review-essay on these matters. He generously gave me carte blanche. In May I began work on the essay in earnest. To the disapproval of my great mentor, Harold Bloom, who felt I should be concentrating on my own career and getting Volume Two ready for publication, I set everything in my life aside and for six months did the research for "Junk Bonds and Corporate Raiders," my *Arion* exposé. I worked through the last twenty years of literary criticism, examining it afresh. What I found was even worse than I expected—a pattern of pretension, incompetence, and naked careerist greed.

The *Arion* essay was completed and submitted in December 1990 and immediately went into production. It appeared in the Spring 1991 issue, which, after a delay due to budgetary constraints, was released in late May. As a panelist invited by P.E.N. to participate in a colloquium on the literary canon at New York University in February 1991, I mentioned in passing that I had written an exposé on the problems in the profession. As the panelists left the stage at the end of the evening, I was approached by Rebecca Sinkler, editor of *The New York Times Book Review*, who introduced herself and asked if she could see the piece for possible excerpting before publication. I gave her the name of *Arion* and told her to contact its editor. I assume the P.E.N. colloquium was also the way *The Chronicle of Higher Education* somehow heard about the upcoming article. It too contacted Herbert Golder and obtained permission to excerpt.

The editors of both the *Book Review* and the *Chronicle* independently selected scattered passages from "Junk Bonds" and strung them together to appeal to their particular audiences. I did not construct the pieces, but I did approve last-minute faxed copies. The articles appeared simultaneously, under headlines never seen by me, in the first week of May 1991 and provoked several groups of highly negative letters, some of which I replied to in the Fall 1991 *Arion*. In early July 1991, the *San Francisco Examiner* published its own excerpting of the exposé as the cover story of its Sunday magazine, *Image*. In November, *Cosmopolitan* magazine, followed by its foreign edition in Greece, reprinted the *Examiner* excerpts. It must be established, in view of the absurd charges and paranoid conspiracy theories of various pea-green minor academics, that neither I nor the editor of *Arion* did any marketing or solicitation for my article. Ideas have their own life and, when the time is right, seem to fly like the wind.

Continuing with my account of the period following the release of *Sexual Personae* the prior year: in April 1990 I received a phone call from the venerable 92nd Street Y in New York City. The director of the "About Women" lecture series had been reading my book and had noted my interest in popular culture. She asked if I would speak on that subject in the fall. On November 29, 1990, I drove to New York with 80 new slides specially made by the University of the Arts and gave my lecture, "Women in Hollywood."

During my appearance at the Y, I spoke warmly about Madonna, a longtime interest of mine. Someone in the audience— a woman editor at a publishing house, apparently—called *The New York Times* the next morning and said there was this woman carrying on about Madonna who would probably be good to discuss the current flap over the banning by MTV of Madonna's new video, "Justify My Love." An op-ed editor promptly called the associate director of Yale University Press, who in turn called me and recommended that I agree to do something for the *Times*. On December 14, 1990, my editorial, "Madonna—Finally, a Real Feminist," appeared. The piece, written in a punchy, satirical style unusual for the op-ed page and accompanied by a large picture of Madonna languishing in a hotel hallway, was the event that first brought me to general public attention. It made me many fans and many enemies, particularly in the old-guard East Coast feminist establishment.

The same week my Madonna piece appeared, but unrelated to it, I received a call from an op-ed editor at *New York Newsday*. He said several people at the newspaper had been reading *Sexual Personae* and had noticed my concern with the theme of rape running through Renaissance and Romantic literature and art. Would I be interested in writing a piece on the current national date-rape controversy? I agreed but said I would have no time to do it until after the holidays. My date-rape article appeared in *Newsday* on Sunday, January 27, 1991. It was picked up by the wire services and reprinted, sometimes in a cut-down version, all over the country.

The *Newsday* piece inspired hysterical, irrational letters from feminists from Alaska to Atlanta, who bizarrely condemned me as "anti-woman" and "pro-rape" for my deviation from the official party line ("Rape is a crime of violence but not of sex," they kept repeating like robots; " 'No' always means 'no' "). It was these letters that convinced me that feminism is in deep trouble, that it is now overrun by Moonies or cultists who are desperate for a religion and who, in their claims of absolute truth, are ready to suppress free thought and free speech. My position on date rape is partly based on my study of *The Faerie Queene*, as detailed in a full chapter of *Sexual Personae*: in 1590, the poet Edmund Spenser already sees that passive, drippy, naïve women constantly get themselves into rape scenarios, while talented, intelligent, alert women, his warrior heroines, spot trouble coming or boldly trounce their male assailants. My feminism stresses courage, independence, self-reliance, and pride.

The third incident in late 1990, unrelated to the other two, was a phone call in November from an editor of *Harper's* magazine, which had published short excerpts from the first chapter of *Sexual Personae* earlier that year. He said the editors had been reading my book and, in view of my adulation in it of image-centered popular culture, wanted to propose a debate between me and Professor Neil Postman of New York University, a media expert and severe, book-centered critic of television. *Harper's* sent Postman's *Amusing Ourselves to Death* to me and *Sexual Personae* to Postman. We both somewhat apprehensively prepared ourselves for combat. In late December, I went to New York and met the wonderfully warm, learned, and articulate Neil Postman and two *Harper's* editors at chic Le Bernardin restaurant. The spirited four-hour debate, taped in the glass-walled Chef's Room, was published in an edited-down form, interspersed with notes of the luxurious dishes of our six-course meal, as the cover story of the March 1991 issue.

That visit to New York made me realize just how surreal my life was becoming, after my long period of privation and neglect. When I drove up to the Sheraton Towers, where *Harper's* had booked me, I was alarmed to have my car and luggage attacked and spirited away by a swarm of bellboys. I staggered confused and luggage-less around the huge, gleaming lobby, with no idea of what to do next. It was like a science-fiction story, *When the Sleeper Wakes*. Finally in my plush room on the forty-fourth floor, I looked down in shock and wonder at the dark, sleazy streets of Times Square, where I had wandered, alone and alienated, so many times over so many decades.

The fourth incident in late 1990, again unrelated to the others, was a phone call from John Taylor of *New York* magazine, who was doing an article on the hot new issue of "political correctness" in academe and who had heard from people reading my book that I was opposed to French theory and to the excesses of academic feminism. Taylor's piece appeared as the cover story of the January 21, 1991, issue of *New York*. It contained several pungent quotes from me as well as a large picture, which, I assumed, was a prefiguration of something else then in process at *New York* but which neither Taylor nor I had any inkling of when he originally called me.

After my November 1990 lecture at the 92nd Street Y, a woman came up to me and identified herself as Francesca Stanfill, a novelist and journalist. She said she had been introduced to *Sexual Personae* the prior spring by a friend, Lynn Nesbit, who also attended the lecture (and who a year later would become my literary agent). Stanfill said that she and Nesbit had talked about the book for months and that in early fall she had begun contacting magazines, including *Vogue* and *Vanity Fair*, about the possibility of doing a profile. If she could secure a commitment from a magazine, would I agree to an interview? I said yes and urged her to call me if and when the moment came.

New York magazine, after shelving Stanfill's proposal throughout the fall, gave her the go-ahead in late December, after my Madonna piece appeared in the *Times*. We began weeks of intense phone interviews on my ideas and career, followed by a full-day, marathon, face-to-face session in Philadelphia in late January. As time passed, the *New York* article got longer and longer, because of my other appearances in the media and my involvement in so many political and cultural issues. Finally, it became the cover story, "Woman Warrior," for the March 4, 1991 issue, in which I posed Amazon-like with one of my two swords on the steps of the Philadelphia Museum of Art. The important point in this saga is that the *New York* profile did not originate, as some have ludicrously claimed, as a neoconservative plot by the patriarchy to set feminism back. It began in the enthusiasm of several sophisticated women for another woman's book, which deals with literature, art, and beauty more honestly than feminism has done.

What I am showing is that my sudden notoriety, over a period of two and a half months, was the result not of any orchestrated public relations campaign but of a chance confluence of a number of different national issues and events. All my media appearances and polemical articles and book reviews ultimately stem from the February 1990 publication of *Sexual Personae*, which because of its length, complexity, and unorthodoxy had a delayed impact on the cultural scene. Yale Press, in the understated, gentlemanly tradition of university press publishing, did no publicity aside from the initial press releases and a few ads. The first time there was a real professional publicity operation behind my work was much later, with the release of the paperback of *Sexual Personae* by Vintage Books in September 1991. And I myself, counter to what I am told are widespread suspicions and allegations, did nothing. I simply sat in my crowded, two-room attic apartment doing my work, watching soap operas, getting phone calls, and going to my university office to meet reporters from around the world.

One of the most dramatic evenings of my life occurred four months after the May 1991 publication of "Junk Bonds and Corporate Raiders." As a guest of the Writing Program, I arrived at the Massachusetts Institute of Technology, home institution of David Halperin, the target of my *Arion* exposé, to deliver a lecture called "Crisis in the American Universities." A crowd estimated in the thousands turned out, jammed the corridors, and overflowed into two other halls equipped with television monitors. The event was reported as a news story in the metropolitan edition of *The Boston Globe*. Reading about it the next morning in my hotel lobby, I felt like Faye Dunaway lounging in her mules and white satin negligée, her brand-new Oscar for *Network* glittering among the newspapers on her poolside glass table at dawn.

At M.I.T., I was speaking extemporaneously from notes as part of my effort to restore energy and spontaneity to academic lectures. I oppose the standard practice of reading prepared texts in classroom, conference, or guest lectures, which has simply led to today's exercises in facile wordplay. If there are real ideas, substance rather than sophistry, in a lecture, the speaker should be able to look at the audience, address it directly, and take in its reactions.

The transcript is verbatim from the M.I.T. archival video tape except for glaring grammatical errors, which were corrected, and for my characteristic American litany, now mostly removed, of "Okay, all right?," which I tend to insert, in a rhythm borrowed from Lenny Bruce, when I have goaded the audience into a response. If, as often happens, I started several different staccato sentences in a row, one was selected. When I was drowned out by applause, laughter, or general uproar (a tumultuous noise level not picked up by the podium mike), I sometimes abandoned sentences midway and so have had to supply the missing word or words. Since, in the operatic Italian way, I often act things out rather than verbalizing them, parenthetical stage directions have been added to the text. The meatiest questions were chosen from the question-and-answer period. They are sometimes condensed here, but my answers have been reproduced in full.

CARTOON PERSONAE

"Their fertility rites seem to have been very private and highly demure. This won't be welcome news to Professor Camille Paglia."

Paglia as Madonna. © 1991 by Tim Gabor. Originally appeared in
The American Enterprise.

Fantasy couples: Paglia and rapper Ice Cube.
© 1991 by Bob Eckstein.
Originally appeared in *The Village Voice.*

"Don't quote me. Out of context it might sound a bit Camille Pagliaish."

PROFILES, INTERVIEWS, DEBATES
EXOTICA

Selected articles on Camille Paglia, listed in chronological order from November 1990 to June 1992. Does not include reviews in the popular press of *Sexual Personae*, most of which appeared in the spring and summer of 1990, after its release by Yale University Press that February. Reviews in scholarly journals are also unlisted here. Annotations by Paglia.

Carlin Romano, "Philadelphia's Academic Bombshell: Camille Paglia's method is 'sensationalism,' and her first book, 'Sexual Personae' is provoking amusement and outrage," *The Philadelphia Inquirer*, November 13, 1990.

John Mascaro, "Camille's Revenge," *Applause* (Public Broadcasting magazine, Philadelphia), January 1991. On cover: "The University of the Arts' Post-Feminist Cultural Commando."

Francesca Stanfill, "Woman Warrior: Sexual Philosopher Camille Paglia Jousts with the Politically Correct," *New York*, cover story, March 4, 1991. Highly accurate, in-depth account of Paglia's history and ideas. Photographs by Harry Benson at the Philadelphia Museum of Art.

"She Wants Her TV! He Wants His Book! A (Mostly) Polite Conversation About Our Image Culture: Camille Paglia and Neil Postman," *Harper's*, cover story, March 1991.

Margery Egan, " 'Woman Warrior' Challenges Feminists to Face Themselves," *The Boston Herald*, March 3, 1991.

Jon Carroll, "Learning to Think Rambunctiously," *San Francisco Chronicle*, March 15, 1991. Calls Paglia "my culture hero of the moment" and compares her to Susie Bright, editor of *On Our Backs*.

Charles Bremner, "Why Can't a Woman Like Her Man More?" *The Times Saturday Review* (London), April 13, 1991. Reprinted as "Men, Madonna, and the Truth about Women" in *The Australian* (Sydney), June 1–2, 1991.

Henry Allen, "Camille Paglia's Mad, Mad Worldview: The 'Sexual Personae' author, venting her scholarly rage," *Washington Post*, April 15, 1991. Reprinted as " 'Female Epic' Born of Furious Isolation," *International Herald Tribune*, April 26, 1991.

J. Eliot Morgan, "Waging the War Against P.C.: Camille Paglia is an Outspoken Critic With Quite a Lot to Say About Harvard Professors," *The Harvard Crimson*, April 18, 1991.

Kang-i Sun Chang, "Paglia's *Sexual Personae:* The Rebellious Devotee of an Alien Underground Religion," *Unitas: A Literary Monthly* (Taiwan), April 1991.

Gail Caldwell, "Hurricane Camille: Learned Lambaster Camille Paglia Takes Aim at Academe—and Attacks From All Sides," *The Boston Globe*, May 2, 1991. Reprinted as " 'Wild Woman' Paglia blasts liberal chic on campuses," *The Columbus Dispatch* (Ohio), June 2, 1991.

"Hot Critic: Camille Paglia," *Rolling Stone*, May 16, 1991. The annual "Hot List" issue.

Diane Winston, "Paglia: An 'Academic Terrorist': Feminist professor adopts aggressive style," *The Baltimore Sun*, May 19, 1991. Reprinted as "Warrior Woman of Academia" in *San Francisco Chronicle*, May 28, 1991, and in *The Seattle Times*, June 2, 1991. Reprinted as "Fire-Eater on Campus," *Hackensack Record* (New Jersey), August 6, 1991.

Gianni Riotta, "Fuochi di Paglia" ("Flames of Paglia"), *Corriere della Sera* (Milan), May 26, 1991. A headline reads: "Io e Madonna faremo fuori Lacan in USA" ("I and Madonna will drive Lacan from America").

Rika Sakuma, "Camille Paglia: Good Thing She's a Woman!" *Crea* (Tokyo), May 1991.

"Media" column, *Ms.*, May/June 1991. "Faux Feminist Award to the new media darling, Camille Paglia."

Alberto Pasolini Zanelli, "La Sorella Minore di Leopardi: Gli Acute Paradossi di Camille Paglia" ("The Little Sister of Leopardi: The

Sharp Paradoxes of Camille Paglia"), *Il Giornale* (Milan), June 13, 1991.

"Wanted: For Intellectual Fraud," cover story, *The Village Voice*, June 18, 1991. Photos of Allan Bloom, Roger Kimball, Eugene Genovese, Dinesh D'Souza, Robert Brustein, Camille Paglia ("Counterfeit Feminist"). Here *The Voice*, strangely taking the side of the academic establishment, denies that "political correctness" exists.

Mark Feeney, "Paglia goes ballistic in BU journal," *The Boston Globe*, June 19, 1991. Describes the just-published academic exposé, "Junk Bonds and Corporate Raiders."

"Rough Trade: Camille Paglia Slaps Academia Around," *San Francisco Examiner, Image* magazine, cover story, July 7, 1991. Inside headline: "A Scholar and a Not-so-gentle Woman: The American university has been taken over by prissy Francophiles, dull-witted thought police and Ken-doll careerists, says Camille Paglia—and it's time to kick some butt." Reprinted in *Cosmopolitan*, November 1991, and in Greek edition of *Cosmopolitan*. Photographs taken at a Philadelphia pornography shop.

"Blutige Zähne und Klauen: Die amerikanische Post-feministin Camille Paglia verstort Liberale und Frauenrechtlerinnen" ("The American post-feminist Camille Paglia stirs up liberals and women's rights defenders"), *Der Spiegel*, No. 29, 1991. Reprinted as *Feministiot lo yislachu la* ("Feminists won't forgive her") in *Ha'aretz* (Tel Aviv), July 24, 1991.

Lee Shepherd, "Camille Paglia: 'Upstate Girl' Challenges Academics," *The Binghamton Press* (Binghamton, New York), July 9, 1991.

Katia Canton, "Feminismo Machista" ("Macho Feminism"), profile of Paglia, *Istoé Senhor* (São Paolo, Brazil), July 10, 1991.

Terry Wheeler, "Sexuality comes naturally to a man from within," *Brutus* (Tokyo), July 15, 1991. Profile of Paglia.

Ann Powers, "Catwoman of Academia: What Does Camille Paglia Want?" *San Francisco Weekly*, July 17, 1991.

Michael Heaton, "Sexual Intellectual: The Radical Feminism of Camille Paglia," *The Plain Dealer Magazine* (Cleveland, Ohio), cover story, July 21, 1991. Inside headline: " 'The only thing that will be remembered about my enemies after they're dead is the nasty things I've said about them.' "

Beatrijs Ritsema, "Machinegeweer: De dwarse denkbeelden van Camille Paglia," ("Machinegun: The Contrary Ideas of Camille Paglia"), *Vrij Nederland* (Amsterdam), July 27, 1991.

Ellen Welty, "Living Dangerously: Confessions of an Ex-Good Girl," *Mademoiselle*, August 1991. Listed as "Forever Bad Girls: Madonna, Sean Young, Camille Paglia, Roseanne Barr."

Celia Farber, interviewer, "Antihero: Scholar Camille Paglia Has Declared War on Contemporary Thinking," published in two parts, *SPIN*, September and October, 1991.

Molly Ivins, "I am the Cosmos," *Mother Jones*, September–October 1991. Attack on Paglia.

Charles A. Radin, "Author Paglia Takes Orthodoxies of Academia to Task in M.I.T. Talk," *The Boston Globe*, September 20, 1991. Account of M.I.T. lecture (transcript in this volume) the previous evening.

Lan N. Nguyen, "Paglia Comes to Cambridge," *The Harvard Crimson*, September 20, 1991. Account of lecture at M.I.T. the previous evening.

Micki Moore, interviewer, "The Anti-Feminist Feminist: Has Camille Paglia Replaced Germaine Greer as the Bad Girl of Feminism?" *The Toronto Sunday Sun*, September 22, 1991.

Brad Miner, "Dances with Wolves," *National Review*, September 23, 1991. Fantasy scene in a topless bar, where Paglia drinks beer and discourses on strip-tease.

Rudy Kikel, "Sex & the Pagan Catholic 'Girl': One Convinced Pagliaddict Confesses to a New Passion," *Bay Windows* (Boston), September 26–October 2, 1991.

Warren Kalbacker, interviewer, "Camille Paglia: the renegade feminist and campus cult heroine lectures us on why she endorses pornography, paganism, and the bracing smell of marine life," *Playboy*, October 1991. Reprinted as "Ideologue of a Pagan Renaissance" in Russian-language *BECTHNK*, cover story, October 16–31, 1991.

Letters, *Yale Alumni Magazine*, October 1991. Paglia attacks Peter Brooks for his role in expediting the "coronation and regime" of Jacques Derrida and Paul de Man.

Matthew Flamm, "The Feminine Mischief," *New York Post*, October 2, 1991. Describes Paglia as "the thorn in the side of contemporary feminism."

M.G. Lord, "This Pinup Drives Eggheads Wild," *Newsday*, October 6, 1991. Calls Paglia "the intellectual pinup of the Nineties," succeeding Mary McCarthy, Ayn Rand, and Susan Sontag.

B. Ruby Rich, "Top Girl," profile and feminist critique of Paglia, *The Village Voice*, October 8, 1991. Headline on cover: "Like a Virgin."

Jim Bencivenga, "Ideas to Shake up Education," profile of Paglia, *The Christian Science Monitor*, October 8, 1991.

Rich Baum, interviewer, "What's Wrong with Feminism? A Conversation with Camille Paglia," *The Cornell Political Forum*, October 1991.

Teresa L. Ebert, "The Politics of the Outrageous," *The Women's Review of Books*, October 1991. Attack on Paglia.

Manuela Cerri Goren, "Uragano Camille: Provocatoria, trasgressiva, irrefrenabile" ("Hurricane Camille: Provocative, transgressive, irrepressible"), *Vogue Italia*, October 1991.

Margaret LeBrun, "Camille Paglia: In Your Face," *Syracuse Herald American*, November 3, 1991.

Mey Zamora, "Camille Paglia, 'La Pornografia es arte' " ("Pornography is art"), *La Vanguardia* (Barcelona), November 3, 1991.

Susie Bright, interviewer, "Girl Talk: Susie Bright Uncovers Camille Paglia," *NYQ*, November 10, 1991. Susie Sexpert declares the bemused Paglia a "butch bottom."

Vera Graaf, "Camille Paglia: Mannerfluchten, Frauen gebaren. Die amerikanische Feministin deutet alle Mythen um" ("Men flee, women give birth. The American feminist rereads all myth against the grain."), *Die Zeit*, November 15, 1991.

Georgette Gouvela, "Attracting Opposites: Feminist Camille Paglia draws seemingly odd artistic comparisons," syndicated Gannett Suburban Newspapers interview, published November 24, 1991.

Dana Kennedy, "Streetwise Feminism," syndicated Associated Press profile of Camille Paglia, *Anchorage Daily News* (Alaska), November 26, 1991. Interview taped in lobby of Algonquin Hotel, New York City.

Forum, *Arion*, Fall 1991. Paglia replies to her critics (Robert Scholes, et al.) after "Junk Bonds and Corporate Raiders."

Tom Smith, "Sex and Our Quarrel with Nature: An Interview with Camille Paglia" (recorded at WAMC, Albany, New York), *24 Hours*, magazine of Australian Broadcasting Corporation Radio (Sydney), November 1991.

Barrie Greene, "As Nasty as She Wants to Be: Camille Paglia Speaks Out at M.I.T.," *The Harvard Salient*, November 1991.

James Bowman, "Perplexed by Sex? Two Controversial Intellectuals, Robert Bly and Camille Paglia, Want to Change the Way You Think about Male and Female Roles," *The American Enterprise*, November/December 1991. Reprint of "Roles Apart," *Daily Telegraph* (London), August 24, 1991.

D. Denison, "The Interview: Camille Paglia," *The Boston Globe Magazine*, December 1, 1991.

Katia Canton, "O Mundo fálico de Camille Paglia" and Luis Coelho, "Eis a muher," *Expresso* (Lisbon) ("The phallic world of Camille Paglia"; "This is the woman"), December 7, 1991. Sharp photo by Rita Barros of Paglia in action, waving her fist from the lectern of the New York Public Library.

Suzanne Gerber, interviewer, "View from a Broad: She pooh-poohs feminists and razzes scholars, but Camille Paglia has only praise for TV," *TV Times*, December 14–20, 1991.

Christopher Culwell, "Camille Paglia's *Sexual Personae*: Scholarship Without Flab," *San Francisco Sentinel*, December 26, 1991.

"1991 Faves and Raves," *Entertainment Weekly*, December 27, 1991. Asked for the most memorable moment in entertainment in 1991, Paglia replies: "Metallica performing 'Enter Sandman' and blowing the walls out at the MTV Awards. Rock lives!"

Laurence R. Stains, "Camille Paglia is Seriously Overbooked," *Philadelphia* magazine, January 1992.

Eric Hellman, "Do I Hear St. Camille, Anyone?" *Bay Area Reporter* (San Francisco), January 2, 1992.

Martha Duffy, "The Bête Noire of Feminism: Cultural iconoclast Camille Paglia likes to throw punches, both physical and verbal, against smug formulas and codes of political correctness," *Time*, Profile, January 13, 1992.

Quendrith Johnson, "Superegos: The 12 Biggest Egos in American Art and Entertainment," *The Boston Phoenix*, January 24, 1992. Oliver Stone, Ted Turner, Roseanne Arnold, Madonna, Jeffrey Katzenberg, Camille Paglia, Axl Rose, Jeff Koons, Norman Mailer, Spike Lee, Mandy Patinkin, Bruce Willis.

Steven Petrow, interviewer, "Who is Camille Paglia, and Why is She Saying Those Terrible Things About Us?" *The Advocate*, January 26, 1992.

Gary Dauphin, "Odd Couples," *The Village Voice*, January 28, 1992. Fantasy situation-comedy interracial couples. Cartoon by Bob Eckstein of rapper Ice Cube in African cap and business suit being served breakfast by scowling, apron-clad, spatula-waving Paglia, while the eggs burn. (See illustration.)

Eric Secoy and Meleah Maynard, "Paglia and *Sexual Personae*," *The Minnesota Daily* (University of Minnesota), January 29, 1992. Pro and con positions.

Sandra M. Gilbert, "Freaked Out: Camille Paglia's *Sexual Personae*," *Kenyon Review*, Winter 1992. Attack on Paglia. An article rejected in a prior form by *Tikkun*. In early 1991, Gilbert claimed to a reporter that *Tikkun* did not print her review because she had conclusively demonstrated how "trivial" *Sexual Personae* is.

Frank DiGiacomo, "Gal Pals," Page Six, *The New York Post*, February 1, 1992. Lauren Hutton takes Paglia to the National Motorcycle Show in Manhattan.

Janet Charlton, "Perked Up," *The Star*, February 18, 1992. Paglia tells the tabloid that meeting Lauren Hutton is "the first real perk since my book came out."

Deanne Stillman, "The Many Masks of Camille Paglia: Part Poseur, Part Philosopher, Part Outrageous Neo-Feminist, the Myth-Making Writer Has Brought Sex, Sensationalism, and Rock'n'Roll to the Temple of Academia," *The Los Angeles Times Magazine*, February 16, 1992. On cover: "Camille Paglia: Amazon Punk Philosopher."

Laura Berman, "Feminist Fatale: Woman warrior Camille Paglia is right. Just ask her. The sexual philosopher and intellectual pugilist calls Harvard profs a bunch of 'dopes' and reveres Madonna," *The Detroit News*, February 22, 1992.

"Women We Love: Super-Feminist Camille Paglia," *Japanese Esquire* (Tokyo), February 1992. Profiles of Lauren Bacall, Nancy Cunard, Tina Chow, Camille Paglia.

"Camille Paglia and Suzanne Gordon Meet Face to Face: What happens when you get together two of the most vocal thinkers on women's issues—who disagree on everything?" *Working Woman*, March 1992.

Emily Culbertson, interviewer, "Equal Opportunity Offender: Out-spoken University of the Arts Professor Camille Paglia Explains Her Views on Feminism, Sex, and Rape," *The Daily Pennsylvanian* (University of Pennsylvania, Philadelphia), March 3, 1992.

Jason Grunebaum, "Paglia Critiques Current Structure of Academia," *Brown Daily Herald* (Brown University, Providence, R. I.), March 6, 1992. Account of lecture at Brown the previous evening.

Maria Miro Johnson, "Paglia Offends, Impresses," *The Providence Journal-Bulletin* (Rhode Island), March 6, 1992. Inside headline: " 'Paglia's the name, fumigation's my game'." Account of lecture at Brown University the previous evening. The article begins, "She chewed them up and spat them out."

Maria Miro Johnson, "The Hit Woman of Academia: Did Camille Paglia's rapid-fire rhetoric pierce Brown's bulletproof vest?" *The Providence Sunday Journal*, March 15, 1992. Inside headline: "Paglia takes shots at everyone." Moody photos of a warlike Paglia at the Providence airport, looking like a scene from Godard's *Breathless*.

Naomi Wolf, "Feminist Fatale: A Reply to Camille Paglia," *The New Republic*, March 16, 1992. Attack on Paglia in cover story, "The New Feminists." Paglia replies in Letters, April 13 (where she analyzes current feminism and criticizes Susan Faludi) and again in the May 18 issue.

Reed Woodhouse, "Thinking like a Gay Man: Confessions of a Paglia-Morphous Pervert," *Bay Windows* (Boston), March 19, 1992.

Thomas C. Palmer, Jr., "Bearding the Literary Lions in Their Den," *The Boston Globe*, March 20, 1992. Account of Paglia's lecture (called

"What's Wrong with Harvard?") the previous evening at Sanders Theater, Harvard University.

Rajath Shourie, "Paglia Criticizes Harvard Scholars," *The Harvard Crimson*, March 20, 1992. Inside headline: "Paglia Slams Harvard." Account of the lecture the previous evening.

Marc Wortman, "Keeping the Press Rolling," *Yale Alumni Magazine*, April 1992. Article on Yale University Press, with account of the discovery of Paglia by editor Ellen Graham.

James Wolcott, "Erogenous Stone," *Vanity Fair*, April 1992. Paglia attains nirvana when *Sexual Personae* is quoted ("A true femme fatale is a force of nature") on a spectacular two-page photo of Sharon Stone, the star of *Basic Instinct*, spread out like a tigress.

"Undressing Camille," *Out/Look: National Lesbian and Gay Quarterly*, Spring 1992. Reprint of interview with Susie Bright from November 1991 *NYQ*. On cover: "Susie Bright Tops Camille Paglia."

Carolyn J. Mooney, "Camille Paglia, Academic Guerrilla, Relishes Her Role as Feminist Scourge," *The Chronicle of Higher Education*, April 1, 1992. Inside headline: "Barnstorming Anti-Feminist Treats Harvard to an Evening of Vitriol."

Kyra Straussman, "Why Camille Paglia is my Personal Savior: Or, How I'm Learning to Be a Feminist in the Real World," *In Pittsburgh*, April 1–7, 1992.

Brenda Elias, "Author Blasts Feminist Thought," *The Daily Hampshire Gazette* (Northampton, Massachusetts), April 11, 1992. Account of Paglia's lecture at Smith College the day before.

Emily Culpepper, "Paglia criticizes rise of women's studies programs," *The Williams Record* (Williamstown, Massachusetts), April 14, 1992. Account of Paglia's lecture at Williams College that week.

Courtney Leatherman, "Feminist Scholars Ask Whether Their Sparring Marks Healthy Debate or a Splintering 'Catfight'," *The Chronicle of Higher Education*, April 29, 1992. Paglia is called, to her delight, "the Jerry Brown of academic feminism."

Paula Chin, "Controversy: 'Street Fighting Woman: Academic brawler Camille Paglia takes on the campus establishment'," *People*, April 20, 1992. Asked by *People* for "one shocking picture," Paglia poses, à la *West Side Story*, with her Italian switchblade knife in the train tunnel at Swarthmore College.

Jennifer Yuan, "Summer Reading Selection Altered: Removal of *Sexual Personae* raises questions of censorship and rouses heated controversy." Lauren Klatzkin, "Content Censorship Comes to Conn." *The College Voice* (Connecticut College), April 28, 1992. Accounts of attack on *Sexual Personae* by the Women's Studies Committee and other faculty. An art history professor says the subject matter of the book is "offensive to human beings and especially women." Another professor says of *Sexual Personae*: "It's bad scholarship, illogical, anti-women, hate-literature, as bad as *Mein Kampf* or David Duke."

"The Girl Most Likely: Camille Paglia, Before," *Spy*, May 1992. Reproduction of a tattered newspaper clipping of Paglia's high-school profile in "Meet the Teens," Syracuse *Herald-American*, November 24, 1963, which *Spy* notes was bizarrely the weekend after John F. Kennedy was shot. On cover: "Camille Paglia, Superteen!"

Deirdre Donahue, "Malcontent of Sexual Politics: Paglia's Rebel Persona," *USA Today*, May 12, 1992. Inside headline: "I Was a Sexual Mutant."

Rebecca Nemser, "Banned in Boston?" *Boston Review*, May / July 1992. Profile of Paglia, with account of refusal of *The Boston Phoenix* to publish the article, leading to the resignation of Nemser as art critic.

Donna Minkowitz, "The Newsroom Becomes a Battleground: The Media's Siege on Lesbians," *The Advocate*, May 19, 1992. Gloria Steinem says about Paglia, "Her calling herself a feminist is sort of like a Nazi saying they're not anti-Semitic."

Suzanne Moore, "The Gender Agenda: She makes Martin Scorsese look laid back and Joan Rivers look polite. She's aroused the fury of feminists and the venom of the American academic establishment. She's Professor Camille Paglia and she's also very funny," *Weekend Guardian* (Manchester), May 30–31, 1992.

Janny Groen, "De man werpt zijn cultuur op als barrière tegen vrouwen," *de Volkskrant* (Netherlands), May 30, 1992. Profile of Paglia. ["Man uses culture as a barrier against women."]

Yolanda Gerritsen, "Ik ben een bezeten, totale egoist: Camille Paglia, een controversiële feministe," *Opzij* (feminist monthly,

Netherlands), June 1992. ["I am an obsessive, total egoist: Camille Paglia, a controversial feminist."]

"Sex Talk: The World According to Camille Paglia," *Arena* (Great Britain), Summer 1992. Quotations from *Sexual Personae*.

Lesley White, "CP, Feminist firebrand bent on reversing the evil of PC," *The Sunday Times* (London), June 7, 1992. Section dramatically led off by the tormented Princess of Wales: first serialization of controversial new book by Andrew Morton, after weeks of heavy publicity.

"Sexual Mutant Trawling Classics for a Persona," *The European* (London), June 11–14, 1992.

Emma Brunt, "Sex is aggression, sex is power," *Het Parool* (Amsterdam), June 12, 1992. Profile of Paglia.

Tineke Straatman, "Men are desperate and afflicted by fear," *Nieuwsblad van het Noorden* (Groningen) and *Utrechts Nieuwsblad* (Utrecht), June 12, 1992. Interview with Paglia.

Wilma Nanninga, "Men, this screaming monster is going to save you!" *De Telegraaf* (Amsterdam), June 13, 1992. On Paglia.

Johanna Blommaert, "The philosopher with the little whip: 'My instinct says to break the rules,' " *De Morgen* (Brussels), June 20, 1992. Profile of Paglia.

Mark Vlaminck, "Italian Peasant Owns More Culture Than American Profs," *Het Nieuwsblad* (Antwerp), June 21, 1992. Interview with Paglia.

Thomas Meissgang, "Die Herrschaft der Hure: Mit provokanten Thesen bringt die amerikanische Philosophin Camille Paglia die Frauenbewegung zur Weissglut," *Profil* (Vienna), July 6, 1992. [The Dominion of the Whore: With provocative assertions the American philosopher Camille Paglia brings the feminist movement to white heat."]

INDEX

The index identifies persons referred to but not named in the text. For devotees of indexes, there are also a few jokes.

ACKNOWLEDGMENTS

Some of the essays in this collection were originally published in various newspapers, magazines, and journals.

"Madonna I" originally appeared on the op-ed page of *The New York Times* (December 14, 1990) as "Madonna—Finally a Real Feminist." Copyright © 1990 by The New York Times Company. Reprinted by permission.

"Madonna II" originally appeared in *The Independent Sunday Review* (London, July 21, 1991) as "The Entertainer's New Clothes: Camille Paglia Defends Madonna Against the Feminists."

"Elizabeth Taylor," originally appeared in *Penthouse* (March 1992) as "Hollywood's Pagan Queen: Elizabeth Taylor."

"Rock as Art" originally appeared on the op-ed page of *The New York Times* (April 16, 1992) as "Endangered Rock." Copyright © 1992 by The New York Times Company. Reprinted by permission.

"Homosexuality at the Fin de Siècle" originally appeared in *Esquire* (October 1991) as part of an article entitled "Women on Men: The Uneasy State of Masculinity Now."

"The Joy of Presbyterian Sex" originally appeared in *The New Republic* (December 1991) under the same title. Reprinted by permission of *The New Republic*.

"The Beautiful Decadence of Robert Mapplethorpe" originally appeared in *Tikkun* (November/December 1991) as "The Beautiful Decadence of Robert Mapplethorpe: A Response to Rochelle Gurstein." Paglia and Gurstein's articles appeared together under the heading "Current Debate: High Art or Hard-Core?" Reprinted with permission of *Tikkun*, a bimonthly Jewish critique of politics, culture, and society based in Oakland, California.

"The Strange Case of Clarence Thomas and Anita Hill" originally appeared on the op-ed page of *The Philadelphia Inquirer* (October 21, 1991) as "Hill is Neither Victim nor a Feminist Hero." Reprinted from *The Philadelphia Inquirer*.

"Rape and the Modern Sex War" originally appeared in *Newsday* (January 27, 1991) as "Rape: A Bigger Danger than Feminists Know."

Camille Paglia's interview with Celia Farber, which appears in "The Rape Debate, Continued," pp. 60–66, originally appeared in two parts in *SPIN* Magazine in September and October 1991. Reprinted by permission.

Camille Paglia's interview with Sonya Friedman on *Sonya Live*, December 13, 1991, which appears in "The Rape Debate, Continued," pp. 60–66, is reprinted by permission of Cable News Network. Copyright © 1991 by Cable News Network. All rights reserved.

"Cleopatra Sold Down the River" originally appeared in the *Washington Post Book World* (May 13, 1991) as a review of Lucy Hughes-Hallett's *Cleopatra: Histories, Dreams, and Distortions*. Copyright © 1991 by *The Washington Post*. Reprinted with permission.

"Alice in Muscle Land" originally appeared in the *Boston Globe* (January 27, 1991) as a review of Samuel Wilson Fussell's *Muscle: Confessions of an Unlikely Bodybuilder*.

"The Critic at Graceful Ease" originally appeared in the *Washington Post Book World* (March 10, 1991) as a review of Wendy Lesser's *His Other Half: Men Looking at Women Through Art*. Copyright © 1991 by *The Washington Post*. Reprinted with permission.

"The Big Udder" originally appeared in *The Philadelphia Inquirer* (May 12, 1991) as a review of Suzanne Gordon's *Prisoners of Men's Dreams*. Reprinted from *The Philadelphia Inquirer*.

"Brando Flashing" originally appeared in *The New York Times Book Review* (July 21, 1991) as a review of Richard Schickel's *Brando: A Life in Our Times*. Copyright © 1991 by The New York Times Company. Reprinted by permission.

"What a Drag" originally appeared in the *Boston Globe* (December 15, 1991) as a review of Marjorie Garber's *Vested Interests: Cross-Dressing and Cultural Anxiety*.

"Milton Kessler: A Memoir" originally appeared in *Sulfur* "A Bi-annual of the Whole Art" (Spring 1991) under the same title.

Poems excerpted on pp. 133–35 are from *The Grand Concourse* by Milton Kessler. Copyright © 1990 by Milton Kessler. Published by MSS-New Myths, SUNY at Binghamton, New York. Reprinted by permission of the author.

"Junk Bonds and Corporate Raiders" originally appeared under the same title in *Arion, A Journal of Humanities and the Classics*, Third Series, Vol. I., No. 2, Spring, 1991. Copyright © by the Trustees of Boston University.